Conflict and Control in
the World Economy

Conflict and Control in the World Economy:

Contemporary Economic Realism and Neo-Mercantilism

R. J. Barry Jones

HUMANITIES PRESS INTERNATIONAL, INC.
ATLANTIC HIGHLANDS, N.J.

First published in 1986 in the United States of America by
Humanities Press International, Inc., Atlantic Highlands, NJ07716

© R. J. Barry Jones, 1986

Library of Congress Cataloging-in-Publication Data

Barry Jones, R. J.
Conflict and control in the world economy.
Bibliography: p.
Includes index.
1. Mercantile system.   2. Economic policy. I. Title
HB91.J66 1986   338.9   86-219

ISBN 0-391-03413-8

PRINTED IN GREAT BRITAIN

To all those who have always appreciated the central importance of preserving community in the face of economic realities, particularly the miners of South Wales.

Contents

Preface

This volume reflects a process of reflection upon the nature of the global political economy and national economic policy that was initiated by participation in the early work of the International Political Economy Group, under the initial leadership of Susan Strange. The subsequent intensification of so many of the fundamental problems with which the world economy is faced has merely reinforced the concern that stimulated this process and the conclusions to which it had led.

Particular appreciation must be expressed towards my wife, Stephanie, for her assistance, and forbearance, and to the rest of my family for their patience.

PART I
Introduction

growing currency crises, accelerating inflation, slow

1 Introduction

The nature and condition of the world economy has rarely been more deserving of investigation and analysis. The 'great illusion' of indefinite economic well-being and stability, fostered during the later 1950s and 1960s, was shattered by a succession of shocks that assailed the global economy from the early 1970s onwards. By the mid 1980s the global economy had experienced a most distasteful cocktail of growing currency crises, accelerating inflation, shock oil price increases, the growing indebtedness of a number of Less Developed Countries (LDCs), induced recession, extensive unemployment and widespread fears of a protectionist epidemic.

Responses to these awesome developments have, however, been extremely varied. Many have argued that they constitute a profound crisis that reflects fundamental, structural failings within the contemporary international economic system. However, the pronouncements of the governments of some of the leading Advanced Industrial Countries (AICs) have been such as to suggest that current problems might be overcome through perseverence with a set of relatively straightforward policies.

The responses of analysts of international economic matters have been equally mixed. Orthodox economists have sought solutions to contemporary problems within the mainstream of their chosen 'discipline'. Many others, however, have seen the manifold disorders of the global economy as evidence of serious shortcomings, if not fundamental weaknesses, within widely accepted approaches to the analysis of economic life.

3

The issues, then, are whether the world faces fundamental problems and whether these confront orthodox views of economics with a profound challenge. If there are no pressing problems then further refinements of analysis remain of relatively marginal significance and of more academic than practical importance. However, if profound practical and intellectual challenges have arisen then the exploration of alternative perspectives upon economic reality and approaches to economic policy becomes a matter of the greatest significance and urgency.

THE CONTEMPORARY 'CRISIS'

Widespread currency crises characterized the late 1960s and early 1970s, reflecting both the widespread growth of inflationary pressures and the intensification of international economic competition. The immediate effects of these pressures manifested themselves in the international monetary system. The convertibility of the US dollar into gold was suspended in August 1971 and the Bretton Woods system of fixed currency exchange rates finally collapsed in 1973. Such financial volatility was, however, but a weak foreshadow of what was soon to come in the international economy.

During 1973 and early 1974 the Organization of Petroleum Exporting Countries (OPEC) was able to impose spectacular increases in the price of crude oil: from some $2.50 a barrel in early 1973 to $11.50 a barrel in 1974. This price rise was accompanied by the general reduction of production and embargo of exports to the USA and the Netherlands. The rise was imposed by Middle Eastern oil producers in response to the Arab–Israeli war of late 1973.

There were three immediate and obvious effects of the oil crisis of 1973–4. First, the Arab oil embargo crystallized concerns about the reliability of supplies of this vital energy source and prompted similar sensitivities towards other critical resources. Second, the oil-importing nations of the world were faced with a massively increased oil bill: an estimated additional bill of some $225 billion during the years 1974–7 and lost some $600 billion's worth of economic production.[1]

Third, but by no means least, a number of oil-exporting states found themselves in possession of huge sums of foreign currency which could not be spent immediately and which were placed on deposit in the international banking system. The second wave of substantial oil prices of 1979 merely repeated and intensified these effects.[2]

The oil 'crises' of the mid and late 1970s also had a number of more indirect, but no less significant, effects. Sensitivities about secure supplies stimulated the accelerated exploitation of alternative sources, such as the North Sea. The example of OPEC's success encouraged many *Less Developed Countries* LDCs to believe that similar achievements might be possible in respect of other basic commodities. This, furthermore, prompted hopes that 'commodity power' might form the 'South's' main weapon in a confrontation with the rich 'North' over the structure and functioning of the international economic order. Such possibilities, in turn, merely reinforced the concerns of many in the North over the security of supplies of many important commodities and resources.

The oil price increases of the 1970s also intensified the inflationary tendencies which were already well established in many countries, including some of the leading AICs. Varied, but increasingly frenetic, official efforts to restore monetary stability soon materialized and contributed to the global recession of the early 1980s. The international banks, for their part, embarked upon a hectic search for 'suitable' borrowers for the massive quantities of 'petro-dollars' that had been placed on deposit by the more financially replete of the oil-exporting nations. Such borrowers were discovered in the form of the more promising of the LDCs. Unfortunately, the counter-inflationary (so-called 'monetarist') policies adopted by most of the AICs involved substantial domestic deflation and marked increases in interest rates. The effects of such policies were to induce recession, both domestic and global. Less Developed Countries were particularly hard hit by these developments, for the markets for their exports of basic commodities and their newer manufactured goods were substantially reduced at the precise time that they were seeking increased export earnings to repay their recently acquired debts.

The situation currently facing the world is thus one of serious unemployment within many AICs and LDCs, retarded global economic growth, and the massive indebtedness of many LDCs. The continuing danger of comprehensive default on payments of interest and capital by one or more of the major LDC debtors carries with it a profound threat to the stability, and even the survival, of the international banking system. With such a threat to the banking system of the Western world comes the additional danger of world economic dislocation on an awesome scale.

The threads connecting the dramatic developments of the 1970s and the crises of recession, indebtedness and intensifying friction in the international trading system are thus complex but fairly clear. The central question for both practitioners and analysts, however, is whether the developments of the 1970s were an aberration within an essentially healthy system or, in contrast, symptoms of an inherently flawed world economic system. If the former, then many of the policy measures adopted by Northern governments during the early 1980s could be seen as no more than the bad-tasting, but essentially short-term, medicine necessary to secure a return to order, prosperity and well-being. If, however, the problems were symptoms of deeper ailments, then budgetary restraint, deflation, wholesale 'bloodletting' within public services, and widespread industrial dislocation and rationalization, might have been both misconceived and ultimately futile.

The intellectual difficulty encountered in attempting to answer such a basic question is that the answer is by no means self-presenting. The contemporary global system is a phenomenon of such complexity and dynamism that no theory or approach can be subject to simple and straightforward testing. Any specific event or development within such a complex whole can provide some support for any one of a number of quite different propositions or approaches. Indeed the very ascription of significance to any 'fact' is possible only if it is located within a broader framework of ideas about reality.[3] Thus, the orthodox, 'conservative' economist might see the recent economic policies of many of the AICs as merely the realism and discipline necessary to restore stability to a basically viable and vital economic system. The Marxist, in direct contrast, might view recent policy developments as no more than the desperate, predictable and ultimately futile efforts to stave off the impending collapse of a fundamentally unsound, and even self-destructive, economic system. To the former, every sign of economic improvement is evidence of the soundness of economic orthodoxy:[4] to the latter, such 'signs' mark no more than a temporary remission.

Empirical 'facts' about the world of economic, political and social affairs are thus interpretatively malleable and difficult, if not impossible, to prove or disprove in any simple manner. Acceptability remains, in large part, an essentially social and psychological matter. Established ideas thus appear 'obvious' while the claims of less orthodox approaches arouse suspicion and unease. The exploration of alternative perspectives remains essential, however, both as a corrective to orthodoxies which, once enthroned, dull critical thought and as an insurance against the possibility, if not probability, that current difficulties will compound and overwhelm established perspective and policies. To be unaware of alternatives is to be unarmed in a world of constant change, complexity and difficulty.

PERSPECTIVES UPON THE INTERNATIONAL POLITICAL ECONOMY

The condition of the contemporary international political economy is clearly in need of careful examination. The notion of an international *political economy*, rather than a simple *economy*, reflects a number of considerations. First, economics, both domestic and international, are a major policy concern of political authorities. Second, developments within the economic realm have a substantial impact upon almost all the other areas of policy which are of concern to governments. Third, but slightly more controversial, it can be argued that much of the structure and functioning of the contemporary international economic system is a direct product of the policies and actions of governments in the past and the present. In this last sense, then, a *political* economy is such, precisely because it is a creation of politics and will ever be so!

The three major perspectives upon the contemporary world political economy, the liberal, the Marxist and the 'Economic Realist', with its neo-mercantilist leanings, have developed in response to, and interaction with, one another.[5] These basic approaches have, themselves, generated many variants, each of which attracts committed adherents. The discussion in this book will concentrate upon idealized forms of the liberal and the Economic Realist approaches. The 'Economic Realist' approach has been so titled for two reasons. The approach claims, firstly, to reflect and accommodate the complex set of 'realities' exhibited by the empirical world. The approach, secondly, shares a basic identity of outlook with the 'Realist' theory of international relations, as will be indicated subsequently.

Marxist interpretations will not be considered directly in this study, although the approach that is to be propounded is quite compatible with insights and ideas of a Marxist parentage. Indeed, it well may be that an effective analysis of the structure of the contemporary global political economy must incorporate such notions, irrespective of their origin.

THE MARXIST APPROACH

Marxist analysis of the contemporary global political economy constitutes a powerful and largely self-contained system of ideas and interpretations.[6] Its approach to current 'realities' is systematically critical and, at many points, based upon an analysis of underlying forces and dynamics, many of which are not open to direct and immediate observation.[7] Prescriptively the bulk of prevailing arrangements and institutions are to be repudiated, overthrown and replaced by a new global order based upon socialist (or even communist) principles. Analytically, and predictively, Marxism remains essentially deterministic. The majority of Marxist studies are also somewhat ambivalent in their attitudes towards ideas derived from non-Marxist sources. Many reject such ideas as reactionary rationalizations or obfuscations; a few are willing and able to use such ideas and analytical techniques as complement analysis, irrespective of their formal origin.

The neglect of the Marxist approach in this volume, however, is a result of its epistemological basis and analytical character. Dependence upon non-observable forces and features, while it may be ultimately sound, does face the analyst with numerous difficulties. Determinism is also intellectually and emotionally unpalatable to many. Sympathy must therefore be extended to those who are uneasy with such an approach and would prefer to remain within the realms of the more-or-less observable and prosaic (with whatever epistemological qualifications such notions might warrant).

Practitioners and analysts alike are also faced with the problem that Marxist predictions of socialist transformations, both domestic and global, are necessarily atemporal. Prior to such transformations, which may be long awaited, relations within and between states will reflect non-socialist principles and practices. Indeed, in a world in which socialism has yet to achieve its final triumph, much of the international economic behaviour of nominally socialist states shows little influence of socialist principles. While critical forms of neo-Marxism may be instructive with regard to such 'anomolies', non-Marxist perspectives may have much to offer on prevailing behavioural 'realities'.

LIBERAL THEORY VERSUS ECONOMIC REALISM

The centre of the intellectual and political stage within the societies of the rich, North-Western (structural rather than geographical) quadrant of the modern world is occupied by the liberal analysis of economics, and such influential derivatives as modern neo-classical economic theory. This approach offers a system of ideas and analytical techniques which, by appearing to be extremely rigorous, exerts considerable appeal. It is, however, a theoretical construction which, as will be shown later, has acquired its apparent virtues as a direct result of basic characteristics and assumptions which seriously distance it from the reality to which it is supposed to relate and even correspond.

The classical forerunner of modern liberal economics was, however, developed as a prescriptive programme as well as a statement about the nature of contemporary reality. The prescriptive purpose of Adam Smith was to attack, and hopefully dismantle, the mercantilist economic doctrines that governments were supposedly pursuing at the time of writing *The Wealth of Nations*. This prescriptive–positive fusion has continued to characterize liberal economics, despite the pretensions and claims of many latter-day adherents, throughout its long evolution from classical into modern neo-classical forms.

As liberal economics has evolved through time, experience and continued confrontation with competing approaches, so too has the mercantilist perspective. The reality of systematic mercantilism in the seventeenth and eighteenth centuries has been contested by some historians, who see it as no more than a 'straw-man' invented by writers like Adam Smith for their own polemical purposes.[8] However, many of the policies and practices of the European states of those days did include features that warrant the title 'mercantilist'.

The common purpose of mercantilist measures was to promote the strength and potential power of the state, and its ruler(s), against other communities with which conflicts of interest, and arms, might develop. Initially, classical mercantilism was seen to be primarily 'bullionist'; policy being directed towards the accumulation of bullion, specie and all other readily transportable forms of wealth that might be used for recruiting and sustaining armed forces. Latter, classical mercantilism broadened its vision to include the promotion and protection of the society's general economic strength, and capacity, and the establishment of a strategically advantageous balance of trade with other states.

The classical mercantilist view of the international system thus accords with that of the modern *Realist* school of international relations' analysis, pioneered by E. H. Carr[9] in Britain and Hans J. Morgenthau[10] in North America. Economic policy was to be based upon the certainty of conflict with other societies and the need to ensure that the state was optimally placed to sustain itself in, and through, such eventualities. Unfortunately, the practical implications of such a disposition could be extensive and, as Adam Smith emphasized, encourage governmental involvement in, and interference with, virtually every element of economic and social life. Personal freedom and economic vigour might be suppressed by such rampant mercantilism; possibilities which might best be prevented by the adoption of a liberal, free-enterprise system in which the role of government would be minimal.

Modern Economic Realism perpetuates the concern of classical mercantilism with strategic security but is equally, if not primarily, motivated by a perceived need to promote the economic well-being and stability of the societies which governments serve. Extensive, and often intensive, governmental involvement in many areas of economic and society is a response to the chronic uncertainties of the modern economy, both domestic and global, and complexities of advanced industrial societies and the numerous demands that populations now place upon their rulers. General economic well-being has thus been added to the traditional quest for national security and international influence.

The issue between the liberal and the Economic Realist perspectives upon the global political economy has both empirical and prescriptive aspects. At one level, proponents of the two contrasting approches to economic policy and behaviour assert that theirs offers the best prospect of general stability and well-being. At another level, there is disagreement about the principles upon which the contemporary global economy actually operates.

The latter controversy is particularly interesting and directly germane to this discussion. It is often an explicit assertion, or an implicit assumption, of liberal writers that much of global economic progress of both the late nineteenth century and the post Second World War era was a direct function of the liberal trade system developed and sustained during those periods. Moreover, departures from liberal purity are viewed as economically and politically damaging aberrations. Protectionism is the outstanding departure from the path of economic purity, a perversion of national economic policy that is held to undermine economic efficiency, and well-being, and hence to stimulate political and military conflict between nation states.[11]

Critics of the liberal position, in contrast, reject all these basic arguments. A truly liberal global order, it is contended, has never been more than a fantasy of liberal theory, and ideology, and has certainly not constituted a necessary condition of economic progress. The periods of substantial economic progress in the past were actually characterized by conditions that significantly departed from those envisaged by, or enshrined in, liberal theory. Indeed, Economic Realists would argue that it is precisely those practical departures from the liberal prescription that produced the combination of stability and effective leadership within the system that was necessary for such impressive global economic advance. This, it would be held, is precisely because the liberal approach rests upon a number of fundamental misconceptions and is quite misleading in the picture that it paints of present, and potential, realities.

The lines of battle between the liberal and the Economic Realist are thus clearly drawn. The liberal believes that economic progress, nationally and internationally, is dependent upon the maintenance of a *laissez-faire* domestic economy and international free trade. The Economist Realist believes, in contrast, that effective governmental influence, or even control, over the economy is essential for national economic progress and well-being, while international economic control and regulation are necessary conditions for long-term global stability and prosperity.

Beyond the central axes of dispute, the liberal and the Economic Realist approaches also differ substantially in the way in which they deal with many prominent features of the contemporary global economy. Liberal economic theory, and its neo-classical variant, has never been happy in dealing with monopolies and oligopolies. Much of the appeal of the liberal paradigm rests upon two claims: first, that it establishes that a true *laissez-faire* system ensures the maximum possible satisfaction of the economic wants and needs of the population; and, second, that it is capable of subjecting the realm of economic life to determinate analysis: a form of analysis that establishes what *must* be the ultimate outcome in any identifiable situation. Unfortunately, micro-economic theory demonstrates that monopolies will, by virtue of economic logic rather than mere greed or mendacity, charge more and produce less than would competitive suppliers.[12] The existence of monopolies thus necessitates a reduction of aggregate well-being and satisfaction for the community. Studies of oligopolies, moreover, demonstrate that their behaviour is intrinsically indeterminate.[13] As any casual observer of the behaviour of the oil companies recently in the United Kingdom will know, at times oligopolists engage one another in determined price-cutting competition, at others they lapse into a tacit and harmonious price-stabilizing cartel.

Monopolies and oligopolies, then, are phenomena with which liberal theory would really prefer not to have to deal. Individual economists may study them, but monopolies and oligopolies continue to confront the governing theoretical paradigm with fundamental problems that are both serious and consistently evaded. Thus the existence of monopolies and oligopolies are stated in conventional economics text-books but their development is not explained. Again, their damaging welfare effects tend to be glossed over. Finally, the future prospects of monopolies and oligopolies are barely considered.

The evasive schizophrenia of liberal economics is accentuated when the phenomenon of the multinational, or trans-national, corporation (MNC or TNC) is addressed. Many TNCs are world-wide oligopolists, in fact or in the making, which have profound, and by no means always benign, effects upon the societies within, and between, which they operate. Some liberal economists would, however, treat them as no more than ordinary competitive, free-market enterprises which, by virtue of size and breadth of operation, are able to maximize productive efficiency, put the world's productive resources to their optimal use and, hence, provide consumers with the widest range of goods, and services, at the lowest possible cost. Others, in contrast, express clear apprehensions about the behaviour of such world-striding corporations and their structural impact upon the global system. However, when such critics of TNCs remain firmly within the liberal paradigm their work remains, of necessity, pragmatic and bereft of a systematic basis.

The Economic Realist, or neo-mercantilist, has no such difficulties with TNCs. Their emergence, nature, and behavioural characteristics are quite comprehensible. They are organizations that act precisely in accordance with the expectations of the Realist. In a complex and turbulent world, the TNC seeks size, strength and influence in pursuit of the maximum attainable level of control over its environment. It is no more than another major actor within a formally 'anarchical' global system: an actor that lacks some of the resources of a territorially based nation-state, but which is also free of many of its pressing responsibilities.

The liberal approach remains embarrassed by such common features of the contemporary international scene as the efforts of groups of states to establish control over the global economy, or some sector, and the existence, and activity, of TNCs. The Economic Realist encounters no such difficulty with such enduring aspects of reality.

The analytical strengths and weakness of the liberal and the Economic Realist schools thus differ in type and significance. The liberal approach offers a deductive system of argument and a variety of powerful analytical techniques that, in sum, appear both rigorous and intellectually attractive. In contrast, Economic Realism embraces a bare few fundamental assumptions and deductive arguments. It is, however, able to accommodate far more aspects of reality.

Power and influence are two outstanding features of reality that Economic Realism is better equipped to handle. Liberal economic theory is based upon the analysis of competitive markets in which, by definition, no consumer(s) or supplier(s) is able to influence market developments solely by its own actions. Power and influence are thus excluded, from the outset, in the basic construction of this theory of economics.

Economic Realism, in market contrast, is founded upon the assumption that actors, be they firms, states or coalitions, will seek power and influence within their environment and over those with whom they interact. Economic Realism does not exclude competitive markets, in the way that the liberal

approach denies power and influence. Indeed, perfect competition can be treated as a special case, while gradations of
competitiveness can be defined, identified and analysed as
they appear in the real world. The *analytical power* of
Economic Realism is thus greater than that of neo-classicism
for it can accommodate the content and purview of the latter.
The reverse is not true of the liberal approach, its analytical
rigour notwithstanding.

Liberal theory is also, with one or two particular excep-
tions, consistently condemnatory of protectionist policies.
However, the liberal argument has had a further, and equally
serious influence for it has encouraged excessive concentration upon the more manifest protectionist measures and
other overt forms of governmental intervention to support
national exporters. This has encouraged a form of tunnel-
vision which has often inhibited a proper recognition of the
wide range of policies available to governments that seek to
enhance the economic performance of their communities and
the economic strength of their states. The consequences of
this perceptual disturbance are twofold: the analysis of
contemporary reality is simplified to the point of serious
distortion, while the prescriptions for policy, and policy
makers, are ill founded and often misleading.

THE SUBSEQUENT DISCUSSION

The purpose of this volume is to establish the need for an
Economic Realist perspective upon the political economy, to
identify its content and to explore its wide-ranging implications in the contemporary world. It will be argued that such
a perspective illuminates the neo-mercantilist character of
many of the policies and practices of the governments of
modern societies. This study is, therefore, at one with a
continuing tradition that includes such notable recent publications as Calleo and Rowland's *America and the World
Political Economy*,[14] and Dudley Seers final work, *The
Political Economy of Nationalism*.[15] It will also be contended
that this approach is particularly effective in revealing the
analogous purposes and practices of the transnational cor-

porations that play a major, and growing, role in the global political economy.

The underlying theme of this discussion is that prevailing conditions compel actors within the global political economy to attempt to establish control and influence over their environment, both material and human. The acquisition of many resources and capabilities may be directed towards this end. Various combinations of resources, capabilities and conditions then determine the degree of control that any actor will be able to secure.

Central to the discussion will be the argument that many conventional discussions of state economic behaviour have been unduly narrow in their focus. Attention has often been confined to explicit measures of protection and export promotion. While such policies and practices remain of considerable significance in the contemporary world, governments and their societies also engage in a far wider range of activities that may have a considerable bearing upon industrial performance and general economic well-being. An examination of the range and variety of such policies and practices will be a particular concern of this volume.

This study is also somewhat more stoical in its basic philosophy, and modest in its theoretical pretensions, than much work within the liberal and the Marxist paradigms. Notions of perfection and perfectibility occupy an important, if implicit, place in many such studies. The emotional appeal of such approaches does not, however, provide any guarantee of secure answers to the major issues of the global political economy. Indeed, it is doubtful if such answers can be found for a world of such complexity and not a little intractability.

Theoretical elegance might also prove irresistibly seductive to the unwary. Not only is the real world rather more complex and evasive than many major theoretical approaches acknowledge, but the relationship between human thought and action is also such as to compound the problems confronting analysts. Human activity reveals a simple pattern of linear evolution only to those who are disposed to see such orderly and progressive patterns. Developments in human activity are actually rather more diverse in character, sometimes cyclical, sometimes dialectical and, on occasion, a direct reversal of former lines of evolution.

The complex and variable patterns of development in human activity reflect, in large part, the central role of the ideas that direct human thought and action. The conscious repudiation of past principles of behaviour may, in some cases, lead to changed patterns of activity. The analyst that seeks to identify the principles of human behaviour must accommodate such principles, where they correspond to the activity that is observed, but does so only at the expense of a particular difficulty. The ideas that the analyst develops have a dual status: they may be, at once, central to what is being investigated *and* to the way in which it is studied. This characteristic does not rule out any form of 'social science' as some, like Peter Winch, have argued[16] but does render the enterprise problematical.

Human beings have the 'irritating' habit of arguing about the very principles upon which they are to base their conduct: much of politics is just such a debate. If debate is central to human activity then it must be accommodated by, or reflected in, studies of human activity. Debates amongst participants may, therefore, necessitate parallel debates within, or between, works of analysis. A serious error may, moreover, be committed by those who believe, or pretend, that the human condition, in whole or part, can be fully apprehended by any one theory or approach. Indeed, the more internally rigorous the theory, and the more demanding its fundamental principles, the less is it likely to encompass the full complexity and contentiousness of reality.

This study, then, has two purposes. The first is to contribute to the general, and necessary, debate between contrasting views of the global political economy and the most effective forms of economic activities to be adopted by societies. If the view of the human condition that has been suggested above is sound then such an exercise is, of itself, valuable. However, the second purpose of this study is to identify the many policies and practices that may actually benefit societies. Such an exercise may well be preferable to guidance from theories that, while appearing elegant and relatively powerful, fail to do full justice to a world of such complexity and intractability that the 'second best', and even 'third best', remain characteristic of reality.

NOTES

1. D. Pirages, *Global Ecopolitics: The New Context for International Relations*, (Belmont, Cal.: Duxbury, 1978) pp. 124 and 125. *See also* H. Askari and J. T. Cummings, *Oil, OCED, and the Third World: A Vicious Triangle* (Austin, Texas: Center for Middle Eastern Studies, 1978) pp. 1–11; and Edith Penrose, 'Oil and international relations', *British Journal of International Studies*, Vol. 2 (1976) pp. 41–50.
2. J. E. Spero, *The Politics of International Economic Relations*, (London: George Allen and Unwin, 2nd edn., 1982) pp. 265–70.
3. *See* the discussions in the chapters by R. J. Barry Jones, John Maclean and Richard Little, in Barry Buzan and R. J. Barry Jones (eds.), *Change and the Study of International Relations: The Evaded Dimension*, (London: Frances Pinter, 1981).
4. *See*, for instance, the eulogy to monetarism by Alan Walters in *The Economist*, 4 May 1985, pp. 19–23.
5. Not all writers in the field follow this classification. Many offer 'structuralism' as an additional major perspective to the liberal and Marxist. *See*, for instance, D. H. Blake and R. S. Walters, *The Politics of Global Economic Relations*, (Englewood Cliffs, NJ: Prentice-Hall, 1976) and Spero *op. cit*. This 'structuralism', however, is not a theory of the same status, or implication, as the others with which it is arrayed. Economic Realism/neo-mercantilism lacks some of the theoretical rigour of the other approaches but can lay claim to equal historical and practical significance.
6. On which, *see*, M. Barratt Brown, *The Economics of Imperialism* (Harmondsworth: Penguin Books, 1975); R. Owen and Bob Sutcliffe (eds.), *Studies in the Theory of Imperialism*, (London: Longman, 1972); M. C. Howard and J. E. King, *The Political Economy of Marx* (Burnt Mill: Longman, 1975); and A. Gamble, 'Critical political economy,' pp. 64–89 in R. J. Barry Jones (ed.), *Perspectives on Political Economy: Alternatives to the Economics of Depression*, (London: Frances Pinter, 1983).
7. *See* John Maclean, 'Marxist epistemology, explanations of 'change' and the study of international relations', pp. 46–67 in Buzan and Jones *op. cit*.
8. *See* D. C. Coleman, 'Introduction', esp. p. 4, and 'Eli Heckscher and the idea of mercantilism' esp. pp. 92–3, in D. C. Coleman (ed.), *Revision in Mercantilism* (London: Methuen, 1969).
9. E. H. Carr, *The Twenty Years' Crisis: An Introduction to the Study of International Relations*, (London: Macmillan, 2nd edn., 1946).

10. Hans J. Morgenthau, *Politics Among Nations: The Struggle for Power and Peace*, (New York: Alfred Knopf, 4th edn., 1967).
11. For a clear presentation, and critical discussion, of this view *see* Barry Buzan, 'Economic structure and international security', *International Organization*, Vol. 38 (Autumn 1984), pp. 597–624.
12. *See*, for instance, R. G. Lipsey, *An Introduction to Positive Economics*, (London: Weidenfeld and Nicolson, 1st ed., 1963), Ch. 18.
13. *See*, for instance, Peter Kenyon, 'Pricing', pp. 34–45 in A. S. Eichner (ed.), *A Guide to Post-Keynsian Economics*, (London: Macmillan, 1979); and Joan Robinson, '"Imperfect competition" revisited', pp. 166–81 in Joan Robinson, *Contributions to Modern Economics*, (Oxford: Basil Blackwell, 1978).
14. D. P. Calleo and B. J. Rowland, *America and the World Political Economy: Atlantic Dreams and National Realities*, (Bloomington: Indiana University Press, 1973).
15. Dudley Seers, *The Political Economy of Nationalism*, (Oxford: Oxford University Press, 1983).
16. Peter Winch, *The Idea of a Social Science*, (London: Routledge and Kegan Paul, 1958).

Part II
The Liberal and Economic Realist Approaches
to the Political Economy

2   The Liberal Approach to Economics and the Global Political Economy

The liberal approach to economics has a long and highly influential history. It is a perspective upon economic life that has influenced the policies, and practices, of governments and attracted the intense interest of many of substantial intellectual powers. A phenomenon of such power and influence clearly demands the closest attention and scrutiny.

The sceptic might be suspicious of any system of ideas that so bedazzles some minds and that seems to offer such a clear and rigorous theory of a major part of the human condition. It will be one of the purposes of this chapter to indicate that such scepticism might well be warranted. While the wholesale abandonment of insights generated by liberal economics will certainly not be advocated, it will be argued that analysis should be developed within an alternative framework: a framework into which liberal insights may be incorporated selectively and with due caution.

In any critical examination of a school of thought or a given approach to analysis there is the inevitable question of the reality of that which is being discussed. The difficulty, here, is the boundary that is to be drawn around any approach, and its adherents. In the case of economic analysis it is clear that there are those whose views are difficult to classify in any simple and clear manner. The current positions of many whose origins lie within liberal theory have developed in such a way as to raise serious doubts about their continuing compatibility with the central tenets of that approach. Many of those who might be entitled post-Keynsians, ultra-Keynsians, or, in the North American context, 'institutionalists' have wandered far from the liberal faith in the benign effects of the 'hidden hand' that supposedly operates within an unconstrained *laissez-faire* economic system.

The ability to differentiate schools of thought by high-lighting their differences also assists with the accusation of unfair attributions of belief, or view, to those who are grouped together under a common title. Here, again, the simplest defence of any system of classification may be to establish the marked contrasts of basic outlook that exist between those who have been placed in any one category and those in contrasting categories. On such grounds, liberals are clearly differentiable from Economic Realists or socialists, while neo-classicists may be further distinguished by their unique confidence in general equilibrium analysis and the role of impersonal processes.

A clear view of, and critical approach towards, the liberal approach to economics must, therefore, be based upon some awareness of its central arguments and basic propositions. Only when these have been examined can systematic criticism be undertaken. What follows, then, is an outline of an inevitably simplified model of the liberal position, and a critical re-examination of some of its basic assumptions and arguments.

THE LIBERAL PURPOSE

The liberal perspective shares one central difficulty with many other approaches to economic life: a problematical fusion of positive analysis with normatively based prescription.[1] This intimate blend of statements about the 'is' and the 'ought' was central to the work of the early, classical liberal economists. One of Adam Smith's essential purposes was to criticize mercantilist practices while advocating the adoption of liberal economic policies.

It is quite clear that criticism of alternative approaches to economic analysis and the conduct of economic policy has remained central to the liberal enterprise throughout the long course of its evolution. Mercantilism, and its modern neo-mercantilist variant, and socialism are attacked vigorously for their interference with the free operation of a competitive market, and the damage to economic efficiency and consumer satisfaction that supposedly results. In the case of socialism, additional criticism is directed against its opposition to self-interested behaviour, acquisitive purpose and entrepreneurial spirit. Some confusion is common on this last point, however, for there is no necessary connection between an extremely efficient competitive market system and private property (or, more particularly, the private ownership of the means of production and/or noticeable inequalities in the distribution of wealth and income). This confusion is a product of the wider set of values entertained by many liberal economists and illustrates one of the dangers that follow from the unavoidable role of value-based theory in the development of any observation and analysis.

The fusion of positive and prescriptive analysis is not, however, peculiar to those whose explicit intention is to offer policy recommendations or to promote the realization of personal values through changes in economic policies and practices. Some increasingly influential theories about the inevitable connection between personal values, established ideas and empirical study indicate that it is a delusion to believe that strictly 'objective' analysis and, therefore purely positive theory, is possible.[2]

The complexities of the relationship between personal values, established views and empirical analysis reflect a number of issues. Such issues include the role of personal interests and values, the necessity for theory before embarking upon orderly empirical investigation and, finally, the possible need to incorporate reference to non-observable factors or forces within effective analysis.

It is clear that interests, of one kind or another, direct the initial attention of investigators. It is rare, even within the somewhat rarefied atmosphere of academia, for analysts to devote time and energy to studying matters that they find uninteresting or that they believe to be quite insignificant.

All aspects of human affairs, including economic activity, are areas of considerable, if not overwhelming, complexity. This complexity can be brought under some sort of intellectual control only if it can be simplified from the outset and if means are established for selecting the most salient features for further attention. Unfortunately, the bases of simplication and selection involve the application of ideas about how reality works, and the features that are most significant. Such selectivity and simplification necessarily precedes systematic empirical investigation and amounts to the application of a form of theory. Moreover, such prior theory generally reflects value judgements and orientations: significance is established by views on how reality affects cherished values or how reality might be better moulded so as to ensure their satisfaction. Theory thus directs empirical investigation. Empirical investigation may prompt the subsequent modification, or even transformation, of theory.[3] However, a 'chicken and egg' cycle characterizes the study of human affairs, into which initial entry is facilitated by the individual's earlier enculturalization and formal education.

Many analyses of complex features of human life, finally, employ references to factors and forces which are not immediately observable but which have to be inferred from the occurrence of their supposed effects within observable reality. Most of the references to systems and structures that are made within the social sciences are of such non-observables. Actual experience is always that of actors who exist within, and whose behaviour reflects the influence of, such systems and structures, rather than of the system or structure itself. However, an account of the activities of the actors who have been observed may be fundamentally deficient unless reference is made to the influential non-observables.[4] The significance of non-observables, then, is that they have a complex relationship with apparent reality, are essentially theoretical and are conceived through a complex process of thought and observation.

The liberal analysis of economic life, in whatever form, cannot, therefore, achieve the objectivity which some proponents have claimed and which has been proclaimed in far too many textbooks of economic theory and analysis.[5] The apparent plausibility of many basic liberal economic ideas does not secure them against the difficulties that have been discussed above. Such difficulties do not, however, affect liberal theory any more or less then the contending approaches.

The values that are inherent in the liberal perspective need not be disguised or denied. They demand careful consideration and are open to acceptance or rejection according to the personal inclinations of each student of human affairs. Adam Smith was more than a mere apologist for emergent capitalism, he was also an unashamed, and wholly justified, advocate of fundamental principles of individual liberty.

THE LIBERAL ARGUMENT

The liberal argument can best be understood in terms of three primary elements. First, it offers the identification of characteristics of human economic activity that are held to be common to all people in all places and at all times. Second, it develops an analysis of the implications that such universals of economic behaviour have under a variety of conditions. Third, but by no means least, it specifies the highly desirable consequences, for the population of any community (national or global), of allowing unfettered free-market principles to prevail.

Throughout the analysis, the liberal model rests upon a number of initial assumptions that necessarily, and explicitly, limit its correspondence with reality. The defence of such limiting initial assumptions is that they provide the analysis with its manageability and precision, while still allowing it to generate fruitful insights into economic reality. However, the newcomer should always recall that the initial assumptions of the liberal approach do constitute a substantial, and potentially very serious, simplification of reality.

Much of the liberal argument can be stated in mathematical terms or, as is common in economics textbooks, in graphical form. For those who are conversant, and happy, with such techniques this practice can do much to assist comprehension. However, there are many for whom such procedures are baffling and something of a deterrent. Since this account is intended for readers who may well fall into the latter category it will concentrate upon verbal exposition.

The liberal arguement starts with a vision of an economic society of rational actors. Such actors are rational in that they seek to maximize the benefits obtained from those resources with which they are endowed. Within a complex market economy, the exchange of goods and services is usually facilitated by the use of money. As consumers, rational actors use their income and wealth to purchase the combination of goods and services that provides them with the highest possible level of overall satisfaction of needs and wants.

As producers, rational individuals also seek to use their skills, energies and equipment to produce those goods or services which can be sold for the highest return (or other payments-in-kind) in the market-place: the profits and wages thus accruing being ultimately used to purchase goods and services (or additional equipment with which to enhance productive capabilities, and hence income-earning capacity). Rational consumers will, in general, purchase more of any good or service if its price is lowered and vice versa. Rational producers will, in contrast, generally supply more at a higher price and less at a lower price (as profits are, respectively, raised or lowered).

The magical feature of an unfettered free, competitive market, however, is the way in which it encourages patterns and supply to move into balance with one another. If consumers do not wish to buy the volume of a good—say apples—that has been supplied to the market at the price initially asked, then stocks will remain unsold. If sellers do not wish to make an absolute loss on unsold stocks they will reduce prices to encourage additional sales. Rational consumers will be encouraged to buy more apples because the lower price now makes them more attractive than some of the other goods and services that were previously purchased. Prices will continue to be lowered until a price is reached at which stocks are sold without the formation of queues of unsatisfied potential customers.

In the example under consideration, and under suitable technical conditions, the market gradually moves towards stability. Rational producers will not continue to supply the original volume of apples. They will switch some of their resources to the production of alternative goods, the market prospects of which seem to be more promising. As the level of supply gradually falls, the price will rise once again, for it will be less and less necessary to cut prices to clear surplus stocks. Eventually, the level of supply of apples to the market will (uncontrollable influences aside) be such, and at such a price, as to ensure that all stocks are sold, that there are no queues of unsatisfied customers and that no producer is still supplying apples at a level of profit lower than obtainable through alternative uses of productive resources.

This model of the market for any good or service is the key element in liberal economic theory. Its range is considerable, for an identical analysis can be applied to such apparently diverse phenomena as the demand and supply of labour within an economy, the demand and supply of savings for investment, and the exchange rates of those national currencies that are traded on international money markets.

The real economy constitutes a simultaneous market for the entire range of goods and services being produced and purchased. Adjustments in the market for one item involve adjustments elsewhere, as consumers are encouraged by changing relative prices to adjust the relative balance of their purchases and as producers are encouraged by changing profit levels to redirect their productive resources. Eventually the whole market will be balanced in a condition of *general equilibrium*, albeit through an extremely complex set of evolving individual consumption and production decisions. Such a condition of general equilibrium marks the most efficient—the optimal—deployment of the community's productive resources, for it provides the highest overall level of satisfaction of those popular demands that have been expressed through market demand; and the satisfaction of the people's economic wishes and wants is the exclusive definition of efficiency within the liberal perspective. This notion of general equilibrium now occupies a central place in modern liberal economic theory and is an essential article of faith of neo-classicists.[6]

The extension of the liberal argument to the entire global community involves no serious departure from the account of the achievement of general equilibrium within the domestic market provided above; merely its amplification in a few important areas.[7] The first problem with which international economic relations confronts the liberal approach is the need to explain why communities should have any economic relationships with one another. The initial, and seemingly quite sensible, response of the liberal economic theory was to argue that societies would trade with one another to secure those commodities, goods and services which could not be produced or obtained domestically. Societies would then export some of the goods and services that they were able to produce at home so as to pay for those that they had to import. The principle of this early explanation of international trade was that of *Absolute Advantage*. Unfortunately, the principle of Absolute Advantage fails to account for the complexity of international trade that is actually encountered. The real world reveals patterns of trade in which societies import goods and services that they are quite capable of producing domestically. Indeed, it is the case that some societies both import and export certain goods and services; as does the United Kingdom in the case of motor vehicles. It is, moreover, quite possible for two or more societies to import and export similar goods to one another simultaneously.

The much vaunted principle of *Comparative Advantage*, which will be outlined below, has been advanced to explain the apparent peculiarity of a situation in which societies import those goods and services that they could well produce domestically. Explanations of the more complex patterns of trade in which similar goods and services are traded simultaneously in both directions refer to such features of modern production as brand names, advertising and the general attempt to establish product differentiation, albeit largely illusory. This latter explanation is, however, somewhat insecure and controversial, for the trade pattern in question may be transitional rather than persisting: a symptom of the gradual shift of relative competitiveness between societies rather than a strange, but durable, condition. The discussion will return to this point later in the volume.

Comparative Advantage

The principle of Comparative Advantage is central to the liberal explanation of, and justification for, international trade. It is of sufficient importance to the liberal approach, and of such general interest, as to warrant a brief discussion. The power and subtlety of this principle is that it demonstrates that even where one society is more efficient at producing the entire range of relevant goods and services than any other, there may still be a sound basis for mutually advantageous specialization of production and subsequent trade between the two societies.

The principle of Comparative Advantage can best be explained through the conventional technique of adopting a highly simplified model of reality. The most appropriate model here is that of a world in which there are two societies which initially produce the same two products and do not yet engage in trade with one another. The life of the people of the two societies is simple yet happy. The climate and natural conditions are such as to allow them to secure shelter and produce clothing with relative ease on an individual, or family, basis. All that has to be, and is, produced collectively is wheat and wine.

The first of these two societies—society *A*—is actually more productive and efficient than the other—society *B*. For every day a worker devotes to production within society *A*, eight kilograms of wheat *or* four litres of wine are produced. In contrast, in society *B* one day of effort by one worker produces only three kilograms of wheat or two litres of wine. Since society *A* is clearly more efficient (in terms of output per man day of effort) at producing everything than is society *B*, there would not seem to be a sensible basis for specialization of production and the development of trade. However, the principle of Comparative Advantage belies first appearances in such cases and highlights the very real advantages that could accrue from such a development. The Figures 1.1 and 1.2 are intended to illustrate this possibility.

Figure 1.1 illustrates the overall relationship between productive efficiency in society *A* and society *B*. Figure 1.2, by reducing the figures for society *A* and society *B* to a common base (one litre of wine), allows a more direct comparison of the relative efficiency with which wheat and wine are produced within society *A* and the relative efficiency with which they are produced within society *B*: the compari-

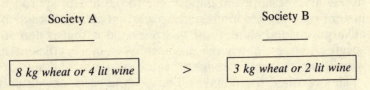

Note: > indicates the greater efficiency and productivity of society A over society B (in terms of output per man day worked)

Figure 1.1: The overall levels of productive efficiency in societies A and B.

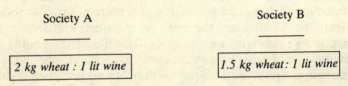

Note: The values have been obtained by reducing the figures for productivity of society A and society B to the common based of one litre of wine: that is by dividing society A's figures through by four and society B's figures by two. This, while appearing arbitrary, is legitimate, here, because it is no longer the overall levels of efficiency of the two societies that are now of interest.

Figure 1.2 The comparison of the relative efficiencies of production within society A and society B.

son in which we are interested when considering Comparative Advantage.

Figure 1.2 thus makes it clear that, irrespective of the levels of overall efficiency, society *A* has a particular advantage in the production of wheat. Before trade develops with society *B*, society *A* has, in a sense, to give up two kilograms of wheat whenever one person's labour is devoted to the production of one litre of wine. If it became possible to obtain wine at a 'price' of less than two kilograms of wheat, from some other society, then it would clearly benefit society *A* to give up producing wine domestically, specialize in producing wheat and trade some of the additional wheat for the 'cheaper' foreign-produced wine. In the case illustrated in Figure 1.2 it is possible for such specialization and trade to develop. Society *B*, for its part, recognizes that if it is able to obtain more than one and a half kilograms of wheat for one litre of wine through international trade then it would be advantageous to give up the domestic production of wheat, specialize in wine production and trade some of its additional wine for foreign-produced wheat.

The mutual advantage from specialization and trade, inherent in the example given in Figure 1.2, may best be demonstrated by the arbitary selection of a trade ratio of one and three quarters of a kilogram of wheat for one litre of wine. In the case of society *A*, for each litre of wine that is no longer produced domestically two kilograms of wheat can be produced. However, only one and three quarter kilograms of wheat have to be 'paid' for one litre of wine pruchased from society *B*: society *A* has thus profited by one quarter of a kilogram of wheat from this new pattern of specialized production and international trade. On its side, society *B* now finds that it has to give up only one and a half kilograms of domestically produced wheat for every additional litre of wine now produced, but is able to obtain one and three quarters of a kilogram of wheat when its wine is traded for wheat from society *A*. Society *B* has also profited by one quarter of a kilogram of wheat from the new pattern of production and trade.

For societies *A* and *B* taken together, then, there is mutual benefit and an increase in overall production when specialization and trade develop. The overall level of wine produced and consumed will remain as before specialization and trade. However, the volume of wheat produced and consumed will have increased, with the benefits of that increase being shared between the two societies. The level of benefit that each society enjoys will not necessarily be the same, however, for the exchange ratio of one and three quarter kilograms of wheat for one litre of wine is merely one possibility (albeit the fairest). Any exchange ratio would be possible within the range marked by the limits of two kilograms of wheat for one litre of wine and one and a half kilograms of wheat for one litre of wine.

The real world, of course, exhibits far more complex patterns of trade than that envisaged in this example. Moreover, the great bulk of such trade is facilitated by money rather than direct barter. Simple exchange ratios are, therefore, rarely possible to identify. However, the distribution of the supposed benefits from specialization and trade is a matter of very real concern and controversy, as will be seen later in this discussion.

On a global scale the promptings of Comparative Advantage will, liberal theorists believe, provide the driving force for a general pattern of specialization and trade. Free-market mechanisms will bring about the matching of demand and supply for any given good or service and the system will eventually attain a condition of general equilibrium. At this point, the world's productive resources will be deployed in such a way as to ensure the maximum possible satisfaction of the wants and needs of the human population.

Modern liberal economic theory has not been confined to an explanation of international trade in terms of those patterns of factor endowment that underlie Comparative Advantage and, hence, competitiveness. There have been some further developments that are worthy of note. Heckscher and Ohlin's work on factor endowments has been extended, particularly by theoreticians like Paul Samuelson,[8] T. M. Rybczynski[9] and Harry Johnson,[10] to specify the equalization of the prices (or rewards accorded to) factors of production in different countries that will follow from free trade. This theoretical development, however, remains within the same methodological framework as the original theory of Comparative Advantage and has been the subject of considerable theoretical controversy, particularly with regard to possible variations of supply of factors of production, with changing 'prices', the unequal applicability of production technologies in different countries, and ambiguities in the definition of 'capital'.[11] The empirical evidence for factor price equalization has also been, at best, equivocal.[12]

A lesser refinement of the liberal theory of international trade concerns the opportunities it provides for the satisfaction of varied tastes and the attainment of economies of scale by producers that are highly specialized, or significantly differentiated from their competitors. The principle of Absolute Advantage has long identified the opportunities that international trade provides for the consumption of goods that cannot be produced domestically. This possibility can be extended to cover the consumption of those goods that it would be possible to produce domestically, but for which there might be an inadequate level of demand to justify that production (given the costs of small-scale production). The production of such a good in one country, but for an international market, might then permit production on a scale sufficient to secure sufficient economies to scale to render production 'economically efficient'.

The economies to scale permitted by an international market might not be to the advantage only of those who desired a good that would not otherwise be produced. Such economies might also permit the increased differentiation of products within an industrial sector as producers are able to secure sufficient levels of production, and attendant economies of scale, for more specialized versions of the good. The effect of such differentiation of products should be the greater satisfaction of the particular desires of a larger number of consumers. The clear possibility of such effects indicates that some international trade may well be highly desirable. The argument in this volume is not, therefore, against international trade itself, but about the extent of that trade and the conditions under which it might best take place.

Analytically, liberal theory life purports to identify the powerful mechanisms that underlie and direct economic life—mechanisms, moreover, which will ensure the greatest well-being of all if left to operate unhindered. A number of the processes highlighted by the liberal approach do, certainly, play an important role in many aspects of economic life. However, their centrality is rather more open to question. Moreover, many of the basic assumptions of liberal economic theory are unsound, and many of its purported conclusions are essentially insecure. To differentiate between the fanciful and the fruitful within liberal economic theory therefore requires a critical re-examination of its basic argument, and the suppositions upon which it rests.

CRITICISM OF THE LIBERAL APPROACH TO ECONOMIC LIFE

Liberal economic theory embraces a considerable range of difficulties and shortcomings. The approach rests upon a number of basic assumptions, which vary in their complexity rather than their theoretical importance. Many of these assumptions subject the approach to very serious limitations or, in a significant number of cases, are simply unsound. The procedure adopted here will be to subject a range of such assumptions to critical examination, in order of ascending complexity.

Rationality
Assumptions of rationality, in one guise or another, are central to many theories of economic, social and political behaviour. The liberal approach to economic life, too, is founded upon an assumption of rationality, but rationality defined in such a way as to create serious problems for the realism of the resulting theory.

The question with rationality is that of the range of possibilities to be included within, or excluded from, its purview. Range, here, affects the linked issues of the manageability of the analytical task that is being undertaken and the predictive power of the resultant theory.

If any, and all, purposes of human beings are to be accommodated it becomes possible, though not necessary, for any human action whatsoever to be deemed rational. Such a possibility is sometimes accepted, albeit briefly, in textbook outlines of liberal economic theory but it cannot long be tolerated for it traps the approach in endless tautology: rational behaviour is anything that the individual believes will best serve his, or her, purely personal desires; and actual behaviour, which is not clearly chaotic, is then rational because it reflects what each individual thought would best serve his, or her, personal desires. Such an approach to rationality would render liberal economic theory quite unable to make the kinds of judgements about behaviour to which it aspires.

A definition of rational action that accommodates any and

all human purposes compounds the basic issue of the predictability of human behaviour. No theory of human activity can entirely escape the problem that perfect prediction of individual behaviour requires full knowledge of all the individual's desires, perceptions and understandings that are pertinent to the potential form of behaviour. However the wider the range of desires, relevant perceptions and understandings the more intractable are the problems of confident prediction. Moreover, the wider the range of the behavioural influences that are permitted, the wider is the range of variation in individual behaviour that will have to be accepted. Claims that individual differences disappear in the aggregate will thus become increasingly strained as the range of accepted influences widens.

Liberal economic theory substantially restricts the definition of rationality in its attempt to combat the problems of tautology and manageability to those human purposes that can be realized through economic exchanges: that is, explicit exchanges of given goods and services for other goods and services whether directly, or indirectly through the use of money. In practice, liberal analysis is also much aided by a pragmatic emphasis upon those economic exchanges that involve money. Money is not merely a medium through which exchanges take place and a store of wealth, but is also, and most significantly, a standard measure of value and quantitative measurement. The advance of quantitative studies of modern economic activity has been particularly aided by this rather convenient restriction upon the range of empirical interest and research.

It is important to acknowledge, at this stage of the discussion, that the explicit, and extreme, restriction of purview is wholly legitimate for any social science. The adoption of a clear, albeit narrow, set of initial assumptions is invaluable if an orderly approach to a complex and problematical realm of human activity is to be sustained. Indeed, much can be gained from the development of restrictive, arbitrary and highly formalized models of reality—heuristic models. The internal dynamics of these models can be subjected to detailed investigation and their analytical implications subsequently checked against reality. Such a technique is particularly valuable for exploring the full implications of assumptions which have been made but which might not, otherwise, be fully tested. Alternative visions of reality, or of the forces underlying apparent reality, can also be investigated through such models. The danger of such models and procedures, however, lies in the possible confusion of the model with reality: of trying to force a messy and intractable reality into conformity with an intellectually more satisfying vision.

In the case of liberal economic theory's treatment of rationality, the substantial restriction of those human purposes that can be accommodated is such as to cut the theory off from a major part of that reality which impinges upon, if not actually characterizes, the 'economic'. Worse, in the hands of committed acolytes, such a restrictive approach to 'rationality' soon transforms itself into an implicit illegitimization of all those human purposes that 'threaten' to interfere with the realization of economic rationality. An acknowledged simplification of reality has thus metamorphosed into a critique of reality: Frankenstein's monster, instead of being an extremely poor imitation of a human being, has become the mould for future generations!

In the contrary direction to that of an unduly restrictive conception of rationality, neo-classical 'supply-side' economists have now become enamoured of the concept of 'rational expectations'.[13] This 'catch-all' analytical convenience has served to rationalize many of the observed departures between real developments and the expectations generated by earlier formulations of neo-classical economic theory, including 'monetarism'.

Liberal economic theory's treatment of rationality has been discussed at some length and in some detail both because it is central to the liberal analysis and because its precise nature, and implications, will often be lost upon the unprepared reader. Some of the other assumptions of the liberal model of a well-functioning, competitive, free-market economy are equally basic, but unrealistic and even absurd.

Prominent amongst the assumptions that are central to the liberal economic model are many which, in Charles Kindleberger's trenchant terms, remain 'heroic and unrealis-

tic'.[14] These include: perfect information; perfect competition, including the absence of monopolies, oligopolies,
barriers to entry and the free movement of all mobile factors
of production; a generally equal distribution of wealth and
income; the reality of general equilibrium, whether manifest
or underlying, and the attainability of relative stability within
the empirical economy; and the absence of uncompensatable
negative externalities, paradoxes of rationality and zero-sum
features within the economic realm. It is to such assumptions
that the discussion is now addressed.

Perfect Information

If the promises of the liberal economic model are to be
fulfilled then actors must be equipped with perfect information. Rationality, in liberal economics, is not just a matter
of trying one's best when making decisions; choices must be
correct at all stages. Unless consumers and producers are
fully aware of all the economic possibilities that are open to
them, and of all the consequences of any course of economic
activity that they may take, they will not be able to choose
rationally. Consumers will fail to secure the highest possible
level of satisfaction if inadequate information denies them
the ability to determine their consumption patterns rationally. Consumers will also fail to maximize their satisfactions if
they are prevented from developing an awareness of their
'real' needs and wants: a suppression of true 'consumer
sovereignty'.[15]

Producers will fail to supply that range of goods and
services that are most wanted by consumers if they, in turn,
are unable to make rational decisions about the allocation of
their productive resources. Liberal economic theory's
promise, that a *laissez-faire* economic system will deliver the
maximum level of consumer satisfaction and the optimal
allocation of productive resources, is thus dependent upon
the availability of perfect information to all those involved.

Perfect information may be a central requirement of the
liberal economic model: it remains patently absurd,
however, under all but the most exceptional of circumstances. In the modern, complex economy the range of
potentially pertinent information that confronts the potential

consumer or producer is enormous. Moreover, the individual would probably find such a range of information intellectually unmanageable. Most actors for most of the time are, however, denied access to anything approaching comprehensive information. Information may be located at a distance or remain technically incomprehensible when obtainable. Much pertinent information is, and always has been, kept secret. Most significantly, the information that is often decisive in determining whether an economic choice ultimately proves 'rational' is information about future conditions. Unfortunately perfect information about the future is intrinsically unobtainable. Liberal economic theory is thus confronted by a fundamental problem, a point which will be taken up again later in the discussion.

Perfect Competition
Pefect competition is also essential to the liberal economic model. If prohibitive obstacles confront those who might be able to sell goods and services at the lowest possible cost then inefficient producers wil continue to operate in the marketplace. The higher prices charged by inefficient producers reduce the purchases that consumers can make of other goods and services and hence reduce their general level of satisfaction. Reduced purchases of these other goods and services will lead to a lower than optimal allocation of resources to their production. The excessive use of productive resources by inefficient producers is thus matched by the under-use of resources by producers of other goods and services and a net mis-allocation of productive resources is thus engendered (mis-allocation, that is, relative to the allocation of resources that would occur when all production was as efficient (and cheap) as possible).

Barriers to Entry
Such a mis-allocation of productive resources through inefficient production can be corrected, within a liberal world, only through the emergence of more competitive producers who use resources more efficiently and are thence able to reduce market prices. If the emergence of such efficient competitors is blocked then the economic system will remain

inefficient and fail to generate both the optimal allocation of productive resources and the maximum possible level of consumer satisfaction. Unfortunately, the real world is beset with myriad obstacles to the emergence of more competitive producers within many industries.

One of the more obvious problems facing a potential producer, and one which illustrates the interrelated character of the basic assumptions of liberal economic theory, is that of information. Successful entry into an industry requires a range of information about technical possibilities, support facilities, outlets and market conditions, both current and future, that is both extensive and extremely difficult, indeed often impossible, to obtain.

The capacity to secure appropriate levels of financial capital is also a serious consideration for the would-be producer in the real world. Here again, the many failings of capital markets may seriously inhibit the prospects of those new entrepreneurs who might, if suitably supported, make a substantial mark upon an industry or even create a new industry. Those who are responsible for determining investments or authorizing loans may lack suitable technical knowledge and understanding, be insufficiently aware of market opportunities, or by unduly averse to exposure to risk.

Intentional barriers to entry may also confront potential producers with overwhelming obstacles. Such barriers may be created by other producers, major purchasers (like large retail chains) or governmental and quasi-governmental authorities. The range of motives for erecting such barriers may range from pure greed through to quite proper concerns for the safety of consumers, the protection of the environment or the maintenance of national security.

Factor Mobility

One special condition of a properly functioning competitive economic system is the full *mobility of factors of production*. If the most suitable equipment, skills or labour force cannot be brought to those places at which some form of production might best be undertaken then inefficiency will result. The cost of production will thus be higher where the introduction of the appropriate factors of production is obstructed: inefficient procedures will persist and artificially scarce factors of production will receive unduly high financial rewards (or, in the jargon, rents). This applies as much to the movement of human labour as it does to any other factor of production. It is interesting to note, however, that few but the most dedicated of academic liberal economists are prepared to advocate the completely uncontrolled movement of people in the modern world: those governments that profess the greatest dedication to free-market principles almost invariably fall at this particular fence and are often to be found amongst the most vigorous opponents of immigration, particularly of low-cost labour!

Monopoly and Oligopoly

Whatever the sources of the obstacles that confront the would-be entrant into an industry, or the expanding established producer, they have a number of effects. Inefficient producers may be protected, as has been suggested above. In many cases, barriers to entry may serve to protect one or more firms that have secured a dominant place in the market for a given good or service: a monopoly or an oligopoly. Such firms are able to set market prices rather than being forced to accept whatever price the market determines. Common sense, and a wealth of historical evidence, suggests that such positions of market dominance are often abused, with supply and price being manipulated to the considerable advantage of the firm(s) involved. Indeed, in the case of pure monopoly, analysis demonstrates that it is economically rational for the monopolist to sell less of its good or service at a higher price than would obtain in a competitive market.[16] Unfortunately, when monopolists then act rationally they do so at the expense of the maximization of consumer satisfaction and the optimal use of productive resources.

The case of oligopolies is even more problematical for the liberal economic model. The problem here is that oligopolists are faced with a choice between two alternatives. The first choice is to collaborate with the other oligopolists to form a cartel which will act, in effect, like a monopolist, securing higher prices for a lower level of production and sales. This choice is attractive for it offers the oligopolist the combination of a relatively quiet life and higher profits per unit of output than would be obtained in a competitive market. However, the market share of each oligopolist will have to remain more-or-less constant for such a cartel to remain stable. Unfortunately, dissatisfaction with current market share, or concern over some gradual fall in sales, may tempt the oligopolist towards the second option—that of precipitating a competitive struggle.[17] Such struggles between oligopolists will be both uncomfortable and costly but may bring considerable rewards as enhanced market shares are captured.

The problem for liberal economic theory is that it is quite unable to specify whether oligopolists will, in general, cohere or cleave. Worse, whatever their behaviour, it is likely that the long-run effect will be to the consumers' disadvantage for a cartel will maintain higher prices and lower levels of supply while a competitive struggle may eventually result in either a restored cartel or an actual monopoly. It is possible that an oligopoly could sustain perpetual competition, and hence price or quality benefits to consumers, but the historical evidence would suggest that a mixed pattern of successive collaboration and competition is more probable.

The capacity of producers to deploy their resources in such a way as to ensure the maximization of aggregate satisfaction of consumers will also be dependent upon a number of conditions. The earlier discussion of rationality has already implied that the only satisfactions that can be accommodated within the liberal economic model, and hence maximized, are those that can be secured through market exchanges. This is a clear, and major, limitation upon the purview of the model. However, difficulties are also created by the two loosely related issues of income distribution and human homogeneity.

The Distribution of Wealth and Income

One of the conventional, and generally quite valid, defences of a liberal economic system is its capacity to respond to, and satisfy, a wide range of differences of individual want, taste and preference. However, a society will be able to satisfy the existing pattern of human needs and wants maximally only if all the members of that society have an equal opportunity to express their needs and wants in the market-place. Many ordinary mortals have long suspected that the losses of satisfaction of those who have lower levels of income and wealth, and who are therefore able to purchase less, exceed the extra satisfaction secured from the additional purchases of goods and services by those who are wealthier. A central concept of modern economics—that of marginal utility—comes to the aid of common sense on this potentially sensitive point.

Liberal economic theory holds that, in general, the utility (or benefit) secured from the consumption of any good or service *declines* as more is consumed. The other side of this proposition is that as consumption of any good or service declines the loss of utility (or benefit) will increase progressively. Thus, for the glutton, the benefit secured from an additional potato will be vanishingly small while removing one potato from a pauper will produce an enormous loss of benefit for that unhappy individual. The argument that is here applied to one basic food can equally be applied to the entire range of goods and services that individuals consume and it implies that the lesser satisfactions of the rich are secured at the expense of the considerable losses of satisfaction of the poor.

Many liberals are good defenders of the economic status quo within the richer, *laissez-faire* economies and would not be happy with a notion of marginal utility that condemned substantial inequalities of income and wealth distribution. One defence of such inequalities rests upon what has become known as 'supply-side' economics. Here it is contended that incentives for entrepreneurs are essential for the efforts and investment that are necessary for economic growth and, ultimately, general benefit. If increased inequalities in income and wealth are necessary in the short term, it may well be that income and wealth will become more evenly distributed as the fruits of economic growth are eventually harvested.[18]

A second avenue of escape from the difficulty of inequalities of income and wealth is to introduce the argument that human beings are substantially heterogeneous: that they are different not only in what they wish to consume but also in the level of satisfaction that they are capable of deriving from various levels and patterns of consumption. This view reduces, essentially, to the proposition that substantial inequalities of purchasing power are acceptable because the marginal benefit actually derived by an extremely wealthy individual from the consumption of, say, a tin of caviar is sufficiently high to at least balance the considerable loss of benefit suffered by the denial to a starving individual of such basic items as a potato or a bread roll.

The assumption of heterogeneous humanity may be convenient for politically conservative liberal economists but it is a departure that generates its own difficulties for the liberal economic model. The problem here is that an economic system that contains people with substantially different wishes may well fail to respond adequately to the entire range of needs and wants. Some needs and wants may be confined to a very few people or may be extremely expensive to satisfy.

Even with a relatively equal distribution of income and wealth, those who have these problematic needs and wants may be unable to mobilize enough effective demand in the market to generate a sufficient level of supply. With a substantially unequal distribution of income and wealth, such goods and services may be those desired by the relatively poor rather than the somewhat more wealthy. If those who want the goods and services in question desire them intensely then it is probable that the system's failure to satisfy them will result in an overall loss of satisfaction, for the alternative goods and services that are actually produced may well provide lower levels of satisfaction to their consumers. Thus, an economic system's satisfaction of one individual's wish for headache tablets is unlikely to offset the loss to another individual who requires an extremely expensive drug in order to control an ailment which is fatal but which is insufficiently common to 'justify' the costs of production.

The central significance of the points that have been made about the unsound basic assumptions of liberal economic theory, and their many implications, is that the criticisms all indicate many of the ways in which a *laissez-faire* system may, in practice, fail to deliver its promise of a maximization of satisfactions and welfare for all the members of an economic community. However, even were the basic assumptions to prove sound, it would still be necessary for the economic system to be able to generate a pattern of general balance, between demand and supply for all goods and services, for welfare to be maximized. The idea of *general equilibrium* thus assumes a position of central importance within modern liberal economic theory and within that form which has become known as neo-classical economic theory.[19]

The notion of general equilibrium carries, as will be seen, a number of important implications. It is to be seen as something as quite different, qualitatively, from the idea of a multiplicity of states of *partial equilibrium*. This lesser condition is quite unexceptionable. At the heart of the notion of a free market is the idea that price movements will bring supply and demand into balance, however ephemeral, and this is precisely what is implied by the term partial equilibrium. Wherever price mechanisms clear markets and leave no unsatisfied customers then partial equilibirum has been achieved, whether it be in the local vegetable market or on international money exchanges. The implications of this concept are not, however, particularly profound.

The idea of partial equilibrium has a clear connection with that of general equilibrium but in no way implies, or entails, its occurrence. Those who wish to entertain the notion of general equilibrium cannot adduce it from the existence of partial equilibria for it is entirely possible that the existence of the latter will not be accompanied by, or contribute to the development of, the former. If partial equilibria exist in half the markets within an economy, but turbulence characterizes the others, then the equilibria of the former will not, in any way, ensure general equilibrium. The idea of general equilibrium must, therefore, be based upon considerations other than the mere existence, at times, of some instances of partial equilibrium.

The Methodology of Comparative Statics
The idea of general equilibrium in neo-classical economic theory is of particularly interest, for it is both a logical

implication of the functioning of a *laissez-faire* economic system, as envisaged by liberal economic theory, and a necessary assumption of the proposition that such a system will deliver welfare maximization. It is, moreover, the one concept that pinpoints one of the fundamental methodological weaknesses of modern liberal and neo-classical economic theory. The most acceptable (though by no means the only) notion of a condition of general equilibrium is one that can apply only to an economy that is at rest: an economy that is static and unchanging. Indeed, the notion of static conditions is entirely consonant with neo-classical economic analysis in which the basic propositions are illustrated by comparing some prior situation with the more desirable situation that may be achieved once the system, or some component part, has been subject to the beneficent influences of free-market economic processes. This approach is the methodology of *comparative statics*.[20]

Analysis which is conducted upon the basis of comparative statics, whether within economics or elsewhere in the social sciences, has certain characteristics. The sources of change are hypothesized from the theoretical framework of the analysis rather than identified through the study of the real world. The processes of change are largely ignored and are certainly not discovered through empirical investigation. In the case of neo-classical economics the costs of change—adjustment, in the technical language—are ignored, for, as will be seen, the methodology allows them to be assumed away. Finally, time is a non-dimension: it is simply not present in a form of analysis which is necessarily timeless.[21]

The development of this criticism of the concept of general equilibrium and of the methodology of comparative statics is necessarily delicate and difficult for it would be absurd to imply that practising economists are actually silly enough to believe that the world can ever be static. It will, however, be argued that the basic set of ideas with which many liberal economists (and particularly neo-classicists) operate reduce to a model which does require just such an assumption. Moreover, it will be suggested that many propositions about economic policy also rest upon such an heroically unrealistic, but usually latent, assumption.

The point can be illustrated best by considering the possibility that the real economy is in constant and substantial movement, indeed of considerable turbulence. If it is assumed that all changes of productive activity involve some identifiable costs to those involved in production—the scrapping of old equipment, the purchase of new capital, the retraining of personnel, the mental effort involved in developing and marketing new products—then the economy as a whole will be benefited only if the post-adjustment improvements to consumer satisfaction and/or producers' profits and wages exceed those costs. In a world of extreme turbulence and constant change, it is possible that there will be insufficient time during which to market the new products and hence recoup the costs incurred. Adjustment in such circumstances would not be justified and would, indeed, be economically irrational (costs exceeding benefits achieved).

The example considered above is, admittedly, extreme. However, once continuous change is admitted, the relationship between the costs of adjustment in patterns of production and the subsequent benefits becomes an uncertain matter. It can no longer be assumed that the benefits will exceed the costs and, indeed, the outcome may well be unfavourable. There is certainly nothing within neo-classical economic theory that permits the logical deduction that benefits will exceed costs under such conditions, and this is serious for an approach that prides itself upon its deductive logic. Indeed, any assertions that ultimate benefits will, in fact, exceed the costs of adjustment are either pure acts of faith or based upon the examination of particular empirical conditions (rather than theoretical analysis).

Only if the resulting condition is assumed to be static can neo-classical economic theory prove, *deductively*, that the benefits of adjustment must exceed costs. Put very simply, a static condition can be assumed to be unchanging *indefinitely*. If a post-adjustment condition generates any benefit, when compared with the pre-adjustment condition, then *any* level of adjustment costs will be covered *eventually*.

The problem of adjustment in a turbulent environment may be illustrated with a simple example. The targeting of field artillery against a fortress may be compared with the problems of firing at fast-flying aircraft and even of engaging in an aerial 'dogfight'. When firing a fixed gun against a fixed target it can be assumed that once appropriate adjustments of aim and range have been made that, ammunition remaining plentiful and other conditions remaining constant, successful shots can be made indefinitely and the efforts made in adjusting aim and range rewarded with the eventual destruction of the fortress. In the case of fast-flying aircraft, the ground-based artillery may make any number of adjustments of aim and range without any guarantee of a successful hit, and success in one hit does little to assure success with subsequent shots. Vast quantities of ammunition may thus be used to little practical effect and prodigious adjustment efforts wasted. In the case of an aerial 'dogfight', the fact that both the target and one's own guns are in constant motion gives rise to the possibility that not only will the target succeed in evading even the best-aimed shots but that one's own flying manoeuvres will actually contribute to missing the target.[22]

The appropriate analogies for the world of real economic activity are those of firing at a fast-flying target or even of engaging in an aerial 'dogfight', whereby one's own best efforts may actually contribute to a 'miss'. Unfortunately, neo-classical economic theory is necessarily constrained to the analogy of the fixed gun firing at the fixed target.

It would, however, be erroneous to assume that general equilibrium is always treated as a static condition that actually manifest itself in the real world. Sophisticated liberal economists clearly recognize the dynamism that is inherent in contemporary economic reality and the implications that this has for theory. General equilibrium therefore has to assume a different, more interesting, but yet more problematical form for such theorists. Rather than presuming a static and actual condition, general equilibrium is now seen to be a tendency, underlying reality. The complex and multifaceted developments apparent in everyday reality are held to be drawn towards this underlying tendency by the processes that are endemic to a *laissez-faire* economic system. The condition of general equilibrium is never achieved but, to the extent that it is approximated, the general welfare is enhanced.

The notion of general equilibrium as an underlying tendency within a laissez-faire economic system certainly avoids the difficulties posed by a conception of this condition as static and actual. However, it draws liberal economic theory onto ever more rocky shores, for it commits it to an epistemology from which many liberal theorists would recoil in horror once aware of its implications. The problem here is that the notion of general equilibrium as an underlying trend in economic reality is to treat general equilibrium as a *non-observable*, but central, feature of, or force within, reality. Something has now been given a central place in liberal economic theory which is not directly amenable to the senses but can be adduced only from a theory which is applied to that reality and which can only be identified indirectly through its purported empirical effects. It is, in other words, not an empirical concept and not amenable to simple empirical verification or falsification.

Such a concept of general equilibrium violates a basic tenet of that positivist epistemology and 'scientific' procedure to which some liberal economists lay such claim. Indeed, liberal economics now falls firmly into the 'realist' school of epistemology.[23] Thus, by adopting an underlying tendency view of general equilibrium liberal economics finds itself sharing with Marxist economics one of those features of the latter which liberal economists are so often keen to criticize.

Whatever the epistemological inclinations of liberal economists, it remains clear that *relative stability* has to be assumed in the economic system if claims that the benefits of adjustment will justify the costs are to be made with any confidence. Such claims can, however, be no more than presumptions and, in the increasingly turbulent world economy now experienced, they increasingly assume the appearance of simple blind faith.

Comparative Advantage and Factor Endowments

The dynamic that underlies the supposed tendency towards general equilibrium within the global economy is, as has been indicated, a manifestation of the principle of *Comparative Advantage*. However, this principle also encounters some serious analytical difficulties. In its contemporary form, as developed by Eli Heckscher and Bertil Ohlin, Comparative Advantage is held to underlie patterns of international economic specialization and trade. Such Comparative Advantage is, in turn, held to rest upon varying patterns of Factor Endowment. Thus, societies are differentially endowed with natural resources, geographical and climatic conditions, capital and skills. They will then tend to specialize in, and export, those goods and services which require greater quantities of those factors of production with which each society is relatively well endowed. Equally, societies will tend to import those goods and services which involve intensive applications of factors of production with which they are poorly endowed.[24]

The need for Heckscher and Ohlin's addition of the notion of Factor Endowments to the principle of Comparative Advantage arose from the tautological character of the original concept. The problem was that Comparative Advantage was supposed to account for observable patterns of specialization and trade, in which societies exported those goods in which they were internationally competitive (for whatever reason) and imported those in which they were internationally uncompetitive. However, the only practical way of establishing the existence of Comparative Advantage was to observe the patterns of competitiveness and trade that actually appeared in practice. Thus it was that explanation was offered in terms of something (Comparative Advantage), the existence of which could be established only by reference to the occurrence of the thing that it was trying to explain (a competitive position internationally). To the question—'What makes a society competitive?'—the principle of Comparative Advantage would have to answer—'The possession of Comparative Advantage'. To the subsequent question—'How do you know that you have a Comparative Advantage?'—the answer would have to be—'When you find that you are competitive internationally'.

The circularity inherent in this outline of Comparative Advantage clearly raises considerable doubts about its analytical and empirical utility. There are two possible avenues of escape from this miasma of tautology. The first is too resort to the kind of 'realist' epistemology that has been discussed earlier in this chapter. It would be valid, within such an approach, to argue that Comparative Advantage constitutes an underlying, non-observable factor within a *laissez-faire* global economy which exerts an influence upon developments, and is partially, but only partially, reflected in any specific patterns of competitiveness that emerge.

Treating Comparative Advantage as a non-observable within a 'realist' approach to economics is not, however, the way in which the concept is normally treated in liberal economics, nor does it tally with the positivist dispositions of many liberal economists. Developing the principle of Comparative Advantage with the idea of differing Factor Endowments appeared, therefore, to offer the most promising avenue of escape from simple tautology. However, while the Heckscher–Ohlin principle of Factor Endowments clearly enhances the original principle, it does not resolve all the difficulties.

The first difficulty with the principle of Factor Endowments reflects the variety of means through which many goods and services may be produced and brought to the consumer. Quite different mixes of the factors of production may be employed equally effectively in the production of any one good or service: one society may employ considerable quantities of machinery in its farming and relatively little human labour; another, in direct contrast, might employ very little agricultural equipment but large numbers of farm workers. What determines the relative competitiveness of the two societies in international markets for agricultural products then will not be their relative endowments of various factors of production but the costs of those factors individually and the combinations required for agricultural production within the two systems. The equation still reduces, therefore, to the unremarkable proposition that a society will be more competitive in producing and trading any good or service if it can bring it to the market at a lower price than its competitors.

The illusory promise of the doctrine of Comparative Advantage, even when enhanced by the Heckscher–Ohlin principle, is more sharply exposed when questions are posed about the nature and origins of those suitable endowments of factors of production that generate Comparative Advantage and, hence, the possibilities of international competitiveness. It is clear that there are some relatively immutable endowments, of geography, resource and climate, that furnish some societies with considerable advantages. Possession of certain scare resources equips a society with an *Absolute Advantage*. Possession of particularly fertile land or an appropriate climate provides some societies with advantages in aspects of agricultural production that come close to being absolute. Thus, while pineapples can be grown in Great Britain they can be done so only under such demanding and expensive conditions as to render it no more than common sense to 'surrender' the pineapple-growing business to societies in which their growth barely requires encouragement.

Byond a number of rather obvious, and largely nature-given, conditions the problem for the doctrine of Comparative Advantage is that the overwhelming majority of the pertinent factors of production are man-made. Capital equipment is manufactured and accumulated by human beings. The economic infrastructure is developed and sustained by human beings. Skills, techniques, knowledge and specific competences are developed, acquired and transmitted by human beings. Those attitudes and values that are germane to the process of economic production are also generated, and transmitted from generation to generation, within human societies. Not only are such central elements created by human beings, they are also far from unchanging or unchangeable.

If endowments with factors of production were given for all time, or even for relatively long periods of time, then the analytical framework within which many modern liberal economists work might have something useful to say about the patterns of economic development to which societies would be best advised to direct themselves. However, many societies have demonstrated the extent to which Factor Endowments can be entirely transformed by human effort and, quite frequently, the direction of their governments. The most careful examination of any society's current pattern of Factor Endowment will do little, therefore, than to

establish one or two of the more obvious considerations and
limitations, the identification of which has never previously
required any study, whatsoever, of economic theory. The
concepts of Comparative Advantage cannot transcend this
fundamental weakness, however, for it is rooted in a
methodology which acts as an intellectual barrier to detailed
consideration of the issues of fundamental, and continuous,
change and development.

The problems with the doctrines of Comparative Advantage and Factor Endowments can thus be illustrated by the
imaginary example of the modern, liberal economist who is
transported in time and place to mid-nineteenth-century
Japan. What, on the basis of modern trade theory, would our
worthy economist recommend, or even expect: a future of
even greater specialization in in-shore fishing, rice growing,
fan manufacture, wood carvings, formalized art and an
interesting sideline in fearsome weaponry?

It is the poverty of much of modern liberal economics, and
of neo-classical theory in particular, on the issues of
economic growth and development that marks one of its
more serious shortcomings. Many of the most cogent critics
focus upon this issue, whether the critics be of a Marxist
persuasion[25] or advocates, like Professor David Simpson,[26]
of the virtues of earlier classical liberal economic theory and
analysis.

There are a number of additional conditions which must be
satisfied if the liberal order's promise of maximizing aggregate welfare is to be realized. These conditions are: that
unfettered economic activity does not generate detrimental,
negative externalities for self or others; that there are no
paradoxes of rationality arising from the basic notion of
rational economic activity itself; and, finally, that there are
no other *zero-sum features* attendant upon economic activity
and economic interaction. Unfortunately, there are powerful
arguments that seek to establish that *laissez-faire* economic
activity does, indeed, generate substantial negative
externalities; that serious paradoxes of rationality arise in
economic behaviour, with the effect of significantly reducing
general welfare; and that zero-sum difficulties are relatively
common.

Negative Externalities

It is relatively common for the economic activity of some to generate negative externalities for others. Noise, pollution and general loss of amenity may be imposed upon some by others who are engaged in self-regarding economic behaviour. Such negative externalities may, in principle, be compensated by those who generate them but there is no guarantee that such compensation will be forthcoming unless pressure can be exerted by the victims or by authorities that are prepared to act in their defence. However, where compensation is offered, and is adequate, it will ensure that the benefits of the economic activity that produces negative externalities will be shared fairly between those who have incurred relevant costs.

In the real world there may, however, be many negative externalities which are of such a form as to defy any real restitution. If the environment is irretrievably polluted then no financial settlements between individuals, firms or societies will compensate humanity. Nothing within a purely *laissez-faire* economic system allows such uncompensatable negative externalities to be identified or dealt with. It is possible that the very privatization of purposes and practices, enshrined in liberal economic theory, will encourage a short-term, self-regarding outlook that militates positively against any serious concern with those general losses that are generated.[27] Indeed, as will be argued shortly, a serious paradox of rationality arises on just such issues of economic activity.

Paradoxes of Rationality and Collective Goods

Many situations may generate serious paradoxes of rational action. Rational economic decision making, for instance, requires the possession of comprehensive information. However, the acquisition of information is a costly and time-consuming business. In practice, therefore, it might well be that the costs of acquiring extra information exceed the benefits that such additional information produces for the quality of the decision made. To seek additional information under such circumstances would therefore be economically irrational for costs would exceed benefits. Unfortunately, it may also be unclear, in many real world situations, whether

extra information would, or would not, make a significant
contribution to the quality of decision. Such complications
and uncertainties are just the stuff of the real world that the
basic propositions of liberal economic theory assume away!

Some of the most serious paradoxes of rationality also arise
in the realm of *collective goods*.[28] Economic analysis usually
distinguishes between two kinds of goods or services: private
goods and collective goods. Private goods can be consumed
on a purely individual basis. An ice-cream may be purchased
individually and consumed individually with no other person
allowed to share in its enjoyment. Many private goods can
also be produced and supplied on a highly variable basis, to
meet the varying levels of demand that develop at various
times. The quantities of ice-cream produced may thus be
varied relatively easily and speedily.

Collective goods are quite different phenomena to private
goods. Their essential characteristics are non-excludability
and indivisibility: once such collective goods are produced in,
or supplied for, a community it is all but impossible to
exclude any member of that community from enjoying the
benefits of that collective good or to vary the quantity of
benefit obtained by any individual. Denial of benefits to
individuals is possible only by their exclusion from the
community. The maintenance of a deterrent against
aggression by other states provides a collective good for all its
citizens and does so on non-excludable and indivisible basis.

Collective goods may be differentiated on a number of
other grounds. However, non-excludability and indivisibility
are their definitive characteristics. The interesting situation
that may then be considered is one in which the provision of
such a collective good requires voluntary contributions from
the members of a community. The problem that arises here is
that it may well be rational for any given member of that
community to withhold his, or her, contribution in the hope
that the contributions of others will be sufficient to generate
the collective good. It is important to note here that the
benefit that the individual gains from the provision of the
collective good exceeds the value of that individual's contribution to the provision of the collective good. However the
opportunity of obtaining a 'free ride' allows the individual to

benefit from the collective good without sharing in the cost of its provision and this is clearly a better cost–benefit outcome than that in which the individual does make a costly contribution.[29]

If 'free riding' was practised by only one member of, or a small group within, a community its effects would be morally regretable but might not, in all probability, prove practically disasterous. There are, however, other features of collective goods, and the impact of 'free riding', that render the matter of great practical consequence. The first, and critical, problem is that liberal economic theory is based upon the assumption that everyone is similarly rational. Thus, if it is rational for one member of an economic community to 'free ride' it is equally rational for all others to 'free ride'. If all attempt to 'free ride' then there will be no contributions and no collective goods (or rides), free or otherwise.

Thus the very principles of economic rationality dictate that individuals who seek to improve their cost–benefit outcomes by 'free riding' on the contributions others make for collective goods end up by denying the benefits of those collective goods to all concerned. Unfortunately, an awareness of the possibilities of 'free riding' will undermine the inclinations to make contributions by those who experience some persisting disposition to contribute. Such 'angels' will be faced with the possibility that there will be insufficient total contributions to generate the desired collective good and that their own contributions will therefore prove fruitless. Worse still, it might be difficult, if not impossible, to recover the futile contributions that have been made. Volunteers who go out at night to mend a failing sea-wall, but who find that they have done so in inadequate numbers, will not be able to recoup their efforts when the sea eventually overwhelms the defences. It is quite irrational, by the tenets of economic rationality, to incur costs without attendant benefits. The risk of such an outcome will, therefore, merely reinforce other temptations to withhold costly contributions to the provision of collective goods, whatever their intrinsic desirability.

Those who are familiar with formal game theory will recognize the parallel between the Prisoner's Dilemma, 'free-riding' calculations and the defensive withholding of contributions. The normal outcome of such conditions will also be familiar; that of generating a mutually disadvantageous outcome in which all are denied a benefit that would have been secured had all acted in an appropriate manner.

The real world provides a mixed picture of success and failure of cooperation. Two keys to successful cooperation are suggested by the analysis of collective action. The first is that special condition in which narrow calculations of self-interest actually do encourage all economically rational actors to make their costly contributions to the provision of collective goods. This situation obtains when each such individual is convinced that his, or her, contribution is marginally decisive: that if the contribution is not made there will be insufficient contributions, overall, to bring the collective good into being but that if the contribution is made there will be just sufficient contributions, with no significant surplus.

The decision that the individual has to make under such conditions is now identical to a choice to purchase a private good: if the contribution is made the collective good is created and a net benefit enjoyed; if the contribution is not made there will be no collective good and a net benefit will have been forgone. There is no opportunity to 'free ride' successfully in this situation. In the absence of an alternative use of the contribution, which would bring higher benefits, it is economically rational for the individual to contribute and thereby secure the benefit of the collective good.[30]

The difficulty with such a solution to the problem of 'free riding' is that every one of those who have to contribute, to bring total contributions up to a suitable level, has to be equally and simultaneously convinced that their contribution is marginally decisive. This is a serious socio-psychological problem to which formal logic has nothing to contribute. Logic indicates that the nature and size of the relevant community has no effect upon the nature of the decisional dilemma. Real world considerations, however, suggest that the nature and size of a group, or community, will be decisive in establishing the pattern of 'inter-subjectivity' that is necessary to secure sufficient contributions.

The second key to the solution of 'free-rider' problems is provided by an examination of those other conditions which might, if present, counteract such mutually damaging tendencies. These counterveiling conditions amount, in effect, to sources of *associated costs and benefits*: associated in that these costs or benefits arise in consequence of making, or withholding, contributions to a collective good but are not the direct benefits, or contributional costs, of that collective good itself. The strengths of these associated costs or benefits may be such as to persuade an individual to contribute to the costs of a collective good that is not actually valued (or not valued as highly as the costs contributed).

The range and sources of the associated costs and benefits that may suppress, and overwhelm, 'free-rider' tendencies is considerable. Individuals may be influenced by their concern to ensure continued membership of a valued social group to contribute to its collective undertakings. A deeply held belief or value system might emphasize the importance of making potentially costly contributions to valuable social goods, such as the patriotism that persuades so many to volunteer in time of war. In some circumstances it is possible for some actors, or agencies, to arrange for contributors to collective goods to receive 'side payments'—other rewards which are conditional upon, but additional to, the primary benefits of the collective good (as with the social and health facilities which many American trade unions offer their members, but which are additional to the unions' primary concern with conditions and pay at work).[31] Finally, contributions may be enforced by some sufficiently compelling agency, as in the case of governments that extract taxes from recalcitrant citizens.[32]

It is the range of sources of associated costs and benefits within domestic society that underlies the frequency with which successful cooperation, and contribution to collective goods, is observed at that level of human activity. At the international level the picture is far less encouraging. Some associated costs and benefits can be mobilized in the areas of limited cooperation between relatively small numbers of states, and other transnational actors, as in the cases of alliances, issue-focused 'clubs' of states, and cartels of commodity producers or distributors.

At the global level it has, unfortunately, been impossible to develop any of the sets of associated costs and benefits discussed above. Effective cooperation on matters of substance have therefore proved extremely difficult, if not impossible, and their fruits somewhat tenuous. The best efforts of many well-intentioned individuals and states, over considerable periods of time, have not succeeded in securing a significant measure of global disarmament, an effective Collective Security system, or a new and more equitable international economic order.

Zeri-Sum Features and Positional Goods

Inhabitants of the real world economy are also faced with situations in which some of their needs and wants can be satisfied only at the expense of the satisfactions of others. Zero-sum features thus arise in a number of areas of economic activity, most clearly in the realms of *positional goods*.[33] The problem with such positional goods is that part, if not the sum of their value to individuals is a direct function of their unavailability to others. Some of the more obvious positional goods—such as positions of status—are excluded from the purview of liberal economic theory by its explicit restriction of focus. They are, however, of considerable significance to some people and are matters which have an important interrelationship with many aspects of economic life.

Other positional goods, and ones which cannot be excluded from the purview of liberal economic theory, are those in which practical conditions mean that the enjoyments of some involve the denial of those enjoyments to others. In crowded communities a premium may attach to properties which have a view that does not include other property. With limited space, however, the clear views of some involve the denial of clear views to others. Indeed, in many areas such a clear view can be secured only at the expense of even more crowded living conditions, and ever more cluttered views, for others. Satisfaction of the demand for positional goods has implications for aggregate value satisfactions similar to the effects of inequalities of wealth and income.

CONCLUSIONS

The purpose of this chapter has been to demonstrate both the major strengths and weaknesses of the liberal approach to economics. An outline of the principal elements of the liberal model of competitive, free-market economic activity, both domestic and international, has, hopefully, suggested something of the appeal of this approach. It should also have indicated how liberal theory illuminates many areas of empirical reality. The criticism of the liberal approach should, however, serve to highlight the many difficulties generated by its core assumptions and basic methodology.

The basic assumptions of the liberal approach to the analysis of economics are serious simplifications of, and unsound assumptions about, important aspects of reality. Its core methodology of comparative statics is also profoundly inadequate, and seriously misleading, as a basis for analysing a dynamic and turbulent global economy. The central concept of rational action also generates paradoxes which undermine the theory's claim to prescribe arrangements that can ensure the maximization of general welfare.

The implication of this critical discussion of the liberal model is that the adoption of an alternative view of economics, and approach to economic policy, can be justified on the basis of the clear shortcomings of the liberal approach itself. It is possible to adopt an approach that is consistent with Economic Realism, or neo-mercantilism broadly defined, as a 'second-best' policy that acknowledges the perversity and mendacity of human agencies which encourages illiberal practices. However, it may equally be that human beings, and their governments, behave in ways that do not accord with liberal tenets, not because they are stupid or perverse, but because the tenets of the liberal position are themselves insecure in the ways that have been suggested in this chapter.

The arguments in the following chapters will not depend upon the argument that the liberal model is inherently flawed. The argument in favour of Economic Realism, or neo-mercantilism, can be founded equally effectively upon a theoretical criticism of the liberal approach or upon a description of prevailing realities, whatever their origin. However, it has been the purpose of this chapter to suggest that human obduracy in the face of such a compelling doctrine as liberal economic theory may not be entirely the fault of the human beings!

NOTES

1. For a brief summary *see* Andrew Gamble, 'Critical political economy', pp. 64–89 in R. J. Barry Jones (ed.), *Perspectives on Political Economy: Alternatives to the Economics of Depression*, (London: Frances Pinter, 1983).
2. *See* the contributions by R. J. Barry Jones and Richard Little in Barry Buzan and R. J. Barry Jones (eds.), *Change and the Study of International Relations: The Evaded Dimension*, (London: Frances Pinter, 1981).
3. Such changes may be undertaken somewhat less readily than might be supposed, however. *See*: T. S. Kuhn, *The Structure of Scientific Revolutions*, (Chicago: Chicago University Press, 1962); and Leon Festinger, *A Theory of Cognitive Dissonance*, (Evanston, Ill.: Row, Peterson, 1957).
4. *See* John Maclean, 'Marxist epistemology, explanations of "change" and the study of international relations', pp. 46–67 in Buzan and Jones *op. cit.*
5. *See*, for instance, the title of Richard Lipsey's famous introductory text, *An Introduction to Positive Economics*, (London: Weidenfeld and Nicolson, 1963).
6. On the nature and significance of this notion of 'general equilibrium' *see*, in particular, John Hicks, *Causality in Economics*, (Oxford: Basil Blackwell, 1979), Ch. IV; and Phyllis Dean, *The Evolution of Economic Ideas*, (Cambridge: Cambridge University Press, 1978), esp. Ch. 7; and for an interesting discussion of its current status *see* Frank Hahn, 'General equilibrum theory', in D. Bell and I. Kristol (eds.), *The Crisis in Economic Theory*, (New York: Basic Books, 1981), pp. 123–38.
7. For a general discussion *see* C. P. Kindleberger, *International Economics*, (Homewood, Ill.: Irwin, 5th edn., 1973) esp. Chs. 2, 3 and 4: and P. T. Ellsworth, *The International Economy*, (New York: Collier-Macmillan, 1964) esp. Ch. 10.
8. *See*, in particular, Paul A. Samuelson, 'International factor-price equalization once again', *The Economic Journal*, Vol. LIX, No. 234 (June, 1949), pp. 181–97 reprinted in R. E. Caves and H. G. Johnson, *Readings in International Economics*, for the American Economic Association, (London: George Allen and Unwin, 1968), pp. 58–71.

9. T. M. Rybczynski, 'Factor endowment and relative commodity prices', *Economica*, Vol. XXII, no. 84 (November, 1955), pp. 336–41, reprinted in Caves and Johnson, *op. cit.*, pp. 72–7.

10. Harry G. Johnson, 'Factor endowments, international trade and factor prices', *The Manchester School of Economics and Social Studies*, Vol. XXV, No. 3 (September, 1957), pp. 270–83, reprinted in Caves and Johnson, *op. cit.*, pp. 78–89.

11. See, Chris Edwards, *The Fragmented World: Competing Perspectives on Trade, Money and Crisis*, (London: Methuen, 1985), esp. pp. 29–38.

12. *Ibid.*; and *see also* C. P. Kindleberger, *International Economics*, (Homewood, Illinois; Richard Irwin, (5th ed.), 1973), pp. 472–3.

13. *See* Mark H. Willes, ' "Rational expectations" as a counterrevolution', in Bell and Kristol, *The Crisis in Economic Theory op. cit.* pp. 81–96; and for a surprisingly sceptical review of 'rational expectations' *see* the brief 'Expecting the future', *The Economist*, 20 October 1984, pp. 19–20.

14. C. P. Kindleberger, *Power and Money: The Politics of International Economics and the Economics of International Politics*, (New York: Basic Books, 1970), p. 19.

15. For a critique of the notion of 'consumer sovereignty', in particular, *see* S. Mohun, 'Consumer sovereignty', pp. 57–75 in F. Green and P. Nore, (eds.), *Economics: An Anti-Text*, (London: Macmillan, 1977).

16. Lipsey *op. cit.* Chs. 18 and 19; and Joan Robinson, ' "Imperfect competition" revisited', pp. 166–81, in Joan Robinson, *Contributions to Modern Economics*, (Oxford: Basil Blackwell, 1978).

17. *ibid.: see also* P. Kenyon, 'Pricing', pp. 34–45 in A. S. Eichner (ed.), *A Guide to Post-Keynsian Economics*, (London: Macmillan, 1979).

18. For some surveys of 'supply-side' economic doctrines *see* the essays by D. Regan, G. Gilder, E. Meadows, A. Lafer and G. Perry, and I. Kristol, in *Economic Impact*, No. 35 (1981/3), pp. 8–35.

19. Phyllis Deane *op cit.* Ch. 7.

20. Hicks *op. cit.* Ch. IV.

21. Many of these points are suggested by N. Kaldor in 'The irrelevance of equilibrium economics', *Economic Journal*, Vol. 82 (December 1972) pp. 1237–55.

22. Technically speaking, unsuitable, but far from impossible, 'elasticities of supply' would also produce this outcome.

23. *See* Maclean *op. cit.*

24. Kindleberger, *International Economics*, *op. cit.* Ch. 2.

25. *See*, for instance, A. Bose, *Marxian and Post-Marxian Political Economy* (New York: Monthly Review Press, 1957).

26. D. Simpson, *The Political Economy of Growth*, (Oxford: Basil Blackwell, 1983).

27. Fred Hirsch, *Social Limits to Growth*, (London: Routledge and Kegan Paul, 1977), esp. Ch. 5.

28. For a discussion of collective goods *see*: Mancur Olson, *The Logic of*

Collective Action: Public Goods and the Theory of Groups, (Cambridge: Cambridge University Press, 1965); and N. Frohlich and J. A. Oppenheimer, *Modern Political Economy*, (Englewood Cliffs: Prentice-Hall, 1978) esp. Ch. 2.

29. N. Frohlich and J. A. Oppenheimer, 'I get by with a little help from my friends', *World Politics*, Vol. 20 (1970) pp. 104–20.

30. *ibid.*

31. On such factors, *see* Olson *op. cit.*

32. *See* N. Frohlich, J. A. Oppenheimer and O. R. Young, *Political Leadership and Collective Goods*, (Princetown, NJ: Princeton University Press, 1971).

33. Hirsch *op. cit.* Ch. 3.

3   The Realist View of Economic Life and Contemporary Neo-Mercantilism

There are many views of economic life that contrast profoundly with the liberal perspective. The Marxist approach, in one variant or another, is one major alternative. The Realist view of economic life is less developed theoretically than the liberal or the Marxist approaches but remains highly significant. Realist views of economics underlie any academic studies, are reflected in the 'institutionalist' school of economic analysis and underlie many aspects of economic policy. Such a view is also essential if a neo-mercantilist approach to international economic relations is to have any coherent foundation.

At the outset it is, however, worth repeating that a Realist approach to economics does not entail the exclusion of any insights drawn from either liberal economics or Marxist economic analysis. The Realist approach is, rather, a broad-ranging and eclectic perspective developed from a number of basic propositions about human existence, the role of control and influence in human affairs, the nature and significance of communities and their cultures and, hence, the essential character of all relationships between societies, whether 'political' or 'economic'. The Realist approach also accepts that there are many, real gains to be secured from international trade, if it is conducted judiciously.

The view of Economic Realism that is to be presented in this chapter is located firmly within a tradition that has persisted throughout the late nineteenth and twentieth centuries. During the late nineteenth century, this approach towards the management of national economic and industrial policy was given its most developed expression by the

German political economist Friedrich List, in an argument that identified the central importance of industry and advocated systematic, if essentially temporary, protection for a country's infant industries. The successful promotion of national industries required, as many later writers have also argued, the preservation or development of suitable institutions and socio-economic structures.[1]

THE BASIC PROPOSITIONS OF ECONOMIC REALISM

The Realist approach does not see economic activity as separated, or fundamentally different, from other basic aspects of human existence. Rather, the economic is merely one, albeit important, facet with many features in common with the other major areas of human activity.

Individual human beings are confronted by a world of considerable turbulence and uncertainty, with attendant threats to their well-being, both physical and psychological. An orderly and happy existence is impossible under such conditions. A major priority is to bring such turbulence and uncertainty under control. Control may assume many forms and may be pursued through many means. However, it remains a fundamental human objective which must be achieved if existence is to transcend mere hand-to-mouth subsistence.[2]

The environment of each individual has human and non-human aspects, both of which may be brought under control by a variety of means. The behaviour of others can be controlled through the establishment of personal influence. Brute force might coerce others, at times, and form the basis of a crude form of power. Rarely, however, will it be possible for any individual to assert his, or her, will over others without some measure of relatively voluntary compliance. Long-standing patterns of association between human beings create the conditions of such voluntary compliance. Proven competence will be acknowledged and form the basis of purely personal authority. Established societies will often have well-developed authority roles, the incumbents of which will receive a measure of automatic deference.[3]

Societies are not, however, merely the sources and repositories of collectively acknowledged authority. Societies also generate and transmit shared patterns of understanding and shared expectations that underlie the capacities of some individuals, or groups, to establish more coercive forms of control over other members of the same society. However, the capacity for coercion may remain latent, or unused, for much of the time. Compliance, under such circumstances, is therefore based more upon perceptions of capacity for, and expectations of, coercion; such perceptions and expectations being considerably influenced by established, socially derived norms and understandings.[4]

The authority and power of individuals and sub-groups is not, however, the sole contribution of society to the generation of human control. Societies are also, themselves, extremely powerful mechanisms for collective self-control. As societies develop they establish numerous rules for, and shared expectations about, behaviour. These are embodied within the basic culture of any society and create the framework of behavioural stability within which each individual is then able to operate. Such rules and expectations are, *par excellence*, means by which the uncertainty, turbulence and threat, that would otherwise confront human beings throughout their daily lives, are reduced to manageable proportions. Indeed, much of the competition or conflict that is encountered within established societies is influenced by the basic cultural rules and understandings[5] without which such competition or conflict would soon become 'nasty, brutish and short'![6].

The constant social collaboration that is implicit in the acquisition of shared cultures is but one aspect of the extensive cooperation and coordination that is necessary between human beings. The attempt to control the non-human environment, beyond all but the most primitive levels, also required collaboration, as early man soon found when hunting, cultivating or building, and as socialist and anarchist theories have long argued.[7] However, while such human cooperation may be necessary, and even vital, it does encounter difficulties. Individuals may well wish to shirk their duty, withhold their contribution, and generally 'free ride' on the efforts of others. This, as will be seen in more detail later, may create serious problems for any collectivity. Societies have, therefore, developed suitable sanctions, culturally based prescriptive and proscriptive values and a range of 'institutions' to counter such tendencies. Government, and its associated structures of 'law and order', are outstanding examples of such institutions.[8]

Human society and culture does not, however, always conform to the cohesive picture suggested above. Three issues remain outstanding. The first problem is that modern societies have become far too complex for cultures alone to prescribe effectively for all situations. There are many areas within contemporary society, therefore, in which individuals and groups may be relatively unconstrained and able to exploit the absence of effective collective control. The second difficulty is that some societies may positively prescribe a lack of clear and strong control in some areas of activity. Individuals may thus be set free in some aspects of social and personal behaviour; individuals and groups might, for instance, be presented with an unregulated market within which to undertake aspects of their economic activity. Third, and finally, there is the serious problem posed by the multiplicity of societies in the contemporary international system and their quite apparent lack of a shared culture: a feature which forms the backdrop to much of the subsequent discussion.

THE ECONOMIC IMPLICATIONS OF THE REALIST POSITION

The primary implication of the propositions about the human condition that have here been labelled Realist is that people will organize to establish advantageous patterns of control over their environments. The scope of such organization has no logical limits but does encounter boundaries created by geography, technology, the apparent demands of certain situations and issues and, by no means least, the historical conditioning of identifiable human groups. The corollary of this proposition is that human beings can rarely, if ever, be expected to forego opportunities to preserve, or enhance, environmental control voluntarily. Roberto Michels' 'iron law of oligarchy'[9] is thus but a special case of a wider, and most powerful, drive towards organized control.

The pursuit of control may be defensive or offensive. However, the proposition that 'the best means of defence is offence' suggests that the empirical differentiation of the two modes, or motivations, is far from easy. Some individuals or groups will seek means of overcoming adverse patterns of control; others will seek to enhance favourable conditions; while yet others will pursue enhanced capabilities with which to pre-empt, or overcome, anticipated difficulties.

The conditions which will prompt individuals and groups to undertake conscious and explicit efforts to enhance their capabilities for control will also be highly variable. Cultures largely determine human purposes and goals, beyond those of basic survival. The means through which people believe that such purposes may be pursued will also be culturally defined (even to the point of excluding quite edible foods from normal consumption, as the prohibition of various meats in some cultures illustrates). Efforts to secure additional control will be prompted by the emergence of conditions, whether actual or perceived, which threaten the successful pursuit of established goals.

The security, moreover, that is pursued through the establishment of control is significantly, if not primarily, subjective. There are therefore no clear limits to the degree of control with which any individuals or groups will be content.[10] Practical calculations of the unwarranted costs of developing additional capacities for control may well exert a moderating influence but at a point which cannot be pre-determined with any analytical precision.

Culture-bearing human beings, individually and collectively, thus make judgements about tolerable levels of uncertainty, insecurity and turbulence in the environment within which they have to operate. Where acceptable levels of these disturbances are exceeded, efforts will be made to establish control. The extent of such efforts, and the resultant control, can be determined only be those who pursue such control and/or the responses of others with whom relationships exist. Thus it is that societies may well seek to preserve conditions, and associated values, in ways that reduce 'efficiency', by narrow economistic definitions, but which enhance social 'efficiency', by wider, and more valid, criteria.

The perspective outlined in the preceding sections thus reverses the view offered by conventional economic theory. The analytical presumption of liberal, and particularly neo-classical, economics, is that of the atomized individual who enters into relationships of pure exchange with others. In the world of the liberal model there are no communities, classes, trades unions, oligopolies, monopolies or multinational corporations, or none that can be identified as analytically distinct, and theoretically tolerable, phenomena. Where there is grudging recognition of such manifestations it is usually to condemn or discount them as mere aberrations.

In direct contrast to the neo-classical view, the approach developed here identifies all such 'collectivist', non-competitive, and even anti-competitive phenomena as common, natural and, indeed, a fundamental feature of all human existence, including economic activity. Whether people find themselves as consumers or producers, employees or employers, they ultimately discover the necessity for means by which uncertainty, insecurity and turbulence can be controlled. Partial organization will often suffice for such purposes, whether that partial organization be a consumers' association, trade union, cartel or monopoly.[11] Such partial efforts, however, are often insufficient to secure adequate levels of control over substantial segments of the economic environment. Activity has, therefore, to be directed at the level of a whole society.

Politics thus occupy a central place in the development of economic control. Politics are the mechanism through which wide-scale control can be achieved.[12] Political strength can, however, often be achieved only through the construction of a suitably large, or influential, coalition of those with differing, but compatible interests and concerns.[13] Governments, where they emerge, reflect such requirements and aggregations of interests. The character of individual states, again, reflects the long-term evolution of politics and government within each society: a long-term process which, moreover, is intimately involved with the development of that society's culture.

Politics, government and the state thus serve to secure a level of control sufficient to permit orderly and fruitful economic activity, in addition to the other well-established responsibilities in such areas as security and internal order. Each society, however, experiences a historical pattern of economic, political and cultural evolution which, in some highly significant respects, is unique. Political and cultural differences between societies then influence the divergent patterns of subsequent economic activity and development. Current political, governmental and cultural patterns are thus receptacles of past influences which may, or may not, be conducive to economic effectiveness in the present: peculiarities of culture and politics may thus, as is so evident in the contemporary world, facilitate or inhibit economic 'success'.

The 'institutional' framework within which economic activity takes place in any society is thus central to economic performance[14] This 'institutional' framework is wide ranging in its embrace but must be the starting point for any sensible analysis of economic activity within a society. It plays a central role in facilitating orderly economic (and social) activity, as well as constituting a definitive characteristic of a society. In a very real sense, a society's culture, political system, and economic institutions *are* its greatest reality: the sources of protection and succour for its members in the face of a turbulent, politically fragmented and often threatening world.

THE INTERNATIONAL IMPLICATIONS OF ECONOMIC REALISM

The pursuit of control over environmental uncertainty, turbulence and chronic insecurity is as compelling at the international level as it is within domestic society. The need for orderly arrangements is even acknowledged by the majority of liberal economic theorists who deem it desirable to ensure a degree of stability within international monetary markets, and agreed rules for international trade. The Bretton Woods Agreement, of 1944, to establish a new international monetary system for the post-war world and the General Agreement on Tariffs and Trade (GATT), of 1947, gave practical expression to such concerns.[15] However, many liberals are seriously restrictive in the range of such arrangements for control that they will accept as legitimate and desirable. They are also unduly optimistic in their expectations regarding the likelihood of acceptable arrangements or the incidence of conditions under which they may be introduced or maintained.

An Economic Realist perspective regards attempts to establish international control as wholly legitimate in any areas of economic life that manifest such levels of uncertainty and turbulence, actual or potential, as to undermine the well-being of the societies affected. However, Economic Realism is firmly rooted in a recognition of the fragmented character of the international political system, the self-help imperative thus engendered,[16] and, therefore, the formidable difficulties that confront efforts to establish effective cooperation between, and joint control by, nation-states in any important area of activity.

It is here, then, that the fundamental paradox of international relations, both past and present, is encountered. Much of the motivation for international collaboration derives from the need to check disruptive, self-seeking behaviour. However, the effectiveness of international collaboration is, itself, often undermined by states, individually or severally, breaking ranks to secure self-serving advantages over their erstwhile partners: a 'Catch 22' which is precisely illustrated by the Prisoner's Dilemma of formal game theory.

Much of formal game theory amounts to little more than the pursuit of sophisticated solutions to ever more complex issues, which have little if any correspondence to reality but which arise from the theory itself. The Prisoner's Dilemma, in contrast, is an extremely powerful and revealing metaphor for many serious situations in international relations and, indeed, other relationships between two or more actors. At its simplest, this 'game' replicates a situation in which two actors are faced with choices between two courses of action. The outcome for each actor depends, however, not only upon its own choice but also upon the choice that the other actor has made. It is a case, therefore, of interdependent decision making.[17]

Game theoretical analysis is conventionally undertaken with the aid of a matrix and outlined in the example of the Prisoner's Dilemma provided in Figure 3.1. The analysis is conducted in terms of the numerical values of the gains or losses that participants secure when they choose to 'play' one or two (or more) strategies. These values are arbitrarily selected by the game-theoretician in such a way as to allow the dynamics of different kinds of situations to be explored or illustrated.

		Actor A	
		Cooperate	*Defect*
Cooperate		+30 +30	+50 −50
Actor B			
Defect		−50 +50	−20 −20

Figure 3.1: an international Prisoner's Dilemma.

In the 'game' depicted in Figure 3.1, actor A and actor B both have the same choices of action—to cooperate with the other or to defect from cooperative behaviour. The options available to actor A are represented by the two columns (vertical lines) of the matrix. The options available to actor B are then represented by the two rows (horizontal lines) of the matrix. Each box of the matrix indicates what will happen in the case of each of the four possible combinations of choice of action by the two 'players'. Thus the top, left-hand box represents the result when both actor A and actor B chose to cooperate. The top, right-hand box, in contrast, represents the outcome if actor A chooses to defect from cooperation while actor B decides to continue to try to cooperate.

The outcomes—gains or losses—for the two 'players' in

this 'game' are depicted in the following manner. In each box, the figure in the top, right-hand corner is the outcome for actor A; the figure in the lower, left-hand corner is the outcome for actor B. Thus the outcomes in the top, right-hand box are +50 for actor A and −50 for actor B.

The actual outcomes indicated in the Prisoner's Dilemma are, as in all such analytical exercises, arbitrary. However, they have been chosen to illustrate the possibilities that often exist within real international relationships. In the example provided, the values have been selected to illustrate a special kind of situation. Here, both actors benefit from mutual cooperation (+30 outcome each) and, indeed, the joint outcome provides a higher level of overall benefit (+30 plus +30 = +60) than would result from any other set of choices either +50 plus −50 = 0, or −20 plus −20 = −40). Unfortunately, either actor might be tempted to try to increase its gains from +30 to +50 by defecting and giving up cooperative behaviour, while hoping that the other actor will continue to maintain a cooperative form of behaviour. Logically, however, if one actor is so tempted, then so may the other. If both actors attempt, simultaneously, to take advantage of the other by unilaterally defecting then the result will be a shift from the top, left-hand box to the lower, right-hand box in which both actors receive an outcome of −20.

The optimist might well argue that such a clearly mutually disadvantageous outcome, in which gains of +30 for both sides are converted into losses of −20 for both, should caution the 'players' against the temptation to defect from cooperative behaviour. Unfortunately, unless each actor trusts the other absolutely, each will be motivated, not so much by self-seeking greed, but by self-protective anxiety. Self-protection against the danger of seeking to cooperate while the other 'player' defects, and thus finding oneself facing the most costly outcome of −50, may be ensured only by pre-emptive defection. If this anticipatory course is adopted it is possible that an outcome of +50 will be secured, if the other 'player' continues to attempt cooperation, and the worst outcome that can be suffered, should the other actor also defect, is a mere −20: a loss that is substantially lower than the −50 against which protection has been sought by the pre-emptive defection.

International relations, in the real world, are rarely singular, or 'one-off', events. Most international relationships continue over considerable periods of time and thus look more like sequences of Prisoner's Dilemmas. The choice of options within such sequences may well be influenced by considerations of the consequences in future phases of the 'game' and by learning cooperative behaviour in past rounds. However, a degree of uncertainty continues to exist even within such sequential Prisoner's Dilemma games as a 'player' might always decide to take a short-term advantage at the expense of longer-term cooperation.[18] Such a short-term approach might well follow from a disposition to discount the future significantly.[19] Such a possibility is even greater in real international relations where decision-makers are subject to a far wider range of considerations than are incorporated into formal game-theoretical analysis and it may be possible to eliminate the opponent from the game, or even transform the 'game' itself.

Defection from cooperative modes of behaviour is thus a constant temptation in situations that correspond to a Prisoner's Dilemma. Defection, in such a game, promises the highest possible reward, if all goes well, while ensuring the least serious losses, if things go badly. The Prisoner's Dilemma characterizes situations in which actors have to decide whether to make costly (in some sense), but voluntary, contributions to the establishment of conditions, or facilities, that are to the individual's advantage and to the common good (collective goods). The temptation to defect, 'free ride' or defend oneself against the 'free riding' of others, undermines the capacity of collectivities to provide collective goods, however desirable they may be.[20]

Particular conditions might encourage the members of a collectivity to make their costly, voluntary contributions to the provision of a desired collective good, but these conditions are extremely demanding in practice. If each potential contributor is convinced that its contribution will be marginally decisive to the provision of the good, then a contribution might well be made. Here, each actor believes that if its contribution is made, there will be just sufficient total contributions to enable the collective good to be brought into existence: there will be no significant surplus above minimal requiements, nor will there be a shortfall in total contributions. In this situation, the actor contributes because it is rational to incur a cost which is necessary to secure a benefit that exceeds the cost incurred (or any other benefit that could be 'purchased' for the same cost), as has been assumed in this discussion of collective goods. It would be equally irrational, by the criteria of economic rationality, to save the cost if that entailed foregoing the higher benefits that could otherwise have been obtained.[21]

Such a solution to the problems of 'free-riding', and of securing the provision of collective goods, may be fine in logic. It is, however, impossibly demanding in all but the most exceptional of real world situations. The problem is that of ensuring that all those who have to provide their contributions to the collective good are all simultaneously convinced that their contributions are marginally decisive. If they begin to suspect that their contributions might be either superfluous, or that total contributions will prove inadequate, then they will be strongly tempted, and indeed compelled by the logic of economic rationality, to withhold their contributions. There is, therefore, a formidable problem of what sociologists would entitle 'inter-subjectivity' to be resolved before any collectivity can succeed in providing itself with desired collective goods from voluntary contributions. The character and size of any collectivity will, therefore, be decisive in determining actual capacities for the generation of collective goods, as Mancur Olson, the founder of collective goods theory, initially observed.[22]

Many hostile actions can be interpreted as special cases of defection from cooperative, and mutually regarding, behaviour. Attempts to cheat, or to exert coercive influence over, a partner in a generally advantageous relationship is one such example of 'defection'. The problem with many such situations is that they involve a bargaining set, or area of mutual benefit in which the exact share to be gained by each party has yet to be determined. A situation of mutual advantage ('positive-sum', in game theoretical terms) may thus incorporate 'zero-sum' features, in which the struggle for greater shares of the available benefits assumes a 'what you win, I lose' character. Such competition over the proportions of benefits to be awarded to participants is thus capable of degenerating into an antagonistic struggle, in which the more 'powerful' prevail and in which the 'losers' develop an acute sense of resentment. The animosities of such 'losers' might be such as to stimulate efforts to undermine, or even destroy, the very 'game' itself. International confrontations between *status quo* and *revisionist* states have had much of this flavour throughout history.[23]

Involvement in a process of escalating suspicion, insecurity, hostility and antagonism is a further example of the kind of damaging departure from mutually regarding and cooperative behaviour that is all too common in all areas of international relations. Such a process has been evocatively entitled an 'arms race', whether it assumes the form of competitive restrictions upon trade, competitive currency devaluations, the competitive accumulation of armaments, or the simultaneous attempts of actors to establish 'power' over one another. Such a process, particularly in the politico-military sphere, is stimulated not merely by the manifestation of threatening intentions by one or more of the participants, but also by the very lack of security from attack that is characteristic of a fragmented international political system. Anticipation of the 'worst case' often compels societies to make just those 'defensive' preparations, or actions, that might in turn convince potential adversaries that they themselves are the subjects of a potential, or actual, threat. Power may, therefore, be pursued as a preventive measure but actually precipitate an escalatory 'power-struggle'.

Amongst those conditions that can overcome the self-defeating temptation to defect from collectively desirable forms of behaviour are the existence of a belief system, value system, or ideology, that unites the members of a society and obligates them to contribute to the collective well-being[24] or the existence and functioning of a variety of institutions, including governments, that are able to ensure or compel such behaviour from those who might otherwise prove recalcitrant.[25] Such counterveiling factors, or considerations, interestingly do not alter the costs and benefits that are directly associated with the collective good itself: the *direct costs and benefits*. Rather, such influences constitute a set of *associated costs and benefits*: associated in that they do not derive from a collective good itself but are enjoyed, or incurred, as a condition of whether contributions have been made to the costs of a desired collective good. Paying taxes may, or may not, generate collective goods that are desired by those who pay those taxes: the avoidance of imprisonment is, however, a considerable associated benefit to those who might thus be persuaded to pay their taxes.

One of the unfortunate characteristics of the international system, past and present, is that it has been unable to generate sufficient associated costs and benefits at a global level to overcome 'free-rider' tendencies and hence generate desirable collective goods. In particular, the global system has been quite incapable of establishing an unifying, world-wide ideology or an effective world governmental, or quasi-governmental, system. Indeed, the contemporary international system is, if anything, characterized by the most acute ideological division and a marked degree of political fragmentation. Failures of cooperation are, therefore, all too common in contemporary international relations. Indeed, effective cooperation has usually proved possible only where the costs involved are trivial, where some ideological community exists between a small group of states, where a limited area of interest permits some states to exert a quasi-governmental influence over others, or where the momentum established by such conditions in the past has some continuing influence within a changed present.[26]

The problems encountered in developing and sustaining cooperation at the international level can, however, often be overcome within well-established societies. Common beliefs, value systems and ideologies are precisely what a widely shared culture provides for the members of a society. Effective government, furthermore, is both a product of a well-established popular culture and a major protector and propagator of such a culture. Uncertainty, turbulence and insecurity can be reduced to manageable levels within well-functioning societies precisely because of their ability to develop those cultural and/or governmental institutions and mechanisms that ensure constructive collective efforts: the international system, in contrast, is still characterized by threatening uncertainties and instabilities precisely because it has been incapable of generating such cultural and/or governmental resources. Indeed, while it has proved easy to induce a global recession through unilateral 'follow-my-leader' economic policies, it has been far harder to orchestrate the coordinated stimulation of economic recovery and expansion.

The international scene is not, however, marked by the constant turbulence and uncertainty that might have been suggested by the foregoing discussion. States moderate their behaviour for much of the time. International interactions are not one-off 'games', as suggested by the simple Prisoner's Dilemma outlined in this chapter. Knowledge that the 'game' will be played again tomorrow, the day after and the day after that, moderates the behaviour of all but the most determined or deluded states for much of the time. This moderation rarely induces wholly cooperative and self-sacrificial behaviour, as will be demonstrated at some length subsequently. Moderation does, however, often blunt the sharper edges of international behaviour and sustain a measure of mutual regard: a principle of reciprocity[27] which influences, but does not wholly dominate, international relations. The institutionalization of such self-restraining principles of behaviour may, moreover, be desired and underlie the establishment of a range of formalized international arrangements.[28] However, such arrangements require special conditions for the formation and maintenance and cannot therefore ultimately be relied upon for the protection of the interests and well-being of the members of any society.

The ultimate unreliability of any international arrangements thus throws societies back upon their own resources. While total isolation may be unrealistic, and even unhealthy, and autarchy unattainable, societies are ill-advised to expose themselves to substantial risks through international arrangements that might well prove unreliable, or not as helpful as might have been hoped initially. Certainly, any international commitment, or development, that actively threatens the cohesiveness of a society's culture or the effectiveness of its government should be abjured at all costs. The undermining of the very foundations of social order and economic stability cannot be warranted by a blind leap towards the internationalist nirvanas of liberal free-trader or a world socialist order. Indeed, to the Economic Realist it is only a society with an orderly and cohesive domestic system, which has been protected from the wilder storms of the international economic ocean, that will be able to make a substantial long-term contribution to the well-being of others within the contemporary world system.

ECONOMIC REALISM IN THEORY AND PRACTICE

The discussion thus far has concentrated upon the considerations that encourage an Economic Realist view of economic life and the pressures that might prompt the adoption of Economic Realist measures in practice. It is important to note, however, that this discussion is based upon probabilistic rather than deterministic assumptions.[29] Economic Realism, as outlined here, merely highlights the possible responses that societies, and their decision makers, may make to the real world of economics and international relations. There may be a powerful and continuing tendency towards the adoption of these responses and practices but this will vary with time, circumstances, society and ruling regime.

The second major feature of the Economic Realist approach propounded in this chapter is that it lacks, as it must, the deductive and determinate character of neo-classical or, indeed, much of liberal economic theory. The world of economics, and particularly of international economics, will be singularly unsuited to such an approach if reality does, indeed, conform to the picture depicted thus far in this chapter.

As a theoretical structure, therefore, Economic Realism cannot constitute a neat, internally rigorous, deductive system: rather, it provides a mixed portfolio of ideas and perspectives. First, it offers a small number of fundamental propositions about economic and international reality. Second, it surveys a wide-ranging list of societal conditions and institutions, and of governmental arrangements and practices, which might reflect or contribute to Economic Realist requirements. Third, it develops a set of arguments that relate such societal and governmental features to identifiable Economic Realist, and neo-mercantilist, impulses.

It has been argued that the first principle of Economic Realism is that the world is characterized by inherent uncertainty and turbulence and that this prompts positive action to establish control and, hence, ensure a necessary minimum of security for its inhabitants. The precise level of control that will be sought cannot, however, be determined with precision. It is people and societies themselves that will make the judgements about the levels of uncertainty that are acceptable and hence the measures that will be deemed desirable in the pursuit of control. Where competition is not found to be unacceptably disruptive, it may well be tolerated and even encouraged. Where competition is seen to be unhelpful it will be regulated or suppressed. Again, cooperation with others to develop increased control over some area of behaviour, or a part of the environment, will be pursued as far as the involved societies deem it to be desired and the costs justifiable.

It is, however, not merely the frequency of efforts to develop control within, or amongst, societies that varies; the forms of control, and their practical effect, may also differ. A society that is experiencing difficulty in maintaining a healthy balance of external trade may avail itself of a range of measures. Its response may range from the imposition of trade restrictions to a variety of systematic efforts to restore the competitiveness of its industries and internationally traded services.

There is also a cyclical pattern in the relationship between the nature of a society and the practices that it will adopt in responding to the pressures created by an uncertain and turbulent environment. The very culture, and set of institutions, that is to be protected also exerts a considerable influence upon the measures that will be deemed desirable or acceptable. Cultural variation thus underlies much of the variation in the approach of societies to economic and international economic policy. This variation makes it difficult to establish a straightforward correlation between given contextual conditions and identifiable patterns of response.

As a general principle, Economic Realists and neo-mercantilists would contend that modern societies generate increasing pressures for governments to promote the economic well-being of their citizens. Such modern societies are complex and generally democratic. Complexity, and the associated growth of an intimate functional interdependence between individuals, and between sections of society and economy, makes uncertainty and turbulence increasingly intolerable. The advent of democracy also makes government more answerable to popular demands which, whether ill informed and irrational or guided by a ground-swell of common sense, may exert pressures towards governmental intervention in economic life, both domestic and international. Indeed, such pressures may even be felt in those complex industrial societies where formal democracy (in the Western sense) has not been implemented. The costs of disorder, or even in passive resistance, in such a societies may be such as to counsel governments towards a degree of popular responsiveness.[30]

It is not only individuals and societies that respond to environmental uncertainty and turbulence by seeking to establish control and, in this endeavour, generating something akin to a culture or an ideology. Such associations of human beings may assume many forms, including private business enterprises, transnational political movements, world religious organizations and international terrorist groups.[31]

Such non-societal associations, including private business enterprises, often make considerable efforts to develop analogies of ideologies and cultures that have many of the characteristics of political ideologies and cultures. The 'culture' of many of the major multinational corporations is part of the folk-lore, and even demonology, of many students of such world-bestriding enterprises. Many other transnational entities are equally able or keen to engender systems of value, belief and understanding within their adherents that will also have the effect of sustaining members, reducing uncertainties and generally enhancing control.[32]

Private enterprises may thus seek to reduce the uncertainty that stems from an uncontrolled environment. Competition may be a major source of such uncertainty, and its minimization through the establishment of a dominant position within any area of production or trade is often the objective of the more dynamic and effective enterprises. Such a position may be sought individually, through the creation of a monopoly, or collectively through the establishment of an oligopoly or cartel.

Governments may be a further source of difficulty for private enterprises and this, again, may be combated through a variety of means. The capacity to exert pressure upon governments is clearly a major advantage here and may be achieved in a number of ways. A firm may seek to establish a strategically vital position in the economy, the production of a vital good or the supply of the government, itself. Again, firms may act with others to develop industrial pressure groups which can lobby governments directly or seek to exert indirect influence through the manipulation of public opinion. Extensive opportunities to evade, or overcome, governmental pressures are also available to companies that are able to operate on a transnational basis, as will be discussed in greater detail subsequently.

CONCLUSIONS

Economic realism, and its neo-mercantilist corollary, thus offers a significantly different view of economic reality to that offered by both liberal/neo-classical and Marxist theory. Its claims to acceptance rest more upon is essential realism rather than the elegance of its theoretical formulations. It offers not so much a rigorous theory but, rather, a realistic disposition which can permit a less doctrinaire view of, and judgements about, a wide range of policies and practices that are often adopted in the real world.

The Economic Realist/neo-mercantilist approach to economics, and to economic and industrial policy, has powerful implications at all levels of economic life. It will be the purpose of the next section of this study to explore these implications in greater detail. The order in which this will be undertaken, however, reflects a basic premise of the study: that it is difficulties that stem from the nature and functioning of the international system that generate the ultimate pressure for societies, and their governments, to adopt clear and positive measures to ensure their well-being—measures in the economic realm, as well as the more conventionally accepted areas of political and military relations.

Part III thus starts with a more detailed examination of the contemporary international economic system. The purpose here will be to identify those many areas in which governments and other transnational actors seek to impose order upon the system, or some of its component parts. It will, however, be concluded that cooperation and control in international relations continue to encounter substantial obstacles. A powerful pressure is thus maintained upon societies and governments to ensure their own well-being. Subsequent chapters in Part III explore the many areas in which such efforts are directed, and the wide variety of means through which these efforts may be channelled.

NOTES

1. Friedrich List, *The National System of Political Economy*, (London: Longmans, Green and Co., (English Edition) 1922); On List, *see* Eric Roll, *A History of Economic Thought*, (London: Faber and Faber, (4th ed.) 1973), pp. 227–31 and, for more recent works within this general tradition *see* D. P. Calleo and B. J. Rowland, *America and the World Political Economy: Atlantic Dreams and National Realities*, (Bloomington: Indiana University Press, 1973) and Dudley Seers, *The Political Economy of Nationalism*, (Oxford: Oxford University Press, 1983).
2. On entropy and its manifold implications, *see* Norbert Wiener, *The Human Use of Human Beings*, (New York: Houghton Mifflin, 1950).
3. For a most effective discussion of the concept and bases of 'power' and 'authority' *see* Dennis Wrong, *Power: Its Forms, Bases and Uses*, (Oxford: Basil Blackwell, 1979).

4. *See*, for insistance, S. R. Waldman, *Foundations of Political Action: An Exchange Theory of Politics*, (Boston: Little, Brown, 1977), esp. Ch. VI; and R. A. Dahl and C. E. Lindblom, *Politics, Economics and Welfare*, (New York: Harper Row, 1953) esp. Part IV.

5. *See*, especially, F. G. Bailey, *Stratagems and Spoils: A Social Anthropology of Politics*, (Toronto: Copp, Clark, 1969); D. K. Kavanagh, *Political Culture*, (London: Macmillan, 1972); S. Verba, *Small Groups and Political Leadership: A Study of Leadership*, (Princeton, NJ: Princeton University Press, 1961), esp. pp. 29–45 and 54–6; and B. Barry, *Sociologists, Economists and Democracy*, (London: Collier-Macmillan, 1970), esp. Ch. III.

6. With due acknowledgement to Thomas Hobbes, *The Leviathan* (1651, various editions).

7. *See*, for instance, F. Engels, *The Origin of the Family, Private Property and the State*, (original publication, 1884). (Moscow: Foreign Languages Publishing House); Prince Peter Kropotkin, *Mutual Aid: A Factor of Evolution*, (Harmondsworth: Penguin Books, 1939); P.-J. Proudhon, *The Principle of Federation*, trans. R. Vernon, (Toronton: University of Toronto Press, 1979 [originally, Paris 1863]); and G. Woodcock, *Anarchism: A History of Liberation Ideas and Movements*, (New York: The World Publishing Co., 1962).

8. As is the central argument of N. Frohlich, J. A. Oppenheimer and O. R. Young, *Political Leadership and Collective Goods*, (Princeton, NJ: Princeton University Press, 1971).

9. *See* T. B. Bottomore, *Elites and Society*, (London, C. A. Watts, 1964); esp. Ch. 6; and *see also* Dahl and Lindblom *op. cit.* esp. pp. 279–80.

10. As critics of Riker's principle of 'minimum winning coalitions' in alliances have argued. *See*. S. Brams, *Game, Theory in Politics*, (New York: Free Press, 1975), esp. pp. 213–232; and *see also* W. H. Riker, *The Theory of Political Coalitions*, (New Haven: Yale University Press, 1962).

11. *See*, especially, W. J. Samuels, *The Economy as a System of Power*, Vol. 1, (New Brunswick: Transaction Books, 1979), Part 2.

12. *See* Dahl and Lindblom *op. cit.* Ch. 4.

13. Some, albeit partial, illumination of this point is provided by notions of 'political entrepreneurship', *see* N. Frohlich and J. A.a Oppenheimer, *Modern Political Economy*. (Englewood Cliffs, Prentice-Hall, 1978), Ch. 4.

14. An argument which is common to a wide range of economists from American 'institutionalists'—*see* Samuels, *The Economy as a System of Power*, Vol. 1 *op. cit.*; and W. J. Samuels, *The Methodology of Economic Thought*, (New Brunswick: Transaction Books, 1980)—through such classical revivalists as David Simpson, *The Political Economy of Growth*, (Oxford: Basil Blackwell, 1983); through to such marxists as Paul Baran, *The Political Economy of Growth*, (New York: Monthly Review Press, 1957).

15. *See*, in particular, F. Hirsch, M. Doyle, E. L. Morse, *Alternatives to Monetary Disorder*, (New York: McGraw-Hill, 1977), esp. pp. 25–34;

J. E. Spero, *The Politics of International Economic Relations*, (London: George Allen and Unwin, 2nd. edn., 1982), pp. 33–41; R. O. Keohane and J. S. Nye, *Power and Interdependence: World Politics in Transition*, (Boston: Little, Brown, 1977), esp. pp. 78–81; and J. H. Richards, *International Economic Institutions*, (London: Holt, Rinehart and Winston, 1970), Ch. 2.

16. *See*: R. W. Tucker, *The Inequality of Nations*, (New York: Basic Books, 1977), esp. Ch. 1; H. J. Morgenthau, *Politics Among Nations: the Struggle for Power and Peace*, (New York: Alfred Knopf, 4th edn., 1947).

17. On the Prisoner's Dilemma *see*: Brams *op. cit.* pp. 30–9; and M. Nicholson, *Conflict Analysis*, (London: English Universities' Press, 1970), pp. 60–6.

18. Nicholon, *Conflict Analysis op. cit.* esp. pp. 69–70.

19. *See*, particularly, M. Nicholson, 'Co-operation, anarchy and "random" change', in Barry Buzan and R. J. Barry Jones (eds.), *Change and the Study of International Relations*, (London: Frances Pinter, 1981).

20. *See*, especially, Mancur Olson, *The Logic of Collective Action*, (Cambridge: Cambridge University Press, 1965); and Frohlich and Oppenheimer, *Modern Political Economy op. cit.*, esp. Ch. 2. *See also* the discussion in Chapter 2 of this volume.

21. N. Frohlich and J. A. Oppenheimer, 'I get by with a little help from my friends . . .', *World Politics*, Vol. 20 (1970), pp. 104–20.

22. Olson *op. cit.* esp. Ch. 1.

23. For a more formal analysis *see* Nicholson, *Conflict Analysis op. cit.* Ch. 5.

24. Olson *op. cit.*

25. Frohlich, Oppenheimer and Young, *Political Leadership and Collective Goods op. cit.* It is also possible that social or material rewards might secure such contributions. Anarchists, of course, contest the need for such 'Hobbesian' governmental institutions, believing that appropriate cultural and societal norms would suffice; *see*; April Carter, *The Political Theory of Anarchism*, (London: Routledge and Kegan Paul, 1976); and M. Taylor, *Anarchy and Cooperation*, (New York and London: Wiley, 1976).

26. *See* R. O. Keohane, *After Hegemony: Cooperation and Discord in the World Political Economy*, (Princeton: Princeton University Press, 1984).

27. The principal of reciprocity has often been held to underlie the development of behavioural 'norms' in international relations. *See* T. M. Frank and E. Weisband, *Word Politics: Verbal Strategy Among the Superpowers*, (New York: Oxford University Press, 1972).

28. Such arrangements often being termed, somewhat controversially, 'regimes'. *See*, especially, Keohane and Nye, *Power and Interdependence op. cit.*; and Keohane, *After Hegemony op. cit.*

29. For a discussion of probabilism and possibilism *see* H. and M. Sprout, *The Ecological Perspective on Human Affairs*, with Special Reference

to International Politics, (Princeton, NJ: Princeton University Press, 1965); and for a general discussion of philosophy and methodology in international relations *see* J. E. Dougherty and R. L. Pfaltzgraff, *Contending Theories of International Relations*, (Philadelphia: Lippincott, 1971).

30. On the political effect of modern societies *see*: E. L. Morse, *Modernization and the Transformation of International Relations*, (New York: Free Press, 1976), esp. Ch. 1; and H. G. Johnson, 'Mercantilism: past, present, future', in H. G. Johnson (ed.), *The New Mercantilism*, (Oxford: Basil Blackwell, 1974).

31. *See*, especially, R. O. Keohane and J. S. Nye, *Transnational Relations*, (Cambridge, Mass.: Harvard University Press, 1972).

32. There is a vast literature on the multinational corporation, amongst which is: R. E. Mueller and R. J. Barnet, *Global Reach: The Power of the Multinational Corporation*, (New York: Simon and Schuster, 1974); G. Tugenhadt, *The Multinationals*, (London: Eyre and Spottiswoode, 1971); and R. Vernon, *Sovereignty and Bay: the Multinational Spread of US Enterprises*, (London: Longman, 1971).

Part III
Conflict and Control in the Modern World Economy

4 Control and Collaboration in the Global Economy

INTRODUCTION

Many types of actors operate within the global system. Their relative power and influence reflect the conditions under and the issues over which they interact with one another. It has become a commonplace feature of contemporary studies of the global political economy that, in some ways and under such circumstances, multinational corporations are able to exert far more influence than many nation-states, or their governments.

It is the very frequency of frictions and conflicts within international or transnational relations, and the serious potential costs that they generate, that stimulate so many efforts to establish collaboration and control amongst all types of actors within the global system. These efforts, however, are beset by many serious difficulties. The failure of international cooperation is all too common; uncontrolled developments, intensified uncertainty and amplified turbulence all too frequent.

The efforts of some actors to establish control may, moreover, run counter to the similar efforts of others. If nation-states seek to collaborate to regulate and control the activities of multinational corporations, then they may challenge the possible efforts of MNCs, individually or severally, to control economic and political developments to their own advantage. The actions of individually strong nation-states might also be directed towards the loosening, or complete destruction, of cartels of MNCs that may have been acting to the perceived disadvantage of the nation-state. The leading petroleum-producing countries have, in the past, been able to undermine the common front on many issues amongst the major oil companies.[1]

The most interesting feature of efforts to establish control within the global economy, by whomsoever, is their varying level of success. Such endeavours seem to wax and wane as the calculus of relative advantage and salience evolves. The strength and influence of various individual states have varied over time. Collaborative arrangements amongst groups of nation-states have emerged, flourished and then dissolved. Individual transnational actors have, at times, seemed unstoppable in their accumulation of strength and influence, but have then found their further advance serious checked, as with those US motor car companies that occupied such a dominant position within the post-war world economy.[2] Groups of multinational corporations have, again, seemed omnipotent within their chosen spheres of activity but then, as with the major oil companies in the mid 1970s, suddenly been thrown back upon the defensive.

Such fluctuating fortunes in the maintenance of control of areas of the global political economy are of central interest in themselves. However, they also raise critical questions of causality. In short, do conflicts develop between nation-states, or other global actors, because mechanisms of control have weakened or failed, or is it the emergence of serious conflicts of interest between such actors that themselves undermine those capacities for control that have or might have been developed? This issue goes to the heart of the contending views of the character of the political economy and to contrasting interpretations of the post-war economic experience.[3]

INTERNATIONAL ECONOMIC CONTROL: CONTRASTING VIEWS

The need for, or existence of, efforts to develop some forms of control within the global political economy is recognized by all the major theoretical approaches. Such approaches differ over the purpose which such efforts are to serve and the origins of control, when it appears.

Analysts of the liberal and neo-classical persuasion recognize, implicitly or explicitly, the central problem of international economic relationships. A system of free-trade encounters many practical obstacles which may impede its realization. As in the domestic economy, an international order has to be established which reflects the requirements of a well-functioning free-market economy and which protects the necessary rules of orderly economic interaction—the prevention of theft, the honouring of contracts and other such facilitative principles.

Liberal theorists thus envisage a necessary, albeit minimal, political and legal order within which orderly free-market economic activity may be conducted. However, it is the very flourishing of orderly and mutually beneficial free trade amongst societies that is supposed to convince them of the desirability of maintaining amicable political relationships and, where required, move towards a measure of political harmonization, if not association. There is, therefore, the possibility of a self-enclosing circle—benign once a free-trade order has been established, but inhibitory and 'vicious' under non-liberal international conditions.

If theory suggests that the political conditions necessary for a liberal economic order can only be established by the flourishing of that liberal economic order itself, then the theory has to be substantially amplified, modified or even abandoned. A promising line of response to this problem has emerged from the writings of those who emphasize the role of *hegemons* in the establishment of a liberal international economic order[4] and of *international 'regimes'* in its subsequent maintenance and preservation.[5] The essential argument here is that if a hegemon—a dominant state, or very small group of states—emerges within an international system it is possible, if the hegemon is so inclined, for a liberal order to be imposed upon the system through various combinations of force and inducement.

Many of the elements of the liberal order then crystallize into regimes. These institutionalize, to a greater or lesser degree, the 'rules' and decision-making procedures necessary to maintain various components, or *'issue areas'*, of the liberal international economy. These regimes, once established, become valued by their members for the relative order and certainty that they introduce into areas of economic interaction that might otherwise be marked by costly disorder and uncertainty. Such regimes may well therefore persist, and exert an influence, long after the strength and position of the founding hegemon has waned and even disappeared.[6]

The approach of radical and Marxist analysts to international control contrasts sharply with that of liberal theorists. Radicals and Marxists identify the requirements of capitalist enterprises as the driving force of the contemporary economic system. There are differences, however, over the extent to which cooperative control will be engendered and the forms that it will assume.

In the analysis developed by Lenin, the activities of the nation-state were directed by the needs of capitalist systems which, while assuming a monopolistic and oligopolistic form domestically, still remained in competition with foreign capitalist enterprises. Under the special conditions of the late nineteenth and early twentieth centuries, these needs fuelled a revival of imperialism, imperial rivalry and finally brought the conflagration of the First World War. Some ambiguity persisted within Lenin's analysis, however, for it maintained that the capitalist–imperialist powers would put aside rivalry and collaborate to combat such a fundamental threat to capitalism itself as the emergence of a socialist society:[7] a position which gained some support from the wars of intervention against the infant Bolshevik regime in Russia and the later Cold War, but which has been complicated by the good contemporary relations established by number of Western MNCs with many of the Eastern bloc countries.

In the post-war world, the substantial expansion of trade, combined with the steady advance of multinational corporations, has created some uncertainty and disagreement amongst radical and Marxist analysts. Three possibilities have been identified by one student of the field: Imperial Rivalry, in which the growing difficulties confronting states draw them into serious conflict with one another; Ultra-imperialism, in which a coalition of major capitalist states collaborate to manage the system in their joint interests; and, finally, US Super-imperialism, in which the United States of America is able to sustain its leadership, manage the system and preserve itself from the socialist challenge.[8]

While the evolving role of nation-states may be in doubt within radical and Marxist analysis, the multinational corporation is certainly viewed as an agency dedicated to the creation and maintenence of international control. The distinctive feature of the transnational mode of production is the firm's control of production and transactions across national frontiers. Dependence upon transnationally integrated systems of production may expose the multinational corporation to some vulnerabilities and dangers, but these can often be reduced through judicious planning and diversified sourcing of inputs and components. The capacity for effective control may also be substantially enhanced if effective co-operation, explicit or implicit, is possible with the other multinational corporations that are engaged in the same areas of economic activity, as has so often been the case of the oil companies.[9]

The controversial issue concerning the influence of multi-national corporations is whether they fuel rivalry between nation-states or whether, in contrast, they create a pressure for closer and more effective international collabortion, regionally if not globally. Such international collaboration might be stimulated, on the one hand, by the wish of multinational corporations to secure the reduction or elimination of various barriers to trade or, on the other, by public and governmental recognition of the need for more effective regulation of MNC activity.[10]

The view of international cooperation and control taken by the Economic Realist, or the neo-mercantilist, is one of expectation in general, coupled wih pragmatism in detail. The essence of this approach towards economics rests upon the identification of the many motives for, and activities through which, peoples seek to develop and enhance control. International behaviour will, therefore, reflect the particular requirements of specific situations, as perceived by the peoples and governments of the societies involved. Where collaborative control is judged desirable, it will be pursued: where isolated action is deemed preferable, cooperation will be abjured. The Economic Realist, or neo-mercantilist, is also able to incorporate indications, from both liberal and radical analyses, of the conditions which will influence the choices of societies between cooperative responses or autonomous solutions.

Interpretations of the forms of, and impulses towards, control in the global economy thus differ widely. Whatever the significance, however, the contemporary system is replete with, and often dominated by, the pursuit and exercise of control.

CONTEMPORARY INTERNATIONAL ECONOMIC CONTROL—FORMS AND FUNCTIONS

There is widespread agreement that the USA exercised substantial international economic control during the post Second World War era.[11] Such hegemonical influence, albeit qualified and always far from absolute,[12] was wide reaching in its effects. Many of the institutions of the post-war international economic order were formed under the auspices of US leadership. Moreover the post-war recovery of Europe owed a massive debt to the economic assistance provided through the USA's Marshall Plan (European Recovery Program), while that of Japan owed much to the USA's occupation regime.[13]

American support played an important part in the establishment of the two pillars of the post-war liberal economic system, the Bretton Woods international monetary system and the General Agreement on Tariffs and Trade regime. American influence was important in the adoption, and the form, of the Bretton Woods international monetary system.[14] Continuing American support for an international free-trade system was also reflected in the *de-facto* introduction of the General Agreement on Tariffs and Trade 1947) when the compromise provisions of the International Trade Organization were rejected by the US Congress in 1948[15] and the periodic pressure that secured the succession of trade liberalization negotiations throughout the post-war decades.[16]

The post-war era thus witnessed a remarkable period of institution building, the fruits of which ripened, came to harvest in the late 1950s and 1960s and survive to the present day. The contributions of this creative process have not been confined to the formal institutions that resulted. Participation in the management of a range of international economic institutions, including the Organization of Economic Cooperation and Development (OECD), has encouraged the political leaders and bureaucrats of the major economic powers in the habit and expectation of mutual consultation and collaboration. Indeed, the managing groups of such institutions have often attracted the evocative title of 'clubs'. Numerous have been the 'summit meetings' held to discuss the primary economic issues of the day during the post-war era. Thus, the leading western economies responded rapidly to the 1973–4 oil crisis with a special conference in Washington, and the subsequent formation of the International Energy Agency (IEA) and the Conference on International Economic Cooperation (CIEC).[17] The current 'debt crisis' of much of the less developed world has, in like manner, encouraged the work of the 'Paris Club' of representatives of the major creditor countries, and financial institutions, and prompted its evolution into an embryonic world banking consortium.[18]

The USA was thus able to play a central role in the stimulation of many of the institutionalized arrangements (or 'regimes') and habits of political response that were to occupy a central role in the international economy until at least the late 1960s. Paradoxically, however, the very successes of the system promoted by the USA encouraged a number of developments, and the emergence of a number of institutions, that were ultimately to challenge that country's strength and influence.

The remarkable recovery of those metropolitan economies that has been devastated, or severely strained, by the Second World War was, alone, likely to weaken the position and influence of the USA. This possibility was, however, reinforced by early signs of potential collaboration, and even a measure of integration, amongst some of the recovering European nations.

The earliest development that was to post an eventual threat to the special position that the USA occupied in the immediate post-war world was the gradual coming together of a number of European nations. This centripetal process was actively encouraged by US policy makers and supported through the good offices of the body that had been established to oversee the disposal of Marshall Plan funds: the Organization for European Economic Cooperation. The formation of the European Iron and Steel Community in 1952 marked the first substantial step along the path towards an ever-expanding, and increasingly influential, European Economic Community (EEC).

In the Far East, the recovery of Japan was actively promoted by General McArthur's occupation regime. Indeed, Japanese recovery was permitted to develop along its characteristically protectionist pattern, with only the weakest of efforts to impose liberal trade policies and practices, particularly towards imports or foreign companies.[19]

Recovery in both Europe and Japan brought with it the seeds of disharmony within the global political economy, or at least that portion which had been dominated by the USA. The consequences have been the weakening of the mechanisms for effective control of the economic system of the non-communist world, increasing instability in many central aspects of the global economy and the crystallization of myriad international trade disputes amongst the major trading states and groups of states.

European recovery allowed individual European nations to become less dependent upon US largesse, more confident in their views and more assertive in defence of their own interests. General de Gaulle's 1965 decision to convert surplus holdings of US dollars into gold and to reduce France's general holding of dollars was one of the more dramatic early demonstrations of European revitalization.[20] Recovery also made the rapidly emerging EEC an increasingly significant actor upon the international economic scene: as an exporter of growing importance within many international markets, as a bloc capable of erecting substantial barriers against imports from countries outside the Community, and, latterly, as a player of considerable weight and influence within the international monetary system, as the strengths of individual currencies have been amplified through the development of the European Monetary System (EMS) and the European Currency Unit (ECU).

Japan's recovery, in its turn, has led to the major role that that country now plays within the contemporary global economic system and to the dominant position that it now occupies in many international markets. Most critically, Japan's current economic performance has accelerated changes in relative competitiveness, induced widespread economic disruption within many of the other Advanced Industrial Countries and, hence, stimulated growing and widespread pressures for protectionism and allied counter-measures.

The longer-term fruits of the impressive economic recovery of the post-war era were also to be seen, ultimately, in the new self-assertiveness of many less developed, commodity-exporting countries during the 1970s. The protracted economic boom of the late 1950s and 1960s had a number of related effects. Rising economic aspirtions and expectations were stimulated in all quarters of the globe. The growing demand for most raw materials, primary commodities and energy sources underlay a general pattern of steady, and latterly accelerating, price increases.

The 1960s had, however, also seen the crystallization of widespread disappointment with the level and rate of economic development actually achieved by many of the Less Developed Countries. It had been hoped that de-colonization would soon be followed by rapid economic progress in the emergent nations. However, many such countries continued to be confronted by substantial obstacles, both internal and external, to the realization of these expectations.

Many and varied were the internal policy responses of those Less Developed Countries that experienced the frustration of their hopes for rapid economic development. Notably, however, considerable efforts were made to generate appropriate forms of international collaboration, control and pressure. The United Nations has become a more attractive proposition as the progress of decolonization has moved the balance of voting power towards the Less Developed Countries. The imbalance between formal voting strength and financial contributions, and hence ultimate influence, within the UN has, however, limited the achievements that can be secured within that forum. The recent withdrawal of the financial support of the USA from the United Nations Educational, Scientific and Cultural Organization (UNESCO) well illustrates the dangers of steering UN agencies in directions that are unacceptable to its major paymasters.

Collaborative action outside the UN has thus proved attractive, if often disappointing in its results, to the Less Developed Countries in their efforts to influence their economic relationships with the world's richer nations. The so-called Group of 77 was formed by those Less Developed Countries that were determined to confront the world's richer nations with a demand for a more equitable international economic order, which would include the introduction of a range of mechanisms through which major aspects of the international economy, and especially commodity trade, might be regulated and controlled.

The negotiations on a New International Economic Order (NIEO), at the periodic meetings of the United Nations Conference on Trade and Development (UNCTAD), ultimately achieved rather little. An attitude of mind, and a habit of consultation and collaboration, had, however, been born within the 'South'. This disposition has assumed many forms, including the continuing pursuit of a 'South Bank' to facilitate trade and development amongst the LDCs.[21]

Collective action in the pursuit of improved returns from primary exports was also the basis of the formation of many commodity associations and producer cartels during the 1970s. In this process the LDCs were much encouraged by the spectacular example of the most effective, for a time at least, of the producer cartels: the Organisation of Petroleum Exporting Countries (OPEC).

The second half of the 1970s were years of near euphoria over the prospects of agreements and arrangements to regulate the trade and control the prices of many primary commodities that were of major interest to the Less Developed Countries. Two motives have been prominent in the pursuit of effective arrangements for commodity control: the immediate pursuit of stabilized earnings from the production and export of such commodities; and, in the minds of some, the longer-term construction of a source of political pressure upon the world's richer countries. The activity of the late 1970s took place against the background of years of efforts to construct viable arrangements for control, most of which had been disappointing in their achievements.[22] The dramatic increases in the prices of many primary commodities during the last years of the decade, however, stimulated beliefs that an irreversible shift had taken place in the balance of advantage between commodity producers and consumers.[23] Increased revenues and a new source of political power were held to be inevitable consequence of such a development.

The over-inflated hopes of 'commodity power' during the latter 1970s underpinned many of LDCs' expectations of a New International Economic Order in general, and of an effective Integrated Commodities' Programme in particular. Such aspirations were always doomed to confront a number of serious political and economic difficulties. Excessive pressure upon a 'North' that retained overwhelming military strength would always face serious dangers of forceful retaliation. Efforts to secure and maintain commodity prices significantly above long-term trends in 'market prices' would also stimulate the pursuit of alternative sources of supply, the use of substitutes or the introduction of commodity-saving innovations. Such prospective difficulties were, however, cast into the shade by the dramatic collapse of the prices of almost all primary commodities during the early 1980s in the global recession induced by the severely restrictive economic policies of many of the richest nation-states. Such collapsing prices overwhelmed the price-stabilizing systems that had been set up for many of the commodity agreements and soon undermined whatever solidarity had been established amongst the producing nations.[24]

Whatever the ultimate prospects of success, considerable efforts have been devoted to the formation of arrangements for the control of trade in almost every primary commodity, natural material and energy source. Such arrangements have been of two main forms: commodity associations that involve both producer/exporters and consumer/importers in a mutually agreed set of prices and practices; or producer cartels in which a group of producing nations attempts the unilateral management of prices by the limitation of production and the control of exports and, in extreme cases, through the regulation of supplies.

There have been a number of commodity associations, the most prominent amongst which have been the International Tin Agreement, the International Coffee Agreement and the International Cocoa Agreement. Most such agreements have an associated organization to administer their provisions. Commodity producer cartels include the outstanding example of OPEC, in addition to a number of other somewhat less well-known groupings including: copper's Paris-based Conseil Intergouvernemental des Pays Exportateurs de Cuivre (CIPEC), the International Bauxite Association and the Association of Iron Ore Exporting Countries.

General recession has undermined all commodity associations, as has been demonstrated by the recent experience of even such past-powers as OPEC.[25] Others have been undermined by the non-participation of major producing nations, as with the absence of Canada and Brazil from the iron ore organization[26] or by the adoption of measures that have prompted consumers to seek alternative sources or introduce substitutes, as in the case of the mercury organization.[27]

Many Less Developed Countries have also formed regional associations to facilitate internal trade and create a position of greater strength from which to manage relations with external agencies, be they states, groups or states, or transnational corporations TNCs. Such endeavours have met with varying levels of success and some have been rather short-lived. However, examples abound of such groupings of Less Developed Countries, from the Andean Common Market (ANCOM)[28] through to the somewhat struggling Economic Community of West Africa States (Ecowas).[29]

States in the sphere of influence of the Soviet Union have, given their commitment to economic control, internal and external, been used to Soviet direction and coordination through the Council for Mutual Economic Assistance

(CMEA or COMECON). The control of the Soviet Union may have waned during recent years, but each member of the socialist bloc retains tight control over its trade flows, general external economic relations and patterns of inward investment.[30]

The global system also exhibits clear recognition of the necessity for agreement, regulation and control in a number of areas that require technical coordination. The costs of a failure to coordinate activity in such areas as broadcasting, telecommunications, postal services and the use of the world's sea-lanes have long been deemed to be such as to underwrite a number of international regulative bodies.

International technical regulative bodies are not, however, immune from political controversy. The International Telecommunications Union (ITU), and its subsidiary bodies, is one international regulative body that has attracted growing attention during recent years. In an era of communications satellites, and of computer-based information gathering and processing systems, the allocation of broadcasting frequencies and the general control of international communications of all types is of growing significance.[31]

Maritime law, and the control of the use of maritime resources, is another area that has witnessed varying levels of politicization and effective regulation. States have long claimed control of navigation in off-shore waters and the exclusive exploitation of proximate fishing grounds. Ambitions in such directions have, however, often been moderated by the influence of a dominant maritime power, or group of maritime powers, that have maintained an interest in open sea lanes and free access to the great majority of fishing grounds. Such maritime agreements or, most commonly, to uphold conventional principles through forceful action. Recent attempts to establish a new 'regime' for the world's oceans and maritime resources have, however, been complicated by two developments: the issue of access to, and use of, sea-bed natural resources; and the dilution of maritime hegemony by the emergence of a Russian sea-borne challenge to the previously dominant position of the USA.[32]

A measure of control of international economic relationships and developments may also be secured on a bilateral basis. Such arrangements between a pair of states may assume many forms, have a variety of purposes and, at times, pose a serious threat to the liberal's free-trade ideal. The complex motives and implications of such bilateral undertakings are, however, left to a later chapter.

TRANSNATIONAL CONTROL IN THE GLOBAL POLITICAL ECONOMY

Nation-states are, however, not the only actors on the contemporary global stage, for they are joined by such diverse bodies as academic associations, religious organizations, trade union organizations, international terrorist groups and, perhaps most significantly, multinational (or transnational) corporations. While the nominal motive of all business enterprises is the pursuit of profit, this objective has wide-ranging, and often indeterminate, implications for their behaviour in specific situations. Strategic considerations loom large in the calculations of all firms: the more so the larger the business, the more diverse its activities and the more numerous the countries in which it operates.

The strategic calculus of TNCs, and other large enterprises, rests upon three considerations: the expansion of profits, the increase of their size, and the creation of stability. These elements may, at times, complement one another: at other times they may conflict. Under some conditions, growing profits may be used to increase the size of the enterprise. Enlargement may generate increased profits, and expansion may be encouraged by a stable economic context within which to operate. Under differing conditions, however, the attempt to increase profits or expand the size of the enterprise may bring it into conflict with other busines organizations. Such damage to the stability of the firm's economic environment may have highly variable effects upon profits or upon the success of the expansion programme.

A high level of environmental control will clearly be of considerable advantage to any large enterprise that seeks to enhance its profitability or size. Such control can be sought, and secured, in a variety of ways. The sheer size of an enterprise within a given industry may be such as to deter all but the most determined, or foolhardy, of firms from hostile actions or reactions. IBM's position within the mainframe computer industry is often held to be of such size and weight. Certainly, serious competition has either been short-lived, as in the case of the Amdhal Corportion, or sustained only with the support, in one form or another, of the governments of the home countries of such competitors, as in the cases of Japan's Fujitsu or Britain's International Computers Ltd.

The overwhelmingly dominant firm within an industry effectively determines much of the environment within which it has to operate. However, the leading firms of an industry which is not so clearly dominated may also collaborate to control the economic environment within which they operate. Such collaboration may range from formal agreements, however protected from public gaze, through the informal 'clubs' that form within such institutionalized markets as the London Metal Exchange, to tacit accommodation of the purposes, and probable responses, of other leading members of an industry. Collaboration, explicit or tacit, may be directed at price regulation, market sharing[33] or the 'disciplining' of truculent nation-states[34]. Such cooperation is, however, inherently unstable for it may always occur to a participant that circumstances are now such as to provide a favourable opportunity for a substantial, and even decisive, gain at the expense of other collaborators.[35]

The pursuit of enhanced profits or size may thus prompt an enterprise to disrupt actively the stability that has existed hitherto within an industry or some area of economic activity. If the strategy is successful then it may contribute to increased control in the future and hence the ability to prosecute the firm's objectives with greater security. A sudden strategic gamble may thus be prompted by the very wish to reduce the uncertainty that has previously confronted an enterprise.

Transnational corporations would, however, generally prefer a substantial measure of control, and relative stability, to the uncertainty and potential disorder that might result from a serious confrontation with their fellows. A significant part of the TNC's environment may be controlled unilaterally with no more than the tacit restraint of potential competitors. The development of its transnational mode of production enables the TNC to exercise considerable influence, and potential power, over the countries within which it operates. Such transnationalization of economic activity provides the TNC with strategic advantages at all stages of its relationship with any single nation-state.

TNCs are often attractive to nation-states for the capital, technology, know-how, distributional capabilities and market-access advantages that they can furnish. The nation-state's bargaining position is weakened from the outset by the knowledge that, in all but a few cases, the TNC has a number of potential host countries in which it could establish its facilities. TNCs are thus able to play societies off against one another; practising a strategy of 'divide and rule' and extracting the most favourable of conditions from the governments of the countries in which they ultimately establish themselves.

Once a TNC has established itself within a country, however, the power of relationship between the company and its host government may be modified. The TNCs assets are now, in a sense, hostage to the inclinations and interests of the host government. This alteration of the power balance may, however, readily be exaggerated. It is increasingly the case that the facilities established by a TNC in any one country are intended to constitute only a part, and often a very small part, of a highly integrated, transnational production process.

By integrating their facilities in different countries into a tight, transnational system of production, TNCs create a pattern of *induced interdependence*[36] which constrains host societies. National governments now find that the presence they can exert upon a TNC is seriously reduced by the limited utility of the local facilities which are little more than a small part of a wider production process. Nationalization may be pointless if the output of the local facilities cannot be sold because the market is limited to the other subsidiaries of the TNC. The acquisition of such a 'white elephant' would deter all but the most aggrieved or deluded of governments.

Transnationally integrated production, and activity, also

equips the TNC with a further and often quite decisive economic advantage. Shipments of components between the subsidiaries of a TNC in different countries effectively replace genuine international trade by *intra-firm trade*. The 'prices' of the components that are 'traded' across national frontiers in this manner are not established by any genuine international market but are set by the TNC's headquarters. The TNC's tactical pricing policies will be determined by the principles of maximizing the revenues retained within the corporation and preserving the greatest possible flexibility for the organization as a whole. *Transfer pricing* is the term that has been applied to such tactical pricing.

Transfer pricing exemplifies the control that TNCs derive from their very transnational mode of operation. The motives, and techniques, of this practice may be illustrated with reference to the means by which a TNC can minimize the taxes that it pays globally. A suitable example might be that of a corporation that extracts a raw material in one country (country A), refines it in a second (country B) and then packages and sells it to customers in a third (country C). Initially, a similar rate of tax might be levied upon the value added by the MNC's activity within each country (VAT). The corporation might, therefore, have no incentive to manipulate the 'prices' of the shipments to, and from, its three subsidiaries. However, the government of one of the countries might decide to seek higher revenues through an increase of its rate of VAT.

Where rates of VAT differ in the countries in which a TNC operates, it will benefit the TNC to manipulate 'prices' in such a way as to minimize the amount of profit, or value added, that it appears to make within the country with the highest level of tax. If in the case presented here, country B increased its rate of VAT then the corporation has two options. It might instruct its subsidiary in country A to increase the 'price' charged for the raw material sent to the subsidiary in country B. If the subsidiary in country B then continued to charge the subsidiary in country C no more than its previous 'price' for the refined material, then the value added within country B would, apparently, have declined and less tax would be paid to its government. In this example, value added (or 'profit') would have been 'transferred' to country A and tax paid upon it at the appropriate level to that country's government.

The corporation could have achieved the same tax saving by maintaining the prices charged by its subsidiary in country A but reducing the 'prices' charged by the subsidiary in country B for the refined materials that it subsequently sent to the subsidiary in country C. Finally, a combination of increased 'prices' for 'imported' materials and reduced 'prices' for exported goods could subject the value added by the subsidiary in country B to a two-way squeeze. Many plausible excuses may be employed to justify such claimed increases in the prices of inputs or reductions in the prices obtained for outputs. Whatever the claimed reasons, or the point at which the tactical manipulation of prices is undertaken, a significant tax saving is secured by the parent company and, most significantly, secured in a relatively invisible manner.

The relative invisibility of the manipulation facilitated by transfer pricing is highly significant and constitutes a potentially invaluable weapon in the armoury of the TNC. Funds may also be moved across national frontiers without the awareness of the governments, or peoples, of the countries involved. Such surreptitious movements of financial resources may be motivated by a wish to overcome exchange controls, evade credit restrictions, counter interest rate policies, or to export capital. They exemplify the capacities for advantageous control that accrue to an internally cohesive, but externally secretive, transnational actor when operating within a political fragmented arena. Hitherto, nation-states have generally been equipped with no more than their own resources of intelligence, and political pressure, in their attempts to regulate the behaviour of TNCs. This, as an issue of critical and growing significance within the contemporary global political economy, will be considered in greater detail later in this section.

The advantages that TNCs enjoy in their relationships with many nation-states reflect, in part, the possibilities that a pattern of *oligopolistic competition* creates for both explicit and tacit coordination amongst the firms that are dominant within any world industry. This peculiar market condition encompasses a number of characteristics. Genuine price competition is replaced by a form of pseudo-competition in which labelling, intense advertising and myriad forms of promotion permit the exaggerated differentiation of one firm's products from those of others.[37] Competition through price reductions is avoided if at all possible, and accepted only as a very last resort. Pricing policies are, rather, determined by the process of *administered pricing* in which prices are set by adding an acceptable margin of profit to the anticipated cost of unit production.[38] Any mismatch between demand and supply is not met, as in the theory of the competitive market, by a price reduction but by the reduction of the volume of production and supply.

Within a market characterized by oligopolistic competition firms are not reluctant to increase their market share and hence improve their prospects of increased long-term profitability. Rather, the critical feature of such a condition is that firms recognize the common strategic goal of avoiding mutually damaging developments, such as a price-cutting war. The recognition of mutual strategic interests is also the basis for coordination on a number of other matters. All will be concerned to maintain the secrecy with which they are all able to operate and will, hence, join together in opposition to attempts to establish international rules of disclosure. Individual states that seek to apply pressure against individual members of an international oligopoly may also be subjected to a boycott by the other firms in that industrial area. Indeed, corporations may lobby their home country governments to apply pressure against states that are proving particularly truculent, as exemplified by the USA Hickenlooper Amendment, which prohibits US aid to countries that undertake uncompensated nationalization of the assets of US firms.

Economic forms of pressure are not, unfortunately, the only means available to oligopolistic TNCs in their confrontations with unresponsive national governments. The history of international business has revealed far too many instances of illegitimate pressure and illicit activity. Many examples of this darker side of TNCs may remain no more than chapters in the demonology of radical critics and the tactical polemics of the governments of host countries. However, there is a strong evidence to support the accusations that have been made against oil company lobbying against the Mosadeq regime in post-war Iran, the involvement of the Brookings in destabilization of Guyana in 1964[39] and of ITT's involvement in the overthrow of the Allende regime in Chile in September 1973.[40]

Oligopolistic competition may also encourage, and facilitate, tacit collaboration against those firms that threaten to challenge those that are currently dominant within an international industry. Such collaboration may range from denying newcomers necessary know-how and technologies (in which assistance may be afforded by patent laws) through to coordinate efforts to prevent adequate market access and to stifle the competitive challenge at birth. Such coordination, whether it be tacit or explicit, complements the general, and more technical, barriers to entry that confront any would-be entrant into a well-established, oligopolistic industry.

The pursuit of transnational coordination and control is not confined to the large business corporations. Trade unions have also been forced into a recognition of the substantial disadvantage with which they are faced when, as nationally bound organizations, they seek to deal with increasingly transnational employers. Cooperation between national trade union associations, and between those unions that deal with the same transnational employer, have both been attempted but, as yet, with extremely limited effect.

Many other bodies, organizations and movements also seek to orchestrate the pursuit of their objectives across national frontiers. Religious bodies have long evangelized internationally and sought to influence the morals and behaviour of the populations and governments of many lands. Pressure groups have also campaigned internationally on such specific, but ethically charged, issues as the abolition of slavery, the defence of political prisoners or various forms of aid to the populations of the less wealthy societies. Recent years have witnessed the growing support and influence of a transnational ecological movement, which embraces a variety of associated groups. Finally, the emergence of close international links amongst a diverse range of terrorist organizations has been one of the more ominous examples of the broader movement towards the establishment of transnational coordination and control by whomsoever it may benefit.

CONCLUSIONS

The achievement of control, whether unilaterally or through cooperation with other actors, may bring considerable advantages. Indeed, effective control may be essential for the successful achievement of basic objectives. It is unsurprising, therefore, that the pursuit of control is common to all actors upon the global stage.

The achievement, or maintenance, of effective control is, however, a far from unproblematic matter. The resources necessary for unilateral control may be unattainable. Cooperation with others may, in turn, be undermined either by direct conflicts of interest or by the temptation to defect from collaborative arrangements. Effective control in international relations, moreover, often requires some compliance, however reluctant, by those who are to be controlled.

In the struggle for control, resources that initially appeared sufficient often prove wanting and coalitions that promised clear victory frequently prove inadequate. The calculus of influence and control thus retains a constant element of indeterminacy. Indeed, it is the very ebb and flow of the patterns of power and influence that forms much of the fascination and intellectual challenge of the study of international relations. It is, moreover, this feature of the subject that distinguishes it from the concern with formal, and determinate, model building that holds the attention of too many of the more able minds within the mainstream discipline of economics.

It is the conflicts that may arise between many of the actors on the global scene, and the fatal defections that undermine many of their cooperative efforts, that create the need for communities to look towards their own resources and to avoid becoming over-reliant upon external sources of well-being and succour. The attention of the next chapter thus turns to such conflicts and accompanying tendencies towards damaging defection and discord.

NOTES

1. *See.* A. Sampson, *The Seven Sisters: The Great Oil Companies and the World they Made*, (London: Hodder and Stoughton, 1976), esp. Chs. 11, 12 and 13; and P. R. Odell and L. Vallenilla, *The Pressures of Oil: A Strategy for Economic Revival*, (London: Harper and Row, 1978), esp. Chs. 1, 2, 3 and 5.
2. *See*, especially, G. Bannock, *The Juggernauts: The Age of the Big Corporation*, (London: Weidenfeld and Nicolson, 1973), esp. Part 3.
3. A particularly interesting discussion of which is to be found in Barry Buzan, 'Economic structure and international security', *International Organization*, Vol. 38 (Autumn 1984), pp. 597–624.
4. *See*, especially, R. O. Keohane and J. S. Nye, *Power and Interdependence: World Politics in Transition*, (Boston, Little, Brown, 1977).
5. R. O. Keohane, *After Hegemony: Corportion and Discord in the World Political Economy*, (Princeton: Princeton University Press, 1984).
6. *ibid.*
7. V. I. Lenin, *Imperialism: The Highest Stage of Capitalism*, (London: Lawrence and Wishart, 1948 [originally, Petrograd: 1916]); and *see also* T. Kemp, 'The Marxist theory of imperialism,' and M. Barratt Brown, 'A critique of Marxist theories of imperialism', in R. Owen and B. Sutcliffe (eds.), *Studies in the Theory of Imperialism*, (London: Longman, 1972).
8. *See*, especially, Bob Rowthorne, 'Imperialism in the 1979s: unity or rivalry', in H. Radice (ed.), *International Firms and Modern Imperialism*, (Harmondsworth: Penguin Books, 1975), esp. pp. 31–2.
9. Sampson, *The Seven Sisters op. cit.* esp. Chs. 4 and 5.
10. *See*, especially, E. Mandel, 'International capitalism and "supra-nationality"', in Radice, *International Firms and Modern Imperialism op. cit.*
11. *See*, for example: Keohane and Nye, *Power and Interdependence op. cit.*; Keohane, *After Hegemony op. cit.*; and J. E. Spero, *The Politics of International Economic Relations*, (London: George Allen and Unwin, 2nd edn., 1981), esp. pp. 23–7, 34–45 and 76–81.
12. *See* F. Hirsch, M. Doyle, E. L. Morse, *Alternatives to Monetary Disorder*, (New York: McGraw-Hill, 197), esp. pp. 27–34.
13. Spero *op cit.* esp. pp. 79–80.
14. Keohane and Nye, *Power and Interdependence op. cit.* pp. 78–80.

15. Spero *op. cit.* pp. 75–9.
16. *ibid.* pp. 80–98.
17. *ibid.* pp. 258–9.
18. *See* 'The court of last resort', *South*, (April 1985), p. 75.
19. *See* J. N. Behrman, *US Business and Governments*, (New York: McGraw-Hill, 1971), p. 71–9.
20. Hirsch, Doyle, Morse, *op. cit.* p. 39.
21. On the 'South Bank', *see* the special report 'Putting up the money', *South* (July 1983), pp. 11–15; and 'South Bank Targets Set', *South*, (July 1984), p. 41.
22. *See*: Fiona Gordon-Ashworth, *International Commodity Control: A Contemporary History and Appraisal*, (London: Croom Helm, 1984); and Cheryl Payer, (ed.), *Commodity Trade of the Third World*, (London: Macmillan, 1975).
23. *See*, for example, C. Fred Bergsten, 'Oil is not the exception', in C. Fred Bergsten, *Toward a New International Economic Order; Selected Papers of C. Fred Bergsten, 1972–1974*, (Lexington: Lexington Books, 1975).
24. *See* Gordon-Ashworth *op. cit.*
25. *See* 'OPEC's final split comes another meeting closer', *The Economist*, 2 February 1985, pp. 63–4.
26. Gordon-Ashworth *op. cit*, p. 265.
27. *ibid.* p. 260.
28. On which, *see* D. H. Blake and R. S. Walter, *The Politics of Global Economic Relations*, (Englewood Cliffs, Prentice-Hall, 1976), pp. 114–15, 123 and 171–2.
29. *See* 'East Africa struggles to overcome divisions', *South*, (August 1982), pp. 64–5.
30. *See*: F. D. Holzman and R. Legvold, 'The economics and politics of East–West relations', in C. Fred Bergsten, *World Politics and International Economics*, (Washington DC: Brookings, 1975); and Spero *op. cit.* Ch. 10.
31. *See* John Vogler, 'Interdependence, power and the World Administrative Radio Conference,' in R. J. Barry Jones and Peter Willetts (eds.), *Interdependence on Trial: Studies in the Theory and Practice of Contemporary Interdependence*, (London: Frances Pinter, 1984).
32. *See*: Barry Buzan, *A Sea of Troubles, Adelphi Paper No. 143*, (London: IISS, 1978); and Keohane and Nye, *Power and Interdependence op. cit.* esp. pp. 86–98.
33. *See* G. J. Stigler, 'A theory of oligopoly', in Bruce Russett (ed.), *Economic Theories of International Politics*, (Chicago: Makham, 1968).
34. For example, the case of the Oil Majors' action against Mexico: Sampson, *The Seven Sisters op. cit.* Ch. 4.
35. *See* O. E. Williamson, 'A Dynamic Theory of Interfirm Behavior', in Russett *op. cit.*
36. *See* R. J. Barry Jones, 'The Definition and Identification of Interdependence', in Jones and Willets *op. cit.* esp. pp. 57–8.

37. Joan Robinson, '"Imperfect competition" revisited', in Joan Robinson, *Contributions to Modern Economics*, (Oxford: Basil Blackwell, 1978).
38. P. Kenyon, 'Pricing', in A. S. Eichner, *A Guide to Post-Keynsian Economics*, (London: Macmillan, 1979).
39. Cheddi Jagan, *The West on Trial: My Fight for Guyana's Freedom*, (London: Michael Joseph, 1966), esp. Ch. 17.
40. *See* A. Sampson, *The Secret State: The Secret History of ITT*, (London: Hodder and Stoughton, 1973), esp. pp. 251–6.

5   Conflict and Disharmony in the Global Political Economy

States, and other global actors, can achieve much through the establishment of control over their economic environments. Such control may be achieved unilaterally or through collaboration with others, whether that collaboration be explicit or tacit. Conflict and disharmony may, however, develop when the pursuit of control by some impinges upon the interests and aspirations of others, or when collaboration breaks down and disharmony results.

Conflicts may arise between actors of all types within the international system and the global political economy. States may clash over matters ranging from fundamental issues of principle to transitory squabbles about the relative advantages to be secured from specific relationships. Transnational corporations may also confront one another in the struggle for sources of supply or dominance within specific markets. Other transnational actors also exhibit conflicts of interest that range from competition amongst religious bodies for adherents to the lethal struggles for power and influence between terrorist (or freedom-fighting) groups.

Collaborative arrangements amongst all types of actors may also collapse at any time. The Prisoner's Dilemma, considered in Chapter 3, demonstrates the general temptation towards defection from collaboration. In the empirical world a range of factors and considerations will influence the choice between continued cooperation, explicit or tacit, and defection. The environment within which actors operate is subject to constant change and this may modify their attitudes towards collaboration. Actors, are, moreover, often mere aggregations of individuals and groups, which have their own internal dynamics. External influences and internal developments may thus alter calculations about cooperation and defection.

CONFLICT AND DEFECTION AMONGST STATES

The reality of international relations is somewhere between the extremes of an unrelenting 'Hobbesian' struggle of all against all, and the liberal vision of a benign world of endless peace and harmony founded upon a *lassez-faire* global economy.

The uneven incidence of international conflict challenges most of the simpler, and more dramatic, theories of international conduct. However, the very complexity and ambiguity of much of reality also provides evidence to support all but the most absurd approaches. Indeed, the same empirical evidence can often be employed to justify interpretations that may be diametrically opposed to one another. The infrequent incidence of conflict between societies can, at one and the same time, be 'explained' in terms of the restraints that human society has placed upon the constant human impulse towards aggression and violence. In direct contrast, human beings can be viewed as essentially peace-loving creatures who are sometimes misled into conflict with one another by perverse political institutions and authorities. The conclusion of most judicious analysts of international conflict is that it remains a constant possibility, but a possibility that is only realized by complex set of conditions.[1]

International systems differ in the relative homogeneity, or heterogeneity, of their dominant members and in the sets of basic objectives that states seek through their international conduct.[2] Systems may contain leading members that are broadly similar in their political outlook and international aspirations, or they may manifest sharp internal differences. The implications of such homogeneity or heterogeneity are difficult to establish with precision but fundamental differences of regime or ideology may well make conflicts sharper and more durable, while conversely making collaboration more difficult. Such conclusions must, however, be treated with considerable caution for there are many historical examples of successful collaboration between states that were fundamentally different in some basic respect, as in the case of the alliance of the Soviet Union with the Western democracies during the Second World War.

International systems also tend to be characterized by the gradual spread of at least a few basic values, aspirations and understandings. Members may acquire values and aspirations from others in the system, while experience also encourages them to learn those forms of behaviour that promise the best chances of satisfying such aspirations. International systems that endure over considerable periods of time may thus assume some semblance of a 'society' with a 'culture'.[3] The vision of an international society should not, however, be taken too far for international relations lack most of the essential features and mechanisms that mark real and cohesive human societies.[4] Unfortunately, the 'culture' of any international system may be such as to encourage conflict, in one way or another.

Human culture has proved highly diverse, throughout human history. Some cultures, such as that of feudal Europe, have been positively militaristic. Others have promoted aspirations that have encouraged conflict and furnished 'principles' that might then justify the resultant conflict. The imperial acquisitiveness of the late nineteenth century and its justificatory ideology of 'civilizing mission' well exemplifies such a culture.

One of the central issues within the social sciences generally, and within international relations in particular, is the relationship between the 'subjective' and the 'objective' in human activity. It can be argued that all conflicts within and between human societies are rooted in the perceptions of the actors involved. In its extreme form, this approach attributes all human conflict to the misperceptions of the participants.[5] In complete contrast, some Marxist theorists argue that there are profound, objective forces at work which govern the human condition and establish the foundations of those ideas and perceptions which appear to be the immediate causes of conflicts.[6] Those wishing to avoid the extremes of either position are faced with a complex equation. It is, however an equation which does permit the identification of some bases of conflict as possessing considerable 'reality', given the conditions in which they arise.

The conditions that generate conflicts between societies are both many and variable in their occurrence. The particular issues that appear to be at stake in specific international conflicts may vary with time and situation. Matters that are uncontentious at one time may engender fierce dispute at another. Changing circumstances have thus brought trade issues to the fore of international controversy, and potential conflict, as global economic conditions have changed during the 1970s and 1980s.

Liberal analysis locates the source of international conflict firmly within the political sphere. Even those conflicts that appear to have an economic basis are held to derive from the prior interference of political authorities with the free development of a *laissez-faire* international economic system. Had such interference not taken place, the liberal maintains that the emergence of a mutually beneficial pattern of trade, economic specialization and interdependence would have demonstrated the illusory character of disputes over economic matters and continued the system against political conflicts. The liberal thus rejects, and can certainly not accommodate, the view that developments in the global economy may themselves actually generate serious international conflicts.

Chapter 2 was devoted to a detailed critique of the liberal view of economics in general and of the international economy in particular. At this stage of the discussion, it is sufficient to note that there are two possible arguments that would account for the inability of the liberal approach to accommodate the possibility that economic developments themselves may engender international conflict. The first of these is that the approach is sound, in principle, but limited by its neglect of a number of important features of reality. The second, and more damaging, argument is that the liberal approach is fundamentally unsound and is, therefore, inherently unable to reflect and accommodate much of reality.

A possible shortcoming of the liberal view of economic reality is its neglect of the 'zero-sum' (what one gains the other loses) possibilities inherent in the process whereby the gains of mutually advantageous trade are shared out between participants. Liberal theory is able to claim no more than trade will, under most conditions, be beneficial to all participants: it is unable to demonstrate what the size of the relative benefits are or, indeed, illuminate the processes through which that allocation is determined. Figure 5.1 illustrates the 'bargaining set' that might arise between two parties to a pattern of trade that could be mutually advantageous.

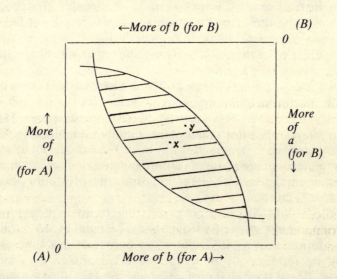

Note: The figure represents two societies—A and B—which produce, and potentially trade, two products—a and b. The trading relationship allows both to obtain a higher level of well-being. The area of mutual improvement in well-being is represented by the shaded area surrounded by the ellipse formed by the two points of intersection between the two curves drawn in the diagram. (Each curve is an indifference curve for one of the two societies—represents a set of combinations of the two products (a and b) with which the society in question would be equally happy—the society is, in short, indifferent as between any of those combinations.)

Figures 5.1: A bargaining set for two trading societies.

The establishment of trade between societies *A* and *B* allows them to move to some point of higher mutual satisfaction, within the shaded area on Figure 5.1. The outcome must, however, be a combination of simultaneous consumption of two goods—*a* and *b*—by both society *A* and society *B*, that is represented by just one point within the shaded area. The critical questions then, are the actual location of that point and the means by which it is to be determined. In an equitable world the outcome might be that represented by point *X*, in which the advantage is shared, reasonably equally, between both societies. If, however, the general power of society *A* has allowed it to impose the outcome represented by position *Y* then society *B* will have secured very little advantage from the trade relationship. Indeed, it may well be that the advantage actually secured will fail to provide adequate compensation, during the foreseeable future, for costs that society *B* has incurred in adjusting to the new pattern of trade.

A society that fails to secure a 'fair' share of the benefits of trade might, ultimately, gain sufficient compensation to justify the costs of adjusting to that pattern of trade. However, the experience of an inequitable relationship, and of the processes by which it has been generated, might well stimulate an acute sense of resentment and, indeed, induce a fundamental sense of alienation from the prevailing international economic order.

The belief that the benefits secured are inadequate might develop at any stage of a society's involvement in any pattern of international trade. Relative advantage at one time may well be replaced by unacceptable disadvantage at a later stage. When the balance of advantage turns against a society its attitude towards the relevant relationship may well change. Efforts may be made to alter the distribution of benefits in a more advantageous way and through a variety of means. In the extreme, the less favoured society may decide that no trade is preferable to the unequal trade with which it is currently presented. Attempts to modify or terminate an international economic relationship may well stimulate political tension and the broadening of potential conflict. The reactions of both the USA and many of the European nations to the growing trade imbalance with Japan illustrates the potentialities for such tension-inducing developments.

The responses of societies to what they believe to be long-standing inequities in the international economic relationships within which they find themselves may also engender tensions and political conflicts. The call for a New International Economic Order by the Less Developed Countries during the 1970s was founded upon the view that the structure of North–South economic relations had been biased to the advantage of the North. The resentments that stimulated this demand were very real, and took little notice of the doubts cast by liberals upon the validity of the South's criticisms of the prevailing pattern of economic relations. The political confrontation between North and South was also very real, despite the false optimism that many invested in the South's prospects of success in extracting major concessions from the North. Indeed, the very concept of the *South* had a symbolic and ideological reality that little reflected the heterogeneity of this loose group of societies in practice.[7] The driving forces of politics are more diffuse, diverse and less determined by 'objective' realities than is often acknowledged in the formulations of liberal, and certainly neo-classical, economic theorists!

It is not only external factors that stimulate societies towards conflict with others. Pressures arising within a nation-state may also prompt antagonistic external behaviour. It has long been a commonplace feature of international politics that regimes often resort to external adventures to deflect domestic criticism, or suppress internal turbulence. The Argentine invasion of the British dependency of the Falkland Islands in 1982 may well exemplify such a departure in policy. There is also some evidence that democratic administrations have sometimes been disposed to define certain international developments as major threats, or pressing crises, as a means of restoring flagging domestic political fortunes.

The pressure to secure economic well-being has also made itself felt, with considerable force, upon modern governments. The obstacles to economic development have, furthermore, been particularly serious for the governments of the LDCs. Such pressures are by no means illegitimate, as is sometimes suggested by the more extreme advocates of free trade, for they represent the real needs that populations need to have satisfied and which can often be satisfied, ultimately, only by their own governments. The problem with such internal pressures is that they often prompt governments to adopt courses of action that threaten to bring them into conflict with other societies.

Conflicts may thus arise between societies whose behaviour is directed by internal needs and forces. However, desirable and mutually advantageous forms of collaboration may also be undermined by such pressures. The desirability of these forms of collaboration may vary and, indeed, may be the subject of considerable theoretical controversy, as in the case of a free-trade system or a system for the effective joint control of TNCs. The motivating considerations may also vary in their legitimacy and may not always be the most elevated, as in the case of the sale of coffee in excess of the International Coffee Agreement quotes by Idi Amin's bankrupt Ugandan regime.

The issue, however, is that societies may often find the pressures for defection from international collaboration, or for entry into conflict with others, virtually irresistable. The governments of all states, being cognizant entities, are, or should be, fully aware of the possibilities that other societies will defect from collaborative arrangements or even precipitate conflict. Decisions about external behaviour and internal policy must, therefore, be taken in the light of such malign possibilities and cannot be based exclusively upon 'best case' expectations about the future behaviour of others. Indeed cooperation, or mutual restraint, in international economic activity can never be fully relied upon because it remains vulnerable to disruption by politically based conflicts or the actions of third parties.

A society may be exposed to considerable danger by a high level of reliance upon international trade and especially upon foreign sources of necessary commodities, goods and services. Such vulnerability is exemplified by the case, albeit largely unavoidable, of Great Britain during the Second World War. Here, substantial dependence upon overseas sources of many basic supplies rendered Britain particularly vulnerable to the maritime blockade that Germany was able to operate with her submarines and aircraft.

General economic vulnerabililty is not, however, the whole story for there may be specific dependencies which can prove extremely serious for societies. Again, the history of Great Britain provides an apt example. Prior to the outbreak of the First World War Britain had 'permitted' her former lead in the production of chemicals to be lost and, indeed, replaced by a growing dependence upon supplies of a number of critical chemicals from the newly competitive producers in Germany. When war then broke out with Germany and her allies in 1914, Britain found herself in the embarrassing position of being denied supplies from Germany of explosives and dyes.[8] Without explosives to propel and charge her munitions, and without dyes for the uniforms of her armed forces, Britain's war effort was somewhat embarrassed until the depredations of recent industrial neglect could be made good.

War is not the only development that can embarass a society that has become over-dependent upon international trade in general, or in some particular aspect. Economic developments can also wreak havoc upon the over-exposed national economy. The effects of the Great Depression of the early 1930s impacted most heavily upon those societies whose exports constituted a higher proportion of their economic activity and who were unable to protect their exports through devices such as Britain's Imperial Preference system.[9] As each society then responded to the crisis by attempting to preserve its domestic industry through protectionist barriers against imports, the damage to those societies that had become heavily dependent upon exports was intensified.

Difficulties may also be created for societies whose policies encourage, or expose them to, high levels of international trade in the absence of serious global economic difficulties. Serious adverse developments may take place which the authorities and publics of some societies fail to recognize because they have adopted a relaxed attitude towards international trade. Unanticipated damage may be particularly great when a society is faced with a competitor that is neither relaxed nor naive about international trade and is, in clear contrast, determined to seize every opportunity to gain a competitive advantage in targeted industries. The collapse of so many Western industries in the face of overwhelming, and often unexpected, Japanese competition, exemplifies the dangers of an unwary approach to international trade.[10]

A naive response to the rhetoric of free-trade may impose damage not only upon inadequately defended Advanced Industrial Countries but also upon Less Developed Countries that are seeking promising areas into which to direct their industrial development. With a generally impoverished domestic population, many LDCs have concluded that development is possible only upon the basis of industries that are orientated, initially at least, towards the markets of the world's richer nations. Unfortunately, success in developing competitive industries has often brought such LDCs into conflict with the very countries to which they wish to export their products. Thus, LDCs like Sri Lanka have found their exports of clothes and textiles to AICs obstructed by the increasingly protectionist Multifibre Arrangement.[11] Again, the Brazilian export-led strategy for growth and development has encountered substantial problems in a world in which protectionist barriers have flourished in the wake of the recession of the early 1980s. A massive debt crisis and savage domestic deflation have been Brazil's reward for relying upon the benefits of international trade.[12]

Specific economic dependencies may also subject societies to particular, and often quite serious, vulnerabilities. Contemporary dependencies upon oil illustrate this danger. The oil embargo of 1973–4 demonstrated the exposure of a number of the AICs to the threat of serious economic disruption in the wake of any interruption of regular shipments of the imported oil upon which they had become so dependent. The early and middle 1980s have, however, revealed the contrasting dangers of over-reliance upon the extraction and exportation of crude oil. A number of societies that found themselves floating upon an oil-based economic boom during the late 1970s and earlier 1980s have been seriously affected by the steady fall in crude oil prices during the mid 1980s.

Many patterns of international economic cooperation and harmony may thus be quite fragile. Indeed, the stability of the whole post-war 'liberal order' may have been built upon foundations that included such ephemeral conditions as: the singular strength of the USA, the phased process of economic recovery and development facilitated by the varying levels of war-time damage experienced by many of the industrialized societies, and the delayed start to serious development by the LDCs that resulted from the slow and phased pattern of decolonization.

The international outlook of societies is therefore, or should be, conditioned by an awareness of the dangerous developments that may well arise within their international economic relationships. Harmonious economic relationships may well be disrupted by political conflicts, by disputes over economic issues or by the myriad temptations to defect from collaborative arrangements. Moreover, societies that are more exposed to the international economy may well be more seriously harmed by such developments. The possibilities of serious harm are a major problem for liberal theorists and the uncritical welcome that they extend to unfettered free trade. They are also a constant concern of judicious political authorities and communities. In the real world, an expectation of the 'second best' may be the wisest course, as even the most doctrinally 'liberal' of contemporary governments have gradually been forced to acknowledge.[13]

CONFLICT AND DEFECTION AMONGST TRANSNATIONAL ACTORS

Conflict and defection from collaborative arrangements are not peculiar to nation-states for they may also be manifest by other types of transnational actors. Given this study's primary focus upon the global political economy, transnational corporations are of the greatest interest here.

The simplest conception of a market economy identifies all business enterprises as being in competition with others in the same area of production and supply. Such competition is a special form of conflict for it often assumes a zero-sum form in which the achievement of a larger share of the market for a good is secured at the expense of some other supplier.

Analysis of the mechanisms of actual competition in the real world reveals a realm of strategic calculation and tactical manoeuvre and an overall picture that resembles that of a physical conflict between determined combatants.

As analysis is further extended, oligopolies emerge and patterns of collaboration, both explicit and tacit, become possibilities. The problem for such forms of collaboration, however, is that the participants remain competitive with one another. Collaboration, then, is no more than a tenuous, and essentially defensive alliance against the 'outside' world. As with all such limited and basically defensive arrangements, a number of developments can disrupt the fragile harmony of the 'alliance'.[14]

Collaborative arrangements between TNCs—oligopolistic cartels of one form or another—may operate to the mutual advantage of all participants and so so for considerable periods of time. This harmonious condition may, however, be undermined by many developments. The calculus of relative advantage of adhering to the arrangement or defecting in pursuit of short-term gains is, itself, unstable. The environment within which the cartel operates may also change and alter calculations. New opportunities may, finally, emerge and face cartel members with powerful temptations to follow their own paths. The history of the oil and petroleum industry illustrates most of these possibilities.

The sale of petroleum to the motorist provides a classic illustration of oligopolistic competition and its inherent instability. The prices charged to normal customers at the petrol pump by the major petroleum distributors are usually the same within any geographical area. Such competition as does occur is undertaken in areas other than price. Advertising may seek to proclaim the peculiar virtues of a given brand of petroleum, despite the virtual identity between any two distributors' fuel. 'Gifts' may be provided for those who purchase certain quantities of petrol. Customers may be given opportunities to play one of a variety of ludicrous games that promise vast, though rarely won, prizes. Distributors may even attempt to offer consistently high facilities at their petrol stations, in an attempt to develop a measure of customer loyalty.

Tacit price maintenance does not always survive within the petrol-distributing cartel, however. Should a major cartel member require a boost in its current revenue levels, or find that it has growing reserves of unsold fuel, it may be tempted to cut prices in order to increase turnover and, hence, revenue earnings. Customer loyalty in the petrol industry seems to have declined markedly in recent years. A reduction in pump prices may therefore stimulate a rapid switch of sales from distributors that have maintained their prices to the supplier that has introduced a price cut. The effect upon those who have attempted to resist the price reduction may soon be so great, in terms of reduced volume of sales and revenue generated, that they too are forced to make commensurate reductions in their parties.

A round of price reductions clearly deprives the petrol companies of profits proportional to the size of the price cut. Unfortunately, such price reductions may not prove to be a discrete event—a process of competitive price cutting, which has no determinate terminal point, may well be precipitated. It is just such a process of mutual blood-letting which is so difficult to stop once started that makes TNCs generally, and the oil corporations in particular, so nervous about any signs of a fissure in their price-maintaining cartel

The process of competitive price cutting, if started, assumes an appearance similar to that of an arms race between opposing military powers. Many conditions determine the pattern of such an 'arms race', or Richardson Process, and the pattern itself may lead to a point of equilibrium at which stability is regained, or result in remorseless escalation.[15] Figures 5.2 and 5.3 illustrate the two forms of 'arms race' process that can develop.

Figure 5.2 illustrates a process of increasing hostility which eventually comes to rest at the point of equilibrium E. In this example, the relationship was stable at the point of origin O. Some disturbance, however, caused actor A to take a hostile action—represented by point IA on actor A's (Expressions of Hostility) axis. The figure then indicates actor B's response to such an expression of hostility by actor A. Actor B's response is identified by moving from position IA horizontally along the dotted line until it intersects with actor B's

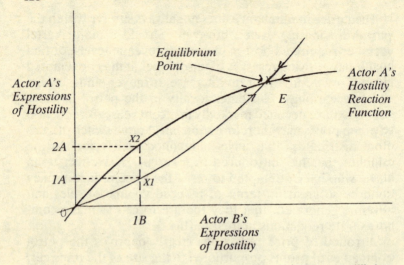

Figure 5.2: A process of increasing hostility (arms race) with an equilibrium point.

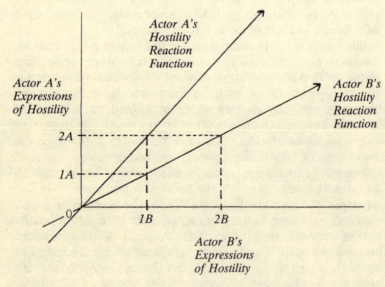

Figure 5.3: An unstable process of escalating hostility (arms race).

Hostility Reaction Function at point *X153*. *Moving down* vertically from this point of intersection, along the broken line, indicates that actor *B* will respond by an expression of hostility represented by point *1B* (on actor *B*'s Expressions of Hostility axis).

A single round of action and reaction is simply demonstrated by Figure 5.2. However, the figure represents the reactions of both actors to *any* expression of hostility by the other. It is possible, therefore, to continue the analysis and establish the response of actor *A* to the level of expression of hostility—*1B*— by actor *B*. This is undertaken by reversing the process outlined in the preceding paragraph but now following the vertical line up from *1B* to the point at which it intersects actor *A*'s Hostility Reaction Function—*X2*. From *X2* the horizontal dotted line intersects actor *A*'s Expression of Hostility axis at point *2A*: the point that represents the expression of hostility that actor *A* will now make in response to actor *B*'s expression of hostility *1B*.

The process of identifying each actors' response to each others' succession of expressions of hostility can be continued. In Figure 5.2 it will be found that the increases of expressed hostility by the two actors diminish gradually until they cease, and become static, at point *E*—the point of equilibrium. The pattern of action and reaction will now be stable unless some external force disturbs the relationship. However, the movements induced by such disturbances will be immediately reversed and the 'system' returned to equilibrium at *E*. Moreover, had the relationship 'overshot' *E* as it developed initially, its further progress would have been arrested and its development turned back towards *E*.

A similar analysis of Figure 5.3 reveals that its dynamic is entirely different from that of Figure 5.2. Should a disturbance now induce actor *A* to make an expression of hostility, represented by point *1A*, then as before actor *B* will respond with an expression of hostility represented by point *1B*. However, actor *A* will respond to this level of expressed hostility by actor *B* with a jump in its level of expressed hostility to *2A*. Actor *B*, in turn, will now respond with an even larger jump in the level of its expressed hostility, to point *2B*. This process of escalation in expressions of hostility will, in theory, continue indefinitely. In practice, however, changes occur at critical stages of such developments: one side may be unable, or unwilling, to continue the escalation; or, both sides may lose patience, become desperate, or simply miscalculate and turn the relationship into something more damaging (war in the case of an arms race proper).

As the discussion of the Prisoner's Dilemma in Chapter 3 indicated, the conditions that will undermine cooperation are not difficult to discover, or generate, in a world of real uncertainty and considerable distrust. A range of internal considerations of changes in external conditions can encourage defection or moves that can, all too easily, precipitate a process of increasingly hostile action and reaction.

External disturbances may assume many forms. Governmental action often precipitates the collapse of collaborative arrangements between TNCs, even when that was not the intention behind the original action. A government might offer one TNC a new opportunity which provides the corporation with additional strength and capability, and thereby encourages it to challenge its erstwhile colleagues. Another opportunity might precipitate conflict between the beneficiary and those that are resentful at having been excluded. The auctioning of Britain's North Sea oil-beds thus drew the major oil companies into a vigorous competitive scramble to secure advantageous shares and promising sectors.

Technological discoveries and innovations may also equip a particular TNC with an advantage which it is tempted to exploit against its fellows. In the case of the oil industry, however, it has been new geographical discoveries of oil sources that have historically been most disruptive. The early exploitation of the Middle East's oil reserves precipitated particularly intense conflicts between the major oil interests and, indeed, between their supporting home country governments.[16]

The considerations, and developments, that may prompt a TNC to break from a delicate collaborative arrangement with others have analogies in other areas of cooperation in the international system. With international terrorist or freedom-fighting groups, the consequences of fragmentation may be lethal for some former colleagues. In the case of other transnational actors, like religious, cultural or intellectual bodies, the effects of crumbling accord may be less spectacular, but not less awkward for those involved. Whatever the context, causes or precise consequences, the calculation of appropriate behaviour remains equally problematical and the results of defection exhibit similar patterns.

CONFLICT BETWEEN STATES AND TRANSNATIONAL ACTORS

The contemporary analysis of international relations has had to accommodate conflicts that did not much concern earlier students in the field. The modern global system is characterized, in good part, by conflicts of interest and activity between societies, on the one hand, and a variety of transnational actors, on the other. A phenomenon that has long historical roots has been massively amplified by the modern communications revolution, in which the movements of both people and information have become rapid, relatively cheap and, hence, commonplace.

A second feature of the post-war era is equally pertinent to the calculus of relationships between societies and transnational actors. Despite the apparent 'shrinkage' of the world, and the associated advance of 'interdependence', the worship of state sovereignty has rarely been more intense. The world today is marked by a plethora of legally recognized states.

The political authorities of modern states are often desperate to maintain control, and promote economic development internally, while preserving the country's dignity externally. A critical paradox is thus established: states are so obsessed with the preservation of their own sovereignty that they undermine effective international collaboration in many important areas of activity; failures of international collaboration in the establishment of effective global regulation and control then allow transnational actors to behave in ways that undermine the real sovereignty of states. The pursuit of sovereignty may, thus, be a self-defeating strategy in a world increasingly bestridden by transnational actors.

Acknowledging the self-defeating character of self-regarding state behaviour in the modern world does nothing, however, to relieve the practical dilemma with which societies are faced. Collaboration amongst states might be desirble, indeed vital, but that itself does nothing to ensure effective collaboration. Indeed, there may be sound, and very real, suspicions that commitment to collaboration might actually worsen a society's position by exposing it to the damage suffered when others defect at critical moments in the history of such arrangements.

Fear of self-damage though naive behaviour is thus a constant check upon the dispositions of states towards many forms of international cooperation and collaboration. Indeed, effective international cooperation may develop only when the lack of such cooperative behaviour generates clear, substantial and unavoidable costs for each, and any, non-cooperating state. In the case of a defensive military alliance, it is the experience of a threat, which carries inherent potential costs and which has to be faced in one way or another, which generates such unavoidable costs for non-collaborators.[17]

Many situations that face modern states lack the apparent clarity of military and security threats. It is quite possible for governments and their peoples to fail to identify the threat that arises from a given quarter or to miscalculate the balance of costs and benefits deriving from certain developments. The relationships between societies and TNCs are replete with examples of both types of error. Failures of state policy towards TNCs partly reflect such errors, and such errors, in turn, are part of the complex balance of power and advantage that develops between the state and the corporation in any confrontation.

When nation-states face TNCs they possess a number of assets which can, in theory, be deployed with considerable effect. In the purely economic sphere, the nation-state may offer the corporation production advantages, market-access advantages, or a combination of the two.[18] Politically, the nation-state is endowed with legal sovereignty over all that exists within its frontiers, has control of a military and police apparatus and should be able to call upon the support of a substantial population.

The assets of a nation-state are, however, far from secure and may often prove to be quite illusory. Production advantages are of little substance if equally good opportunities exist in other countries. Market-access advantages are often overlooked by states, are often qualified by the wish to secure the goods and services being offered by the TNC and may be particularly difficult to withdraw once made available. Politically, sovereignty exists as a reality only where it can be enforced. The military and the police are not always the unquestioning servants of governments, and may sometimes be subverted by the agents of a TNC. The populations of most societies are rarely entirely unified on all issues or in their support of any government. Internal political differences are precisely the material that external agencies such as TNCs can exploit implicitly and, at times, explicitly.

In any potential confrontation with nation-states, TNCs do not appear to have that many inherent advantages. TNCs enjoy no special status in international law and, indeed, are often the subject of considerable suspicion within the global community. TNCs are not entitled to recruit military forces and cannot call upon loyal populations in their conflicts with others. The power and influence of a business enterprise thus appears to be severely limited.

The reality of transnational business, however, contrasts markedly with the politically naive view outlined above. TNCs are able to combine the actual shortcomings of many nation-states with the advantages gleaned from their own transnational mode of operation to construct a potentially powerful armoury of techniques and devices with which to engage geographically anchored societies.

Their transnational mode of operation endows TNCs with invaluable assets. Relocation to 'off-shore' headquarters in countries that impose minimal regulation and negligible taxation is an opportunity that TNCs are exploiting with increasing frequency. Transnational operation allows also the TNC to practice the highly advantageous form of transfer pricing discussed in an earlier section. Transnationality also encourages, and partly facilitates, an unprecedented level of mobility. Corporations develop investment programmes, shift capital, allocate production and marketing shares and move their financial assets with greater flexibility than nationally based firms or, indeed, many earlier international producers.

TNCs are often able to exploit the possibilities for international manoeuvre and flexibility with considerable surreptitiousness. Host states may find that significant developments have taken place without their awareness, let alone approval. However, it may often be to a TNCS's advantage to publicize the possibility of its opportunities for international mobility. States or work forces that are proving awkward on one issue or another may be 'persuaded' to adopt favourable policies by the threat of withdrawal from operation in those countries or of concentration of new investment in other countries or areas of the world. The recent threat by Ford to end the production of motor cars in Europe is a classic example of such a thinly veiled threat to European governments and trade unions alike.[19]

The subsidiaries of contemporary TNCs are increasingly the pawns in a global economic chess game directed, strategically, by the central headquarters. Geographical flexibility is a prime asset which may even be pursued to the point of moving the headquarters from the corporation's traditional home. Sad, indeed, is the corporation that operates transnationally but which finds that its geographical flexibility is limited by the scarcity of the resources that are its business or the location of assets in which it has made a costly investment. Corporations that are fixed by immovable roots may be able to exploit such possibilities as transfer pricing but their bargaining position may be severely limited once the host country understands what is happening and appreciates the potential advantage with which it is endowed.

All is not lost, however, for a TNC that is inescapably committed to operations within given countries. Modern nation-states are, in reality, affected by numerous weakness and disabilities, which may often be to the advantage of TNCs. The shortcomings of nation-states range from objective dependencies to vulnerability to nefarious influences.

Few societies are totally self-sufficient in the resources and capabilities necessary to satisfy the entire range of the needs and wants of their populations. Investment capital may be insufficient to undertake new, and valued, developments. The technical capabilities, and general know-how, available locally may be inadequate in some areas. The ability to develop and sustain a world-wide system of distribution, or to secure appropriate levels of access to necessary markets, may also be beyond many societies for whom exports are economically essential. Such weaknesses may seriously damage the economic development of a society but may often be overcome with the help of a TNC.

TNCs are, characteristically, organizations that are handsomely endowed with capital, technical competence, general know-how and ready-made systems of distribution to, and sales in, most of the world's major markets. The package of assistance that the TNC can offer the beleaguered state may thus be irresistible. The governments of host states may believe, correctly or incorrectly, that the TNC will be able to impose an economic relationship upon them that is, in some sense, exploitative.[20] They may, again, suspect that the relationship, once established, will be open to further manipulation by the corporation. However, the needs of the host society may be such that its leaders conclude that inward investment by a TNC is the lesser of two evils.

Governments, despite their affectations of omniscience, are rarely able to determine policies on the basis of full information, perfect anticipation or, indeed, precise calculation. A veil of ignorance shrouds many of those future developments that will actually determine whether or not a new investment, or economic initiative, will prove to be of benefit to a society. The quality of decision making towards potential investments by TNCs will, however, be reduced by a number of factors. A government may simply be naive about the nature, capabilities and characteristic practices of TNCs. Such a government may well have inflated expectations of the benefits that will be secure from any new TNC venture. Such naivety may, furthermore, be reinforced if a government is entranced by a liberal economic doctrine which itself obstructs full recognition of the many dangers attendant upon transnational business.

Administrative incompetence may also inhibit recognition of a TNC's actual contributions to an economy. Failure to collect taxes efficiently, to ensure appropriate accounting procedures, to monitor financial flows, or to develop adequate intelligence about international industrial and trade conditions may deny a government the ability to make a sound judgement about the benefits secured from the operations of a TNC's subsidiary. Unfortunately, the resources required to satisfy these administrative conditions are so demanding as to be beyond the means of most contemporary nation-states. Indeed, a number of attempts to develop international agencies to monitor the activities of TNCs, under the auspices of such organizations as the United Nations and the European Economic Community, have been stimulated by the recognition by many nation-states of just such difficulties.[21]

The political realities of most nation-states are also such as to undermine seriously their strength in bargaining with, or even confronting, TNCs. The creation of a community that is totally homogeneous in its political views and judgements has not yet been achieved even by such states as Nazi Germany or Mao's China. In less extreme societies, divisions of outlook and opinion abound, even where the basics of belief and fellow-feeling remain common to most citizens. Such political differences are readily exploitable by TNCs and their local allies. Sympathetic governments can be encouraged and rewarded in many ways. Unsympathetic governments can be opposed by opposition groups and parties, whose views can be influenced by the TNCs. Local newspapers may be in the hands of sympathetic owners or, as is the case in many parts of the worlds, owned by TNCs, like Britain's Lonrho, or individuals, such as Rupert Murdoch, who are themselves transnational entrepreneurs. The actual effects of TNCs remain sufficiently complex, and even ambiguous, to permit expressions of approval in even the most unpromising cases.

Unfortunately relationships with legitimate political movements within heterogeneous political communities do not exhaust the possibilities that are open to determined TNCs in their dealings with unresponsive governments. Many factors will influence the forms of activity that a TNC will deem judicious within any society, but suitable conditions have evinced such reprehensible behaviour at the funding of secessionist regimes, as in the case of Union Miniere's funding of Tshombie's breakaway Katanga in the aftermath of Belgium's withdrawal from Zaire[22] and the active support of the violent military coup d'etat against Allende's socialist government in Chile.[23] The behavioural standards of TNCs may well vary according to the area in which they are operating. It is advisable, therefore, for governments to be aware of their rating in such respects when dealing with TNCs.

Subversion by TNCs is not, however, always a matter of conscious political decision. TNCs have often been accused of generating a form of cultural subversion which undermines local beliefs, values and practices, while implanting a Western, materialistic and 'consumerist' outlook. Such views are to be discerned in the writings of many Western critics of TNCs and in the proclamations of the ideologues of such anti-Western movements as Iran's moslem fundamentalism. Empirically, it is clear that TNCs do spread increasingly similar products, and the disposition to acquire them, around the world. Judgements about the desirability, or even acceptability, of such a process are, however, a matter of ideology.

It is both theoretically and empirically possible that, as liberals contend, TNCs do bring considerable economic benefits to the societies in which they operate. There are, however, a number of issues over which conflict may well develop and many conditions that will determine the relative strengths of the two sides in any confrontation.

Societies will be rightly concerned with the effects of TNC activity upon the movement of capital and investment, and upon the location of productive activity. They will wish to secure 'fair' economic returns for their community, however the judgement of what is 'fair' may be made. Governments will also be keenly interested in the impact of TNCs' operations upon global financial flows, in general, and financial flows across their borders, in particular. The extent to which societies are able to tame TNCs and secure beneficial effects is, however, a complex and indeterminate matter.

CONCLUSIONS: COOPERATION, CONFLICT AND THE IMPERATIVE FOR SELF-HELP IN THE CONTEMPORARY INTERNATIONAL ORDER

The essential problem for the state in the contemporary international order is that while cooperation, both explicit and implicit, may be the optimal course there are many serious impediments to such collaboration. Many other types of transnational actor are also confronted by a similar dilemma; they too may be advantaged by cooperation but find that they are strongly tempted to defect or are vulnerable to the consequences of the defection of others.

The issues of cooperation amongst nation-states confronts both liberals and Economic Realists. All but the most naive liberals recognize that the implicit cooperation amongst states that is a necessary condition of orderly international trade is difficult to sustain. Rationality, by pure economic standards, is ambiguous in its implications in this area and, indeed, as the work on collective action suggests, such rationality may be fatal to collaborative behaviour. Dominant leadership and subsequent institution building may, therefore, be necessary conditions for the development and maintenance of a liberal economic order. However, despite the heroic efforts at reassurance of analysts like Robert Keohane,[24] such collaboration may be tenuous and the conditions upon which it rests ephemeral.

The Economic Realist also recognizes that international collaboration to control and regulate the economic environment is highly desirable. However, such analysts also recognize the dilemma to which societies, and their leaders, are subject. Self-sacrifice in the pursuit of collaborative arrangements that fail to materialize is not the basis of sound conduct for Economic Realists. While collaboration, of the right sort, may be the most desirable condition, its attainment should be approached with caution for others may well seize an unfair advantage. Enthusiasm for any form of international collaboration, whether through formal agreement or the tacit acceptance of international trade, should always be tempered and prior regard paid to the protection of one's own society's interests and well-being. Where cooperation is to be attempted it should, moreover, be as well organized as possible and accompanied by clear penalties for defection. The development of many of the institutions and rules of the EEC can be viewed as just such an attempt, albeit cautious, to construct a tighter and more reassuring form of cooperative international association.

Nothing in the Economic Realist's prescription of self-protection, and caution in approaching international collaboration, discords with the actual behaviour of other major actors upon the international and transnational scene. Transnational corporations that failed to pay due regard to such principles would not long survive in the global business jungle. Equally transitory would be the presence of other political, quasi-military and religious organizations that committed themselves hastily to collaborative ventures. Certainly the histories of many of the world's major organized religions would have earned the admiration of Niccolò Machiavelli and indeed, in the shape of the Borgia family, succeeded in stimulating his intellect.

If the fate of societies cannot rest exclusively, or even primarily, upon collaboration with others then measures of self-help assume major significance. In the political realm, the maintenance of military forces has long been recognized as the norm for those states that have a serious regard for their security and sovereignty. The implications of self-help in the economic sphere are, however, more diffuse, complex and, given the intellectual influence of liberal economic theory, a more controversial matter. The recognition of the breadth of economically relevant measures of self-help, and an acknowledgement of their central significance to the well-being of communities in an uncertain world, is, however, a matter of considerable importance. It is to this realm of policy and activity that the attention of the next section of this book is directerd.

NOTES

1. For a standard discussion, *see* K. N. Waltz, *Man, The State and War: A Theoretical Analysis*, (New York: Columbia University Press, 1954).

2. *See*, for instance, the discussion in: K. N. Waltz, *Theory of International Politics*, (Reading, Mass.: Addison-Wesley, 1979), esp. pp. 100–1; and R. J. Barry Jones 'Concepts and models of change in international relations', in Barry Buzan and R. J. Barry Jones (eds.), *Change and the Study of International Relations: The Evaded Dimension*, (London: Frances Pinter, 1981), esp. pp. 16–17.

3. *See* the proximate notions developed by Evan Luard, *Types of International Society*, (New York: Free Press, 1976), esp. Chs. 5, 7, 12 and 13.

4. *See* Roy E. Jones, 'The English School of International Relations: a case for closure', *Review of International Studies*, Vol. 7 (January, 1981), pp. 1–13.

5. *See* J. W. Burton and A. J. R. Groom, C. R. Mitchell, A. V. S. de Reuck, *The Study of World Society: A London Perspective*, (International Studies Association (USA), 1974).

6. *See* the discussion by Andrew Gamble, 'Critical political economy', in R. J. Barry Jones (ed.), *Perspectives on Political Economy*, (London: Frances Pinter, 1983).

7. For an historical survey *see* Charles Jones, *The North–South Dialogue: A Brief History*, (London: Frances Pinter, 1983).

8. *See*, especially, Corelli Barnett, *The Collapse of British Power*, (London: Eyre Methuen, 1972), pp. 85–8.

9. *See* Angus Maddison, 'Economic policy and performance in Europe, 1913–1970', in C. M. Cipolla, *The Twentieth Century, Vol. 2: The Fontana Economic History of Europe*, (London: Fontana, 1976), esp. pp. 457–66.

10. *See* G. C. Allen, *How Japan Competes*, (London: Institute of Economic Affairs, 1978), esp. pp. 11–29.

11. On Britain's position on and role in the MFA *see* G. Shepherd, 'UK economic policies and their implications for Third World countries: the case of textiles and clothing', in A. R. Fiddell, (ed.), *Adjustment or Protectionism: The Challenge to Britain of Third World Industrialisation*, (London: Catholic Institute for International Relations, 1980).

12. *See*, for example, 'Brazil's strategy awry as exports slump', *South*, (September 1982), p. 67.

12. *See*, for instance, the report of the Thatcher Government's late recognition of the need for substantial export credits: 'Thatcher U-turn on export loans', *Guardian*, 22 May 1985, p. 32.

14. *See* J. R. Friedman, C. Bladen, S. Rosen (eds.), *Alliance in International Politics*, (Boston: Allyn and Bacon Inc., 1970), esp. George Liska, 'Alignments and realignments'.

15. On such 'arms races' *see* K. E. Boulding, *Conflict and Defense: A General Theory*, (New York: Harper and Row, 1962), esp. pp. 25–40.

16. A. Sampson, *The Seven Sisters: The Great Oil Companies and the World They Made*, (London: Hodder and Stoughton, 1975), esp. Ch. 4.

17. *See* Mancur Olson and Richard Zeckhauser, 'An economic theory of

alliances', *Review of Economics and Statistics*, Vol. XLVIII (August 1966).

18. *See* R. J. Barry Jones, 'The United Kingdom and transnational corporations', in R. B. Stauffer (ed.), *Transnational Corportions and National Governments*, (Sydney: Centre for the Study of Transnational Corporations, 1985).

19. 'Ford warns it may cut European base', *Guardian*, 30 January 1985, p. 3.

20. On this concept *see* R. Jenkins, *Exploitation*, (London: MacGibbon and Kee Ltd., 1970).

21. *See*, for example, the information on EEC moves in: 'Multinational face controls', *Guardian*, 9 October 1981, p. 17.

22. *See* Kwame Nkrumah, *Neo-Colonialism: The Last Stage of Imperialism*, (London: Heinemann, 1965), esp. Ch. 4.

23. A. Sampson, *The Secret State: The Secret History of ITT*, (London: Hodder and Stoughton, 1973), esp. Ch. 11.

24. R. O. Keohane, *After Hegemony: Coopertion and Discord in the World Political Economy*, (Princeton: Princeton University Press, 1984).

Part IV
Economic Realism and Contemporary
Neo-Mercantilism

6 The Implications of Economic Realism for State Behaviour

INTRODUCTION

A world in which collaboration with others may often be advantageous for all concerned, but rarely invites total confidence, confronts societies with a substantial dilemma. The calculation of the relative advantages and disadvantages of various forms of collaboration may also be complex. Indeed, the balance of advantage and disadvantage may well shift as pertinent conditions alter.

Societies, and their governments, also have to determine not only whether to participate in collaborative arrangements, but also on what terms that collaboration will take place. Liberal theory assumes that impersonal mechanisms produce favourable economic conditions without conscious decision by society or government. This notion illuminates some features of economic life but bears little resemblance to the practices actually adopted by real societies or their governments. It is, moreover, quite clear that dramatic levels of economic progress often owe much to the general policy framework established by governments and to a range of activities in which political authorities have engaged. Competitive international trade may, or may not, promote general well-being: policies intentionally designed to maximize a society's benefits from such a pattern of trade will, however, often secure greater well-being for the home population, whatever the impact upon others.

In the contemporary world, governments that fail to approach all forms of international collaboration, whether they be disarmament agreements, alliances, common markets or 'free-trade' systems, without due caution and reserve may do serious disservice to their populations. It must always be recognized that others may defect àt critical moments or seek unfair advantage. Clear decisions have to be taken, however, not only about whether to participate in collabortive arrangements, but also upon the measures that are necessary if such collaboration is to prove of maximum benefit to a society's citizens. Clarity and caution is also necessary in any relationship with transnational actors that may otherwise be able to exploit the political fragmentation of the contemporary international system.

This section of the study seeks to identify the range of policies, governmental practices and general arrangements that might best equip a society to protect and promote the economic interests of its population. It is not contended that any contemporary society exhibits all of these policies, practices or arrangements. Rather, the purpose is to outline the range of possibilities, to highlight the contribution that each can make, and to indicate, by implication, the possibilities that are open to a society that appears to be failing to gain sufficient benefits from its external economic relationships. There is no suggestion, however, that it would be feasible, or desirable, for any society to adopt the entire range of possibilities or that the adoption of any one is necessarily unproblematical.

POLICIES AND PRACTICES FOR A NEO-MERCANTILIST WORLD

The range of social, economic and political conditions that may have significance for any state's internal economic position and performance is considerable. Indeed, it may be difficult to identify a domestic condition which has no bearing whatsoever upon relative economic strength and performance. Even such essentially personal matters as religious belief and private moral principle may influence economic behaviour and attitudes and, therefore, attract the interest of governments and quasi-governmental institutions.

The wide range of conditions which may bear upon

economic performance, and thereby attract official attention, are not significant merely as isolated factors. Such conditions may also combine together in complex sets, the aggregate effect of which is highly significant for economic performance. Recognition of such interlinkages amongst conditions, and the policies which seek to influence them, may considerably enhance the effectiveness of a government's promotion of economic effectiveness and well-being. While 'totalitarian' systems and regimes might be clearer in the systematic character of their approach to economic and quasi-economic promotion, many other political communities exhibit, or would benefit from, a degree of integration in their approach.

A number of areas of policy relevant to economic performance have long been obvious to even the most casual of observers. Controversy continues to rage over explicit protectionism[1] and, in particular, over the imposition of financial tariffs upon imports. Much of the early attention of the General Agreement on Tariffs and Trade was focused upon just such devices. Increased attention has, however, recently been directed towards the many protectionist practices that fall under the general title of non-tariff barriers to trade (NTBs): devices which may range from the application of 'suitable' health and safety standards, through the acceptance of 'voluntary' limits by would-be exporters to a given country, to the imposition of explicit quantitative quotas upon various types of imports.

A country's trade position can be promoted, not only by protection against imports, but also by the active support of its own exports. A wide variety of mechanisms can be adopted in this area, from direct subsidies to the development of advice and intelligence organizations for the assistance of would-be exporters. As with protectionist measures, the means by which exports may be promoted also vary in their visibility, subtlety and the degree to which they are deemed legitimate within the contemporary international economic community.

Beyond the specific promotion of exports, the general involvement of the government in the development of its industry will clearly be of paramount significance to the preservation of its overall position in the global economy.

The extent to which societies have explicit industrial policies varies, as does the character of those policies. However, most societies have policies with freely acknowledged implications for the preservation and/or development of the country's industrial system and general economy.

Industrial policy is, however, often difficult to differentiate clearly from the general economic policies—both monetary and fiscal (taxation)—that are adopted within any society. Industrial developments clearly require investments and many economic policies exert an influence upon the availability of funds for desirable ventures. Moreover, a buoyant domestic market is often helpful, or even necessary, for successful industrial ventures. Economic policy again has a marked influence upon the general level of domestic demand. Indeed, it may even be possible to influence the demand for a particular type of good or service. Alterations of the levels of tax imposed upon different types of alcoholic drink might, for instance, influence the balance of demand in this area of consumption. Macro-effects are, however, more common and easier to effect than such micro-manipulation of patterns of demand through general fiscal measures.[2]

The contribution of government to a vital and competitive national economy is not, however, limited to the more obvious areas of policy and activity. Most of the characteristics and conditions of a society have some bearing upon its economic performance. The economic infrastructure is a vital component of the overall economic and industrial system: firms require transport, communications, sources of power, water supplies and a host of other services and facilities for their effective functioning. Governments have, therefore, played a growing role in the provision of roads and communications throughout the industrial era.

As the modern economic and industrial system has evolved it has also become increasingly clear that an effective educational system is also a vital necessity. Governments, therefore, have become increasingly involved in the regulation, moderation and, frequently, the direct provision of all levels of education for a growing proportion of their youthful, and sometimes not so youthful, populations.

The general health and well-being of a population also has

a noticeable effect upon its vitality and overall economic capacity. The contribution made by policies that promote fitness and good health is often overlooked within Advanced Industrial Countries. However, the history of these societies has, itself, revealed the serious consequences of inadequate attention to the general health of the population. It is also a problem that bears acutely upon the governments of many of today's Less Developed Countries as they strive to raise general health to a level sufficient to sustain a serious assault upon economic underdevelopment.

The contemporary history of economic development and performance has also provided a clear demonstration of the significance of culture and systems of social principles. Attempts to explain varying levels of economic development or competitiveness without some reference to these powerful forces have proved seriously wanting. Far too many variations in performance cannot be explained satisfactorily in terms only of specific governmental policies, institutions, practices or even governing ideologies. What seems to work in one context does not in another, and the liberal's pursuit of an universalistic perspective encounters another serious obstacle.

Cultures and social principles may define the context within which economic activity takes place; they are, however, far from immutable. The industrial revolutions of the past wrought profound changes upon the cultures of the societies in which they materialized. These changes were, however, relatively slow to crystallize. The leaders of those contemporary countries that are seeking rapid industrialization are, however, faced with the task of inducing simultaneous, or even prior, cultural changes that will render their populations more suited to industrial production and life within modern economies. Similar concerns are also becoming evident within the governments of a number of those more mature industrialized societies that seem to be in danger of embracing a post-industrial culture with, perhaps, excessive and premature enthusiasm. Mrs Thatcher's exhortation of the British people to return to 'Victorian values' is, perhaps, merely one of the more grotesque expressions of such a concern.

The preservation of the political security of their countries and, to that end, the maintenance of an adequate capacity for self-defence, has long been recognized as a major responsibility of governments. Less obvious, however, has been the often intimate connection between military and security matters and the promotion of economic vitality and well-being. This connection goes well beyond the traditional use of military strength to protect, or even seize, sources of important raw materials or other economic assets. The military–economic nexus penetrates a wide area of activity, from the stimulation of arms sales abroad, to the use of military research and development funds, and of subsequent procurement policies, to promote technological innovations and support companies that are important to the national economy.

PRIMARY NEO-MERCANTILIST POLICIES AND PRACTICES

There are a number of policies and practices that are conventionally associated with the neo-mercantilist protection of home industry from imports and with the promotion of a country's exports. The popular concentration of attention upon these measures has, however, distorted the general discussion of the role of the state in the economy, both domestic and global, for such measures are, in fact, merely the more sensational 'tip of the iceberg' of contemporary political economy. The neglect of the role, and significance, of a range of other means and measures had reduced the awareness of some societies of the advantages being secured by others. The quality of the debate about the possible, and desirable, measures that might be adopted in such naive societies is, therefore, commensurately diminished.

The traditional means of the neo-mercantilist promotion of patterns of production and trade that are deemed to be socially advantageous are, nevertheless, common in the modern world, and much debated by students of international trade. The focus of attention has conventionally been upon the imposition of tariffs against competitive imports or goods that are deemed undesirable.

Tariffs

Apart from the imposition of high taxes to reduce the importation of luxury goods in some societies, there are two situations in which tariff barriers have often been erected against imports.[3] The first situation is that of the protection of 'infant industries' against the overwhelming competition from established industries abroad, to which they would otherwise be subject during their gestative phases. The 'infant industries' justification has been much debated by liberal economists, is tolerated by the GATT, and is generally accepted as a legitimate argument in favour of some relatively short-lived measures of protection. Many LDCs protect their developing industries on the basis of such an argument and the history of Japan's post-war industrial advance is an outstanding demonstration of its potential, practical effectiveness.

Protective tariffs have also been established when a society's established industries come under increasingly strong foreign competition, particularly within domestic markets. Such an alteration in the competitive balance may result from the general decline in efficiency of a domestic industry or the emergence of more competitive industries abroad. In either case, the state's authorities may justify a protectionist response with a number of arguments that reflect the range of pressures with which they may be faced.

The most powerful, and least answerable, argument that a state's authorities can mobilize in defence of protective tariffs is that of defending an economic capability that is, in some way, essential to the country's security. The capacity to sustain military operations during time of armed conflict is clearly essential for any society that contemplates such a possibility with any seriousness. Traditionally, it was felt necessary for a power of any significance to be able to provide its forces with the great proportion of its necessary equipment and supplies from domestic sources. Such a principle still applies for a state that wishes to minimize its potential vulnerability to external embargo, blockade or general inability to secure foreign supplies.

'Autarky' is, however, unattainable by most states in the modern world. A careful judgement has to be made, therefore, about the kinds of conflicts that may realistically be expected, rather than deterred, the feasibility of stockpiling adequate resources and therefore the need, if any, for maintaining the ability to ensure domestic sources of supply. Most states are, however, concerned to maintain or develop reasonable levels of general industrial capacity and domestic food supply.

An argument has developed recently that draws a parallel between strategic concerns in the politico-military sphere and strategic considerations in the economic realm. The concern here is with the general 'spill-over' effect upon a nation's industry and economy generated by the presence of enterprises that are in the forefront of innovation in the more advanced, and critical, areas of technology, or with the 'headquarters' effect, in which the headquarters of major corporations supposedly favour local sources of components, supplies and services.

Permanent protection may not always appeal to states. They may well feel, however, that a limited period of protection might provide significant assistance for a particular industry. An 'industrial rebirth' doctrine has thus emerged that parallels the more widely accepted 'infant industry' strategy. The intention here is to provide an umbrella under which failing industries may shelter while undergoing regeneration and the development of a more competitive basis. Time and opportunity might thus be secured for the rationalization of an industry, its re-equipment with the most modern forms of productive technology, the modernization of its product range, the revitalization of its management and the retraining of its work-force. As competitive assaults from abroad are deflected, so too a healthy domestic market is guaranteed to domestic producers. Once the home industry has regrouped effectively, the gates to international competition can be reopened without disastrous consequences.

A government might also be concerned about the effects upon the country's balance of payments of the rapid collapse of a domestic industry in the face of growing foreign competition. Timing may be everything in this matter, for the speed of change in the patterns of relative competitiveness in the world economy have increased considerably during recent decades. The speed with which a domestic industry is eclipsed may therefore be dramatic, as in the cases of the swamping of the British motor cycle industry, and the near collapse of the British colour television industry, in the face of the Japanese assault of the late 1960s and 1970s and early 1980s. Even in the situations in which the affected country is able to switch its industrial resources successfully to new areas of production such redeployment may take time: time during which serious balance of payments problems may be suffered as exports are lost and imports grow. A government may, therefore, be rightly concerned to slow the rate at which such a competitive assault is experienced, if not to actually deflect some of its long-term impact.

The problem facing a government is even more serious if it entertains some doubts about the switch of productive resources in response to changes in the international competitiveness of any established industries. Liberal theory, by making the heroically absurd assumptions that were examined in Chapter 2, and by resting upon the misleading methodology of comparative statics, is able to assume that such adjustments will be both automatic and of acceptable cost. Where a government, in contrast, fears that a suitable redeployment of productive resources may be much delayed, and difficult to ensure, then it may well be tempted to protect threatened industries by tariffs and avoid long-term, chronic domestic unemployment.

Protectionist measures may also be adopted in defence of specific communities or characteristic features of the 'national way of life'. The French have been particularly keen to adopt a range of policies, including protective tariffs, to sustain agriculture, rural communities and their traditional way of life. Such policies have been sustained both at national level and through the influence that France has been able to exert upon policies of the wider EEC.

Protective tariffs are not, however, without their critics and indeed real drawbacks. Liberals acknowledge that the preservation of politico-military security is a legitimate, and at times pressing, consideration in the determination of economic and industrial policy. This general principle, however, does not mean that liberals accord unconditional approval to any policies or practices that are justified in terms of security, for such concerns have no clear a priori limits. Indeed, it is just this insatiable characteristic of the security argument that prompts many liberals to cast doubt upon all but the most unambiguous of such claims, whether they be advanced in the area of economics or personal liberties and freedoms.[4]

Arguments about the strategic economic contribution of selective tariffs rest upon even more controversial grounds than those of politico-military security. Liberal theory is unable to accommodate such a notion because of its failure to incorporate the concern with the 'institutional' framework within which economic activity, and particularly industrial innovation, takes place. Here, the modern liberal view, and neo-classical theory in particular, is at odds with both classical economic theory[5] and the approach of Institutionalist and 'ultra-Keynesian' schools of economics.[6] Liberal theory is thus unable to entertain such notions at a formal level. In practice, however, even those governments that have the highest nominal commitment to neo-classical economic principles exhibit a noticeable sensitivity toward the condition of their countries' most technologically critical industries, as the continuing concern of Mrs Thatcher's Conservative Government towards Britain's electronics and computing industry has illustrated. The real issue, then, is not whether strategic economic concerns are such as to warrant some expression in policy, but how far such concerns should mould policy.

The danger with protectionism is that it may merely inhibit necessary patterns of economic adjustment or sustain ill-conceived ventures. If a given national industry lacks long-term viability then it may be advisable to permit if not actually encourage change as rapidly as possible. There is some evidence that Japan has achieved considerable success in encouraging a movement away from areas like shipbuilding, with released productive resources being redeployed in more promising directions.[7]

The inadvisability of protecting declining domestic industries by substantial tariffs may be compounded if the effect is merely to cushion inefficient enterprises indefinitely. Tariffs, under such conditions, bring tax revenue to the government and a range of apparent benefits to those who are engaged in the protected industries. The owners of the affected enterprises are able to secure acceptable levels of profit without having to make costly investments or introduce possible desirable changes in products, management, staffing or sales techniques. The managers in such businesses are able to enjoy an existence of greater comfort, complacency and, possibly, higher salaries than would otherwise be the case. The workers in such firms may also be able to retain inefficient techniques, practices and attitudes. The costs of such tariffs are placed, in contrast, upon the domestic consumers of the protected goods, who will have to pay higher prices, and upon their producers abroad, whose sales, profits or employment prospects will be damaged.

In summary, then, protective tariffs are often criticized for arresting necessary economic adjustment, for favouring special interest groups within the protected society, be they industrialists or workers, and for harming the interests of both domestic consumers and foreign producers. Moreover, the higher prices of protected goods and services will displace a certain amount of demand from the rest of the range of goods and services that is available within the domestic economy. Producers of these other goods and services will therefore find their interests damaged by the protection that has been accorded to others. Worse, such unprotected producers may find that reduced demand prevents them from developing a scale of production that would actually allow them to reduce costs, devote more research and development to improve the quality of their products and, ultimately, achieve a possible increase of their own export markets.

Non-Tariff Barriers
Non-tariff barriers (NTBs) do not, as such, produce a direct financial contribution to the exchequer of the country that erects them. The direct contribution that non-tariff barriers can make to the preservation and promotion of domestic industry, however, is broadly similar to that of financial tariffs.[8] The difficulties generated by such devices are also

akin to those produced by tariffs. The character of the NTBs, their explicit acknowledgement, and the nature of their justification, however, varies considerably from country to country.

NTBs can emerge from almost any regulations that are developed to control the quality or content of goods and services. Indeed, they may even be created by the very existence, and operating procedures, of the administrative systems that are established to oversee quite legitimate controls. The paperwork, administrative producers and plethora of regulations that often confront a would-be exporter to some countries is such as to deter all but the most determined or desperate. The reasons for such administrative obstacles are highly varied, and include the concern of many socialist countries to regulate ideologically suspect imports; the wish, often strong in many LDCs, to provide opportunities for white-collar workers; and the clear wish, exemplified in the case of Japan, to create substantial albeit covert obstacles to competitive imports.[9]

In some cases it is, thus, quite possible for serious NTBs to emerge from quite real, and legitimate, concerns. Regulations to limit the levels of exhaust emission from motor cars, to control the incidence of transmittable diseases in agricultural and dairy products, to ensure that childrens' toys are manufactured safely and hygienically, or to ensure that financial services are run on a sound, and responsible basis are all examples that may well result in the establishment of effective NTBs against exports from some countries. Unfortunately, it is often impossible to discriminate between those regulations that serve real concerns and proper efforts to improve well-being, and those that are introduced or applied with increased vigour merely to obstruct imports.

Recent moves to revitalize the GATT have placed particular emphasis upon NTBs, as well as the parallel issue of persisting, and substantial, restrictions upon international trade in 'services'. However, the ambiguous basis upon which so many NTBs are built faces such international conferences with serious difficulties. Financial tariffs remain clear and unambiguous obstacles to imports. Many NTBs, in contrast, rest upon considerations that states can claim to be both quite legitimate and fully proper areas of domestic political concern and action. The spectre of interference with states' sovereignty is thus raised as soon as serious criticisms of NTBs are advanced.

NTBs have, however, been employed as undeniably serious barriers to imports by some countries. Within Europe, the manipulation of NTBs to undermine many of the internal free-trade requirements of the Community has been extensive. Britain has sought to use national health regulations to restrict inflows of Continental milk. France, for her part, has deployed her health regulations against incoming British lamb. Many regulations also restrict imports of a range of products from outside the European Community.

In the world of NTBs, the Japanese are past masters. The regulations covering the conditions that must be satisfied, and the paperwork that must be completed, to import goods that are competitive with Japan's own industries are awesome. Moreover, the regulations and necessary paperwork are amenable to rapid change, so that an importer may yet find that the satisfaction of past requirements is no guarantee of successful entry of his goods when they actually arrive on Japanese soil. Such last-minute frustration, however, presumes that bureaucratic requirements have at some stage been apparently satisfied. This condition itself is, however, not always that easy to ensure for the Japanese bureaucracy will often prove itself to be peculiarly labyrinthe in its procedure, and tortuous in its rate of progress.

NTBs are, therefore, at once a most significant issue for those who seek the further liberalization of international trade but also the most complex of issues to confront those who are charged with the negotiation and imposition of new rules and regulations. Indeed, it is difficult to see how any effective control of NTBs will be possible without violating many of the real responsibilities that state authorities still have to fulfill towards their populations.

Quotas

A particularly contentious form of NTB is that of quotas imposed upon imports of some specific goods or services, or those deriving from an identified country. Such quotas may appeal to governments that perceive dangers for specific domestic industries or, indeed, general threats to the home economy. Quotas on specific types of imports may be highly specific, with little effect upon the rest of a country's import trade. Quotas can also be more specific than tariffs by being applied selectively against the exports from countries that seem to pose a special threat or to be taking particular advantage of prevailing trade arrangements.

Liberals see quotas as particularly clear and unacceptable violations of the principles of free trade. The possibility of geographical specificity, indeed, makes such quotas a singularly direct violation of the GATT's 'most favoured nation' principle: the principle that a state must offer to all other states the same terms for trading as it offers to the most favoured of its trading partners. Selective discrimination clearly violates such a principle and confronts the liberal with the vision of the progressive destruction of the free-trade order, as discrimination proliferates, reciprocates and intensifies.

Selective quotas upon given types of imports or upon the exports of a given country are, however, a practical possibility for states that are experiencing serious, and unacceptable, threats to domestic industries. The speed and intensity of a competitive assault can be moderated by quotas, and domestic industry provided with a breathing space in which to improve its competitiveness. The general impact of another trading nation can also be dampened by geographically selective quotas. It is interesting to note, in this respect, that Japan secured an agreement to restrain Italian car imports, when the Japanese car industry seemed vulnerable to foreign competition in 1953, and that this same agreement now protects Italy's car industry from the Japanese assault that has proved so irresistable elsewhere.[10]

Quotas may, however, stimulate developments that were not, initially, fully anticipated or even desired. Geographically specific quotas have prompted a complex pattern of manipulation of 'countries of origin'. Clothing and textiles have to be shipped from countries that have exhausted their quotas under the Multifibre Arrangement to other countries that have not. The goods are then relabelled and shipped once more to the lucrative markets of Western Europe and North America. Japanese car manufacturers are seeking to exceed their basic quotas of cars to be shipped into countries like Britain by exporting additional cars from plants in countries like Australia.[11] Again, many Japanese car manufacturers have discovered a sudden and unprecedented enthusiasm for establishing manufacturing (or, more properly, assembly) facilities in Great Britain. The primary motive for this is to evade EEC quotas by undertaking production within the Community's frontiers.[12]

Quotas are often most significant, however, as bargaining counters. International trade negotiations often involve threats of quotas, or are accepted in the form of 'voluntary' export restrictions. When quotas are threatened, the subjects often offer diverse concessions that range from voluntary restrictions upon exports to the opening of domestic markets to exports from the threatening state.[13] It was such concessions that American legislators were seeking through their deliberations on trade restrictions against Japan during early 1985.[14]

Bilateralism

Many of the most pressing issues within the contemporary global trade system are now handled through direct negotiations and bargains, both formal and tacit, between two clearly identifiable sides. The parties to such bilateral negotiations and arrangements may be nation-states, groups of states or a mixture of the two. Britain has thus engaged in bilateral negotiations with various countries at one time or another.[15] At other times, Britain has been but part of a collective EEC effort.[16] The bilateral negotiations of the United States vary considerably, sometimes involving isolated tasks with the Japanese,[17] sometimes confrontations with Europe and, at other times, alliances with European nations against Japan. Indeed, Japan and the United States have even been known to make common cause against the European nations![18]

Bilateralism is anathema to the letter and spirit of the General Agreement on Tariffs and Trade. It is, however, an enduring characteristic of all forms of international relationships. States often precede multilateral negotiations with prior consulations with those who are likely to prove influential or helpful. Moreover, states will continue to believe that many of the most pressing international difficulties may best be managed through direct contact with those with whom problems have arisen. Bilateralism is thus an ever-present opportunity for states, a frequently invaluable facility, and a 'sin' only in the eyes of those who are doctrinally disposed so to judge such forms of behaviour.

Bilateralism is not merely convenient, it also allows states to exploit the various strengths and capabilities through which advantages might be secured. The asymmetrical, and imbalanced, patterns of interdependence that characterize so many relationships within the contemporary international political economy are a major source of such strengths and advantages.[19]

It is the very imbalance of Japan's trade relationships with her other partners within the advanced industrial world that renders her vulnerable to the imposition, or threatened imposition, of quotas or 'voluntary restraints'. Table 6.1 and 6.2 indicate the dimensions of this imbalance.

The serious dependence of many LDCs upon the AICs, not only for markets for their products but also for aid, capital, modern technology and, most commonly overlooked, many basic foodstuffs, also renders them open to the demands that the identified countries may wish to place upon them. Quotas against manufactured goods, or the systematic discrimination practised by many AICs against commodities refined within their source LDCs, have, therefore, to be accepted with little more than nominal protest.[20]

Such are the financial and general economic pressures under which many LDCs find themselves in the contemporary world that a special form of bilateralism has found increasing favour and exploitation. Where balance-of-payments and currency problems are particularly acute, some countries have found it useful to resort to barter trade. Barter allows direct control over imports, thus eliminating unnecessary luxuries, while guaranteeing that such imports are matched by exports. Balance-of-payments problems are avoided, currency shortages by-passed, necessary goods secured, and outlets for products assured.[21]

Table 6.1: Imbalances in Japan's trade with other Advanced Industrial Countries and regions.

%ages of exports sent to one another 1977			
USA to Japan	8.8%;	Japan to USA	24.7%
EEC to Japan	0.9%;	Japan to EEC	10.8%

Source: UNCTAD Handbook of International Trade and Development Statistics, 1979, (New York: United Nations, 1979), Table 3.1, pp. 86–92.

Table 6.2: The value of Japan's exports to and imports from selected Advanced Industrial Countries—1983.

Country/region	$US billions	
	Exports to:	Imports from:
United Kingdom	4,983	1,940
France	2,010	1,302
West Germany	5,877	2,414
Europe (total)	29,896	12,838
USA	42,829	24,647

Source: Statistical Handbook of Japan, 1984, (Tokyo: Statistical Bureau, Prime Minister's Office, 1984).

Barter trade is not, however, free from serious short-comings. Trade, which may be quite difficult and time consuming to organize, is restricted to the parties to the barter and to the goods they are able to offer one another. The flexibility of the arrangement may, however, be considerably increased if simple barter trade is expanded into a more complex pattern of 'counter trade'. Here, bilateral barters are expanded into a wider network of exchanges of commodities and goods. Specialized agencies negotiate the potential exchanges prior to final agreement and the start of shipments. Agreement is reached when a taker can be found for all the shipments that are necessary to produce a final balance. Such 'counter-trade' is, however, even more demanding to organize than simple barter trade and, for that reason, even more difficult to bring to a satisfactory conclusion.[22]

Protection from imports is, however, but one side of the coin of primary neo-mercantilism in the contemporary world. The domestic economy, and its component industries, may also be much assisted by policies and practices designed to promote exports.

Export Promotion
The support and promotion of a country's exports is a common phenomenon in the modern world. It is also a complex matter for a very wide range of governmental policies and practices may have a bearing upon the inclination, and capacity, of a country's industries to secure foreign markets. Many of these more diverse policies and practices will be considered in a later chapter. Attention will be confined, at this stage, to those forms of governmental activity that have an intentional role in export promotion.

Many of the policies and practices adopted by a number of the world's leading industrial societies are explicitly directed towards the promotion of exports. Governments often recognize the importance of providing intending exporters with good information about the countries in which it is hoped to sell goods and services and about their particular economic needs. Formal agencies of government, like overseas diplomatic missions, may be used to accumulate such information, and encouragement given to other helpful agencies that are formally outside the governmental structure, like chambers of commerce and trade associations.

Overseas diplomatic missions may also be employed in the direct promotion of a country's exports. Recent studies such as the official Berrill report of the British diplomatic service have placed considerable emphasis upon the growing importance of the commercial side of its work and upon the need for overseas representatiaves to be more attuned to this aspect of their work. Permanent establishments upon foreign soil may be supplemented by the formal, and often quite elaborate, trade missions that states now commonly employ in their pursuit of increased markets in given countries or regions.

Exporting brings additional business risks to the trader. Governments often act to reduce such risks by the provision of what amounts to an official insurance scheme. Such arrangements are usually directed towards the non-payment of bills by importers and assume the form of export guarantees. Exporters pay a relatively modest premium to an agency which will then reimburse them to the value of the goods exported should importers default. Such arrangements are, in general, much to be welcomed and attract controversy only to the extent that exporters in many LDCs claim that the general poverty of their home countries prohibits their governments from providing export guarantees on a scale to match that of the AICs. Many of the LDCs' leading firms thus claim that even with export guarantees of the AICs are able to secure an unfair competitive advantage.

Export guarantees are, however, often combined with a practice that is far more controversial: export credits. Such credits are frequently offered to potential importing countries, may assume one of a variety of forms and are often associated with other financial and trade arrangements. The combination of export credits with various forms of economic aid is a particularly controversial matter within the contemporary global political economy.

The primary purpose of export credits is to induce a potential importer to purchase goods from the credit-granting country by providing finance on more generous terms than would be available from purely commercial sources.[23] Low rates of interest on outstanding loans are the main feature of these credits, with rates as low as 5 per cent below commercial levels. The scale of export credits has been considerable, in the past, with a peak world value of some US$8–10 billion in the period 1979–81.[24] However, negotiations amongst the leading industrial countries, within the Organization for Economic Cooperation and Development (OECD), in December 1983 produced a 'gentlemen's agreement' to restrict such credits substantially.[25]

The 'gentlemen's agreement' over export credits has not resolved the issues raised by this form of export promotion. The recipients of such credits have objected strenuously to the proposed control and restriction of what they see as a significant form of 'aid', albeit of a peculiar variety.[26] The providers of such credits have also sought to evade the formal limitations imposed by the 1983 agreement by turning increasingly to 'mixed credits', in which export credits are associated with grants of conventional aid. Such mixed credits were pioneered by France in the 1970s, are now practiced by a large number of AICs in pursuit of large orders and contracts in the Developing World. The proportion of outright aid in such 'mixed credits' grew to some 37 per cent by late 1983.[27]

The contemporary practice of the industrialized states is thus to promote export through a complex mixture of insurance for exporters, subsidized loans to importing states and outright aid. Many of the AICs have organizations devoted to the administration of mixed credits and export insurance. Britain has an Export Credit Guarantee Department; France operates its official Banque Francaise du Commerce Exterieur, with insurance arranged by the private, but approved, Compagnie Francaise d'Assurance pour le Commerce Exterieur; West Germany offers mixed credits through Kreditanstalt für Wiederaufbau, and insurance through the private Hermes Kreditversicherung AG; Italy administers mixed credits through the Instituto Centrale per il Credito a Medio Termine (Medio-credito) and insurance is obtainable from the Sezione Speciale per l'Assicuranzione del Credito all'Esportizone (Sace); and the Japanese maintain their Export–Import Bank for the general support of exports and as a vehicle for the provision of up to 55 per cent of official finance for exports.[28]

The growing use of 'mixed credits' has aroused the ire of the USA and prompted a threat to outbid its competitors by increasing the aid component of such packages to a level that would prove prohibitively expensive.[29] However, the USA has its own Export–Import Bank which organizes mixed credits in association with the USAs main aid organization, the Agency for International Development (AID).[30]

Clear and direct support for a country's exports does not exhaust the possibilities that are open to governments. A wide range of other policies and practices have a substantial bearing upon export performance. Many of these policies and practices have their own justification in terms of domestic requirements. They may, however, be adopted with some regard to their implications for export performance and, most certainly, for their effect upon the ability of industry to defend its home markets.

A variety of tax advantages may be accorded to exporting firms. Such advantages range from the removal of value added taxes from exports, to the rather more dubious practice of relieving exporters of some part of their national insurance bill (or analogous charges). Such tax incentives are, however, no more that one aspect of the wide range of governmental policies and activities that can produce incentives, or a more supportive context, for exporters.

CONCLUSIONS

Primary neo-mercantilist policies can make, and indeed have often made, a considerable contribution to the economic well-being of societies. A variety of protectionist measures, including tariffs, quotas and non-tariff barriers, have been used with considerable success to cushion infant industries or to provide an umbrella under which competitiveness can be restored in the face of growing international competition.

The threat of such measures are also common in international trade negotiations. Countries may be persuaded to moderate their exports to another country by the possibility that trade barriers will be imposed. Agreements can also be reached on restraints that remain within acceptable, if not ideal, limits. Bilateral negotiations between major trading partners, be they single states or groupings such as the EEC, are also the mechanism through which many such 'understandings' are reached. This bilateralism, however, strikes at the heart of the universalism which underlies the GATT and its associated arrangements.

A wide variety of measures may also be adopted to support and promote a country's exports. Such practices range through insurance schemes, credits and direct subsidies. Controversy has been generated by many of these practices, with intense international negotiations focused upon export credits. As the increasing use of mixed credits has illustrated, however, the impulse towards neo-mercantilist practices flourishes in the shadows of even the most determined endeavours to secure agreed limitation and loyal adherence to more universalistic principles.

Reality continues to confront even those governments that would favour the total abolition of all neo-mercantilist policies and practices. A wide range of domestic conditions, and thereby governmental policy, continue to have a profound influence upon the international competitiveness and economic well-being of societies. Behaviour that is effectively neo-mercantilist is, therefore, extremely widespread in the modern world and governments cannot ignore the benefits that others secure when such behaviour is effectively orchestrated. In their turn, therefore, governments are forced to recognize an obligation to develop their policies and activities in neo-mercantilist directions. The mixed record of success of governments in this respect does little to qualify their commitment in this direction.

NOTES

1. *See*, for instance, Brian Hindley and Eri Nicolaides, *Taking the New Protectionism Seriously*, (London: Trade Policy Research Centre, 1983).
2. For a discussion of marco-economic policy *see* M. Stewart, *Controlling the Economic Future: Policy Dilemmas for a Shrinking World*, (Brighton: Wheatsheaf Books, 1983), Ch. 2.
3. On tariffs generally, *see* P. T. Ellsworth, *The International Economy*, (New York: Collier-Macmillan, 3rd edn., 1964), Ch. 13.
4. *See*, for instance, Charles K. Rowley, '*The Political Economy of the Public Sector*', in R. J. Barry Jones (ed.), *Perspectives on Political Economy: Alternatives to the Economics of Depression*, (London: Frances Pinter, 1983).
5. *See* D. Simpson, *The Political Economy of Growth*, (Oxford: Basil Blackwell, 1983).
6. *See*: W. J. Samuels (ed.), *The Economy as a System of Power*, 2 vols., (New Brunswick: Transaction Books, 1979); and A. S. Eichner, (ed.), *A Guide to Post-Keynsian Economics*, (London: Macmillan, 1979).
7. *See*, for instance, Charles Smith, 'Japan and the new industrial countries of East Asia', in P. Norbury and G. Bowna (eds.), *Business in Japan*, (London: Macmillan, 2nd edn., 1980), esp. pp. 25–6.
8. On NTBs *see* C. P. Kindleberger, *International Economics* (Homewood, Ill.: Irwin, 5th edn., 1973), pp. 122–6.
9. On Japan's NTBs against British pig-meat products, *see* 'Tebbit pushes

pork on Japan', *Guardian*, 18 April 1985, p. 23; and on her general NTBs see 'Why Britain is bamboozled by a bamboo barrier', *Guardian*, 21 October 1980, p. 19.

10. *See* the report 'Dog eat dog', *The Economist*, 2 March 1985, p. 10, in a special survey on the motor industry.

11. 'Tokyo may import Australian vehicles', *Guardian*, 15 July 1982, p. 12.

12. 'Nissan cast as cuckoo in the nest', *Guardian*, 1 February 1984, p. 19.

13. *See* 'Japan eases car import rules', *Guardian*, 8 March 1984, p. 22.

14. *See*: 'Look out, Japan, the Americans are coming', *The Economist*, 30 March 1985, pp. 43–4; and 'Trade pressure on Japan', *Guardian*, 2 April 1985, p. 21.

15. *See*: 'Talks with Korea on trade imbalance', *Guardian*, 27 June 1980, p. 15; 'Cut shoe exports, Brazil told', *Guardian*, 4 July 1980, p. 14; 'UK warns France and Japan on Trade', *Guardian*, 22 January 1982, p. 18; 'Jenkin threatens car sanctions over Japanese imbalance', *Guardian*, 26 January 1983, p. 14.

16. *See*: 'EEC retaliates against US steel imports ban', *Guardian*, 29 November 1984, p. 18; and 'EEC eyes Far East steel talks', *Guardian*, 30 March 1985.

17. *See* 'Japan tries to head off US trade war', *Guardian*, 30 March 1985.

18. *See* 'Japan and US seek new talks, *Guardian*, 20 May 1984, p. 16.

19. *See* R. J. Barry Jones, 'The definition and identification of interdependence', in R. J. Barry Jones (ed.), *Interdependence on Trial: Studies in the Theory and Reality of Contemporary Interdependence*, (London: Frances Pinter, 1984).

20. ibid. esp. pp. 47–55.

21. *See* 'Revamping the glass bead business', *South*, (March 1985), pp. 55–6.

22. *See*: 'Better ball bearings than bad debts', *The Economist*, 15 December 1984, p. 69; and reports in *South*, (March 1985), pp. 55–60.

23. *See* 'Staving off a trade war', *South*, July 1982, pp. 66–7.

24. *See* 'Billions at stake in the export credit shake-up', *South*, December 1983, pp. 81–3.

25. *ibid*.

26. *ibid*.

27. *See* 'Missing it over credits', *South*, February 1985, pp. 56–7.

28. *ibid*.

29. *ibid*. and *see also* 'Gentlemen, please!', *The Economist*, 8 September 1984, pp. 16–18.

30. *ibid*.

7 Secondary Neo-Mercantilist Policies and Practices: Domestic

INTRODUCTION

The range of policies and practices that have relevance for the international competitiveness, and general economic well-being, of a society may be very wide. Few, indeed, are the areas of governmental activity, or social condition, that have no economic significance. Where a policy or practice may have a bearing upon economic vitality, it is likely that some government somewhere will, at some time, seek to exploit the possibilities thus offered.

The variety of the policies and practices that may be germane to a society's economic performance is considerable. Explicit economic and industrial policies are clearly of the greatest potential importance. Many societies have also recognized the powerful role of their educational and training systems with policies aimed at securing the contribution that can be made by such services. Health provisions are also salient to economic performance, for a weak and diseased population is unlikely to make an effective and vital work force. The performance of people at all levels of a socio-economic system will also be significantly influenced by their basic beliefs and values. Norms of public behaviour, social principles and moral beliefs may, therefore, be matters of considerable interest to governments that wish to create or maintain a suitable social environment for economic progress.

ECONOMIC POLICY

The general economic policy of any government is directed towards a number of objectives. Governments have long acknowledged a responsibility to sustain as stable a financial system as possible. A stable financial system, within which substantive economic activity can take place, also requires a stable currency.

The maintenance of economic activity has also been held to require a sound and supportive legal framework. Liberals, from the time of Adam Smith onwards, have recognized this essential responsibility of government. Liberals have, however, often sought to limit governmental involvement in the economy to the preservation of financial probity and a stable currency and the maintenance of a suitable legal framework.

Many governments in the modern world have, however, undertaken quite a wide range of activity directed towards the promotion of industrial development and general economic well-being, with accompanying tendencies towards overtly neo-mercantilist measures.[1] Post-war policies reflected a widespread belief that an optimal basis for the direction of the national economy was to be found in the measures for macro-economic management advocated by John Maynard Keynes.

During the period of post-war economic recovery, Keynesian techniques did seem to work well. Governments found that they were able to promote sustained growth through the periodic stimulation of domestic demand. However, the very process of recovery itself generated forces that were ultimately to undermine confidence in Keynesian management. Recovery brought revived international competitiveness and a substantial increase in international financial liquidity, at a time of growing popular expectations of never-ending improvements in prosperity and economic well-being. By the mid 1960s, therefore, a number of quite serious problems were being experienced by some of the Advanced Industrial Countries and making their macro-economic management policies appear less effective, and robust, than had once been believed.

By the mid 1960s the rates of economic growth achieved by the industrialized countries began to diverge quite substantially, with that of countries like Great Britain falling significantly behind many of the others. Currency crises were also experienced by a number of the AICs, as they struggled to maintain fixed exchange rates at a time of substantial increases in the quantities, and mobility, of internationally liquid financial resources. Defence of currency values became, for countries like Great Britain, an exercise in self-immolation. An era of 'stop go' economic policy was born in which economic growth would be seriously interrupted by deflationary policies introduced to deflect some sudden surge in adverse currency speculation.[2]

'Stop go' policy is the inverse of the kind of national economic policy required for the effective support of industrial development. The previous calculations of enterprises are undone and unprofitable investments rendered loss making as costs are increased by rising interest rates and as demand for the goods produced is reduced. Future plans are also interrupted as business managers reconsider the wisdom of costly investments and risky initiatives in a depressed economic climate. Such 'stop go' economic policies probably contributed quite significantly to Britain's long-term loss of industrial vitality during the 1960s, in particular, and resultant surrender of competitiveness to societies that had no intention of damaging themselves in such manner.[3]

A totally consistent and rigorous economic policy may be an unattainable ideal. However, many governments have managed to maintain policies that are more consistently helpful to industry and, hence, economic progress.

The general framework of a country's fiscal and monetary policy exerts a considerable influence upon economic vitality and industrial effectiveness. The contribution of such policies will, however, depend upon the general approach of a government towards industrial development. Where private initiatives are seen to be the primary, if not the sole, source of productive investment, then fiscal policy can encourage investment and entrepreneurship. Where, in contrast, state institutions are believed to be best suited to the promotion of industrial development, then fiscal policy can be directed towards the generation of the highest possible revenues for public investments.

FISCAL POLICY

Private industrial investments can be encouraged by a variety of tax policies and measures. The USA has long maintained a fiscal atmosphere that is conducive to private investment, particularly in new enterprises. A number of devices have been adopted, including 'tax holidays', in which taxation upon earnings from new investments may be delayed for some initial period, or by arrangements that allow individuals or organizations to offset losses from high-risk investments against profits made from other, perhaps safer, interests. In a society which is already more attuned to speculative investment, such encouragements have done much to sustain the impressive levels of investment in new technology enterprises witnessed in the USA during recent decades.

The level and pattern of taxation will also have an influence upon overall economic demand. Tax reductions stimulate domestic demand and may, therefore, provide improved opportunities for domestic producers, if they are suitably responsive and/or accompanied by other policies that limit 'leakage' into additional imports.

The general pattern of taxation will also influence the structure of demand, for it will alter the relative levels of disposable income of members of different socio-economic groups. The system of income tax might be such as to impose increasing levels of taxation upon higher levels of income and wealth. Such a progressive system would reduce the level of demand for luxury goods and services while enhancing the relative level of demand for basic foods and goods. In contrast, the highly regressive tax system that would result from abolishing income and wealth taxes in favour of comprehensive purchase taxes (or VAT) would leave the less wealthy members of the community paying a higher proportion of their incomes as taxes while the richer sections retained a higher proportion of their income for personal consumption. Such a situation would dampen demand for basics while expanding the demand for luxuries.

In the absence of compensatory export opportunities, alterations in the structure of domestic demand will affect the markets for home producers. Those that face falling demand will have to reduce output. Such reductions of output may reduce the efficiency of production and may endanger the financial viability of the enterprise. Firms that experience increasing demand will be encouraged to expand output, may be stimulated to increase investment and may well find that they have achieved new economies of scale which make them even more competitive, domestically and internationally.

The reduction of domestic demand for certain goods and services is not, however, automatically disadvantageous. Firms may be stimulated to diversify into the production of new goods or services that are more promising than their traditional products. Again, a firm faced with a drop in domestic demand might dictate itself to the pursuit of new, or expanded, markets abroad and hence make an increased contribution to the national balance of trade and payments.

Fiscal policy is not, however, merely a mechanism for the manipulation of economic activity within a society. It is also the means through which governments secure the resources required for a range of domestic policies and programmes. The financial needs of such programmes sometimes prompt governments to adopt tax policies that are actually discordant with the industrial needs of a society and even those needs as perceived by the government itself.

MONETARY POLICY

It is not only taxation policy that can exert a significant effect upon the general level and structure of industrial activity within a society. Monetary policy, which liberals have long identified as a major responsibility of governments, may also have considerable, if unintended, effects upon domestic economic activity.[4]

A government may implement its monetary policies through a variety of means, the regulation of banking and credit practices, the manipulation of interest rates, and the management of the relationship between its own income and expenditure.

The control and regulation of banking, credit and allied financial services may have mixed motives. The primary concern of governments is to ensure that banking and financial services are generally performed responsibly. A stable financial sector is, in turn, essential to a stable and well-functioning economy and industrial system. Alterations in the rules governing banking and credit operations will, however, have a significant effect upon the supply of money within an economy. If the rules governing the generation of credit by agencies outside the official system are eased then it is likely that monetary expansion will occur and that it will become increasingly difficult for governments to control money supply through the means that have conventionally been available.

The easing of rules governing the generation of credit may, however, be favoured by governments that wish to see a new flexibility introduced into the economy and, thereby, new sources of demand for industry. As with so many devices, however, there may be a serious cost in terms of diminished official control over the money supply.

The manipulation of the interest rate is one of the more immediate instruments of a government's monetary policy and source of influence over general economic activity. Governments often have the formal authority to set interest rates for banks, and other credit agencies. Governments and their central banks are, moreover, usually the 'lenders of last resort' to the financial system and hence able to exert considerable influence upon the rates at which the wiser members of the banking system will be prepared to lend funds to others.

Governmental action to secure an increase in the prevailing interest rate will usually have deflationary objectives. The sources and significance of inflation within any economy are a matter of considerable, and intense, controversy.[5] However, governments have often sought to reduce the enthusiasm of individuals and firms to borrow funds from banks and credit agencies by promoting an increase in interest rates and thereby making it more expensive to borrow. This, within some interpretations, is then held to impose general check upon inflationary pressures within the economy.[6]

Interest manipulation has not, however, been confined to deflationary purposes. Official encouragement for lower rates has often been intended to stimulate an increase of activity within an economy. In Keynesian theory, although primarily focused upon fiscal policies, such measures could be invaluable, particularly within an economy with significant levels of unused, or underemployed, productive resources.

Recent experience, in countries like Great Britain, has demonstrated that significant, unanticipated and adverse movements in domestic interest rates can have drastic consequences for firms. As the monetarist experiments of Mrs Thatcher's incoming Conservative Government in 1979 proved, firms that had borrowed in order to invest in new equipment or products or to develop new markets were severely affected by sharp and substantial increases in the rates of interest that they now had to cover. Moreover, high British interest rates attracted financial inflows elevated the value of the pound sterling, undermined British industrial competitiveness and further damaged those firms that were heavily reliant upon export markets, or were particularly vulnerable to competition from imports.

Interest rate manipulation is not the only source of monetary policy and influence. The overall relationship between the government's income, from taxes, assorted levies and borrowings at home or abroad, and its expenditure is also a major source of monetary expansion or contraction. If governments spend more than they receive, then a significant contribution is automatically made to the growth of the money supply within the country. An imbalance between governmental receipts of taxes, and levies, and their expenditure is a norm within the modern world. However, governments may seek to balance that gap through borrowing. Such borrowing, if it is not to be met by 'printing money', constitutes a debt for future repayment and may 'crowd out' other forms of borrowing and thereby valuable forms of investment. Such inflationary and 'crowding out' effects are much deprecated by 'monetarists' and 'supply-side' economists, who often call for balanced budgets.

Deficit financing may contribute as much of an economic stimulus to an economy that has unemployed resources as a reduction in the interest rate. Traditional Keynesians have not, therefore, been nervous of advocating imbalanced governmental finances under suitable conditions. Governmental borrowing has been recommended, not merely to finance budget deficits, but also to secure funds for government-supported investments. Indeed, there are many who feel that such governmental activity is essential to make good the failings of private investment and innovation within a number of economies.

EXCHANGE RATE POLICY

A government's approach to the management of the international value of its country's currency is also of great importance. Exchange rate manipulation has become an increasingly complex matter as the level of mobile funds has risen dramatically during recent decades.[7]

International movements of funds can be rapid and substantial, with considerable effects upon the exchange values of the currencies involved. Indeed, this substantial increase in international liquidity was one of the major sources of the collapse of the post-war, Bretton Woods fixed-exchange-rate system during the early 1970s. Many factors and considerations influence those whose decisions determine the movements of such internationally liquid funds.

The general tenor of economic policy influences the overall view that international money managers, and speculators, take towards a national economy. A reduction of general confidence may induce a substantial outflow of funds and thence a significant fall in the international value of a currency.

Shorter-term developments in economic and monetary policy may also have a marked influence upon financial movements and, therefore, currency values. The interest rate movements that have been discussed earlier have a rapid and sharp influence upon such financial flows. Increases in rates attract funds and boost currency values. The reverse effect is generally produced by a reduction in a country's interest rates.

Developments in a country's economy that are beyond the

short-term control of government may also have a noticeable effect upon the value of a country's currency. The advent of North Sea oil has provided a general boost for the value of Britain's currency: a boost that was dramatic during the earliest years of the 1980s and which, despite occasional set-backs, may persist. The effect that such stimulus to currency values have upon a country's economy and industry may not, however, be particularly beneficial, as the fate of a wide section of British industry in the early 1980s demonstrated.

Governments were committed to maintaining the values of their currencies within specified limits by the Bretton Woods Agreement of 1944, on a post-war international monetary system. This 'regime' lasted from 1945 until its effective abandonment in 1971. States have now adopted a variety of approaches towards the management of exchange rates.

A policy of a truly 'free-floating' exchange rate has rarely been maintained for a protracted period of time. Most states have opted for a compromise between fixed and freely-floating exchange rates. Some governments have pursued policies of 'responsible' or 'managed floating', in which their practice has been to intervene in international money markets only to maintain the value of their currencies within rather wide limits: indeed, limits that have often not been specified in advance.

While interest rate manipulation continues to offer governments one means of seeking influence over the value of their currencies, market intervention has continued to be the initial response of governments, and their monetary authorities, when faced with serious movements in currency values. The value of a country's currency can be depressed by increasing the quantity offered for sale internationally: alternatively, its value sustained by the use of accumulated reserves of gold, other currencies, or the IMF's Special Drawing Rights (SDRs) to purchase it on international markets.

The longer-term management of a country's exchange rate is also influenced by a broad range of economic and industrial policies. Specific mechanisms may also provide a government with significant sources of influence. Exchange controls have often been used to control inflows and outflows of funds. Many countries continue to impose such controls, including France, Italy and the overwhelming majority of developing countries.

Exchange controls are generally condemned by liberals as a serious interference with free international economic activity. There has, therefore, been continuing pressure for the abolition of exchange controls by those leading economic powers, like the USA, that subscribe to such liberal economic doctrines. Mrs Thatcher's Conservative Government promptly abolished Britain's structure of exchange controls on assuming power in 1979 and opened the floodgates on a massive exodus of capital from the country.[8] A dramatic collapse in the value of the pound was avoided only because of the counter-influence of Britain's new oil earnings.

A number of states have sought a more collectivist approach to the management of currency values, through linking their currencies with those of other countries within some region or some international association. Prominent members of the European Community have experimented with a variety of arrangements of growing formality. The European Monetary System (EMS) was established by agreement between the then German Chancellor, Helmut Schmidt, and French President, Giscard d'Estaing, in 1979 to coordinate the relative values of the major European currencies. Currency values were then to be maintained within an agreed limits of relative value: the so-called European monetary 'Snake'. Most of the leading members of the EEC have now joined the EMS, with the exception of Great Britain.[9]

The EMS is intended to combine the economic and financial strengths of its members. Adverse influences upon the currency of one member of the EMS may well be compensated by favourable influences upon that of another. The cumulative weight of the EMS in the international monetary system might also be far greater than could be achieved by any one European country acting alone: a matter of growing urgency in a world of ever more dominated by the fate of the US dollar and the remorseless advance of the Japanese yen.[10] This is one of the considerations that lies behind the steady promotion of the European Currency Unit (ECU), initially a device for internal accounting within the EEC, as a form of internationally acceptable currency. The emergence of the ECU as a full international currency, however, waits upon mechanisms for clearing instruments denominated in ECUs and acceptance by some, including the German monetary authorities.[11]

The attempt to promote industrial development through the manipulation of exchange rates may, however, run into the particular problem of the differential rates at which such developments exert an influence. Increases in interest rates may have a rapid and quite dramatic effect upon the financial viability of firms. Rapid movements in exchange rates may also have a reasonably rapid effect upon the profitability and competitiveness of exporters. Measures intended to stimulate additional investments, the development of new products or the pursuit of new markets may, however, take a considerable time to have their effect. Managers need to be convinced that conditions are now more promising and that they will remain so for a period of time sufficient to justify additional efforts, costs and, possibly, risks. Substantial lags may, indeed, mean that intended effects are swamped by other developments well before they come to fruition.

Whatever the means adopted, the objective of a country's exchange rate policy should be to minimize the damage that can be inflicted upon the domestic economy by the increasingly volatile movements of currency values in the world's money markets. It is also possible that a country's industrial progress can be promoted through the judicious management of its exchange rate: an optimal level might ensure that a country's exports are competitively priced at the same time that its necessary imports do not become too expensive.[12]

INDUSTRIAL AND DEVELOPMENT POLICY

Industrial and development policies are widely pursued by governments of all persuasions and declared purposes. While varying considerably in their content, and explicit acknowledgement, such policies play a central and critical role in the contemporary global political economy, despite their neglect, and even deprecation, by 'ultra-liberal' ideologues.

Doctrine exerts an obvious influence upon the general approach of a government towards industrial and development policy. Many of the more extreme socialist regimes have experimented with complete governmental control of industry. Ownership of the means of production has been vested in the state, plans for the economy developed on a regular basis and production targets set for individual enterprises. As the history of the Soviet Union has demonstrated, impressive levels and rates of development can be achieved under such a system, but at the cost of considerable wastage and, in many cases, growing rigidities. Few amongst the Socialist countries of the modern world have not now experimented with the introduction of greater flexibility within their economies and greater self-determination, on one basis or another, for their individual enterprises.

The opposite extreme would be the case of the regime that felt no obligations whatsoever to involve itself in the development of its economy and industrial system, beyond that of sustaining a suitable financial and legal framework. However, such a possibility has remained no more than a fantasy of some neo-classical and 'ultra-liberal' theorists, for all governments have exceeded such limits in some significant areas of activity.

Most countries and governments thus sustain an approach that falls somewhere between the extremes of all-embracing state Socialism and ultra *laissez faire*. The situation in most states, therefore, is that of a mixed economy with variable levels of governmental intervention. The EEC, and its authoritative agencies, has shown clear signs of developing and increasingly interventionist and *dirigiste* approach towards its industries.

Planning

General economic and industrial planning, in one form or another, may be undertaken by a government. The British Labour Government of 1964–70 toyed with a National Plan, to be implemented primarily by a new Department of Economic Affairs. This venture was, however, short-lived as the government was rapidly 'blown off course' by serious balance of payments and exchange rate difficulties externally and by determined civil service resistance internally.[13] From the early 1960s, therefore, overall 'planning' in Britain has been largely confined to the reporting and advisory activities of the National Economic Development Council and Office (NEDC and NEDO).[14] In marked contrast, Japan has demonstrated a cpacity to deploy a wide variety of mechanisms, including the famous Ministry for International Trade and Industry (MITI), to achieve a remarkably high level of economic and industrial coordination and consequential success.[15]

The Role of Nationalized Industries and Public Investment
Governments may also be able to exert a considerable influence upon the national economy through the industries and other services that they own, or control, individually or through such umbrella organizations as Italy's Institute per la Riconstruzione Industriale. Nationalized industries, which are far more widespread in the modern world than is commonly supposed or generally admitted, may be strategically central. They may supply basic materials to much of the rest of industry and/or be major consumers. State-owned mining industries have been major suppliers of energy to national industries and a major consumer of steel products and a range of associated equipment. The railway systems of most countries are also owned wholly, or in large part, by the state and are, again, a major contibutor to the economy and its industrial system. Such state-owned heavy industries are joined by a wide range of services that are provided by state authorities and that may be major consumers of the products of important sectors of a society's industrial system, as with the educational system's consumption of books and a wide range of educational materials.

Neo-liberal sentiments have, however, ushered in a period of enthusiasm for de-nationalization, or 'privatization', in some AICs. Large nationalized industries can, it is argued, be better managed by private industry, become increasingly efficient and, therefore, make a greater contribution to the vitality of the economy. Britain has been particularly prone to this fashion, with Mrs Thatcher's Conservative Government selling a number of major industries to the 'public', outstanding amongst which have been the sale of the telephone service—British Telecom—in 1984 and the continuing plans for the sale of British Airways. The conservative, 'Liberal' Government of Japan has exhibited similar tendencies, with the development of plans for the sale of its own telecommunications system.

A related opportunity is the use of public investment to support the economy overall or particular industrial sectors that are in particular need of assistance. Such programmes of expenditure, it is argued, create jobs, support industries and provide society with intrinsically valuable facilities and conditions. Authoritative bodies like the Organization for Economic Cooperation and Development are prepared to lend their approval to such programmes in countries like Britain which experience chronic unemployment of labour and productive resources[16] and which have many public facilities, including roads, drains, and public housing stock, in acute need of restoration.

Many conservative governments are, however, deeply hostile to such programmes of public expenditure and infrastructure investment. They believe that the real effect would be to add considerably to the total bill for public expenditure, an addition that would have to be met either from inflationary deficit financing, additional public borrowing, with its 'crowding out effects', or from additional taxes upon those whose activity they wish to encourage with financial incentives, not penalties. Such projects would, it is argued, contribute no more than a temporary boost to employment. The only large-scale projects which such governments will contemplate are those, like the scheme for a fixed link across the English Channel, which might be financed exclusively by the private sector[17] or those, like the new Falklands airport, which have military–strategic 'justifications'.

Regulation and Control

Governments may also employ their legislative powers in attempts to influence the pattern and performance of economic and industrial activity. Much regulation reflects a genuine concern with public well-being or the health and safety of those at work, as with Britain's pioneering nineteenth-century factory acts. The standards of practice of many service industries, including financial, insurance and many professional services, may also be ensured through such regulation. Maintaining the quality of products, of services and of conditions of work may all contribute to the vitality of a country's industries.

Regulation may, however, have significant disadvantages. It is notoriously vulnerable to improper use as a form of non-tariff barrier against imports, particularly in the area of livestock and foodstuffs. Regulation is also believed, by 'neo-liberals', to suppress much of the vitality of the economic and industrial system by ensnaring entrepreneurs with endless controls, paperwork and, most seriously, additional costs. Deregulation has therefore become one of the shibboleths of modern 'neo-liberal' governments, especially that of President Reagan in the USA.

A particular area of regulation, and controversy, concerns the organization of industry. Many countries have well-established organizations and procedures for investigating and controlling excessive concentration within their industries. Britain's Monopolies and Mergers Commission is but one example. The EEC, as a supranational authority, has also developed an increasingly effective and influential cartel-busting organization, DG4.[18] The principle behind such agencies is the preservation of a competitive structure within any industry and, hence, competition and efficiency.

The view that a competitive condition is essential in any industry is, however, vulnerable both to developments in prevailing conditions and to changes in governmental doctrine. In marked contrast, the general approach of some neo-liberal governments, like that of Reagan in the USA, has been to reverse the thrust of official influence in the field of industial organization.

The Reagan administration has, under the influence of its neo-liberal doctrines, been seized by the notion that the USA's anti-trust (anti-monopoly) legislation has actually inhibited developments within industries that would be beneficial to the much-heralded 'supply-side' revolution. The regime's influence has, therefore, been cast in favour of many mergers and take-overs that would previously have been blocked by the authorities.[19]

Prices and Incomes Policy

Prices and Incomes policies have sometimes been seen as playing a vital part in efforts to control inflation, retain international competitiveness and, perhaps most significantly, develop a harmonious and constructive atmosphere within the industrial system. Proposals for such policies encounter arguments concerning their political feasibility and their economic effectiveness. Politically, it is argued that the very conditions of industrial unrest and inflationary pressure that often prompt contemplation of prices and incomes policies make such policies impossible to implement effectively.

Critics of Prices and Incomes policies contend that they have a number of fatal shortcomings. When effective, such policies merely distort conditions within the labour market; wages cannot move with sufficient speed and magnitude to correct imbalances that have arisen between the supply of, and demand for, various types of abilities and skills. Such freezing of labour mobility will, in turn, have detrimental consequences for an economy's most promising and dynamic industries.

Prices and Incomes policies are, however, reasonably easy to evade by determined employers. Valued employees can be attracted and rewarded in ways that are beyond the scope of the Prices and Incomes policy, and its implementing authority. Thus, attempts to maintain Prices and Incomes policies in Britain during the 1970s spawned, unintentionally, myriad forms of non-financial rewards for managerial employees within private industry. Finally, it is often argued that Prices and Incomes policies merely build up pressure for a wages' explosion which follows upon the ultimate, and inevitable, collapse of the experiment. The Prices and Incomes policy of recent French governments have certainly been of limited duration and effectiveness.[20]

Many of these criticisms of Prices and Incomes policy have some empirical support. However, there is evidence that judicious experiments with such policies can have a highly beneficial, and relatively long-lasting, effect upon the structure and performance of a country's economy and industrial system. During early post-war decades the long-lived Social Democrat Government of Sweden developed a 'solidaristic' wage policy, requiring relatively equal pay in all industrial sectors, as part of a wider policy which sought a combination of economy security for employees with enhanced economic efficiency, and international competitiveness, for the country's industry. Such a wage policy favoured the more efficient and profitable firms while squeezing the less effective, which were forced to improve their performance or go out of business. The consequence of such a policy was the stimulation of those major firms that have actually preserved a Swedish presence on international markets and the promotion of a considerable level of social and industrial harmony.[21] Such policies may not be able to survive indefinitely, but their contibution to longer-term industrial strength and economic well-being may be profound, as Sweden's case has demonstrated.[22]

Humanitarian and economic arguments have also been advanced to support governmentally enforced minimum wage laws and regulations. Such measures, which have been much promoted by organizations like the International Labour Organization, are held to mitigate against extremes of poverty and economic exploitation whilst promoting efficiency, as employers seek to use their more expensive labour more effectively. Such policies run counter to the views of governments, like that of Mrs Thatcher in Britain or President Reagan in the USA, which contend that employment can be generated only if people are free and willing to price themselves into jobs by accepting low wages.[23] Some governments, like Mrs Thatcher's, have therefore withdrawn from international minimum wage agreements.[24]

Selective Intervention and Sectoral Support
Selective forms of industrial support are also available to governments. Such selectivity may be *ad hoc* as governments are drawn into the provision of survival support for industries or enterprises that are faced with overwhelming pressures.

Even governments that have turned their faces determinedly against state intervention or systematic industrial subsidies, like Mrs Thatcher's British Government, have encountered irresistible pressures to extend financial lifelines to troubled enterprises, from the British Leyland motor company to the British Steel Corporation,[25] and been drawn into abortive efforts to preserve the much-favoured Laker Airways.[26]

Consistent support may also be extended to specific sectors of a country's industry. The philosophical and political constraints under which states often operate, outside the Socialist block, make sectoral support a more acceptable and common practice than attempts to intervene comprehensively throughout the economy and its industrial system.

Many LDCs have adopted conscious and clear policies of support for the development of a range of basic industries. Within the AICs, greater attention has been directed towards the advanced technology industries, upon which long-term economic prospects are held to rest. This concern has stretched from an Europe-wide wish to preserve a presence in consumer-orientated industries like video-recorders[27] and video-disc players[28] through to an almost universal concern to maintain an industrial capability in the broad field of information and communications technology.

Sectoral support for advanced industries has focused upon a number of clear front-runners: information and communications technology, robotics and various computer-based industrial facilities, biotechnology, advanced transport, and materials technology.

Information and computer technologies will be considered in greater detail later in this volume. However, there have been a number of departures worthy of particular note: Britain's appointment of a Minister for Information Technology; Britain's five-year, £25 million programme for support for the fibre-optics industry, initiated in mid 1981;[29] an Anglo-French agreement on view-data transmission standards in March 1981;[30] the famous French programme of replacing telephone directories with French-built, on-line computer terminals;[31] and the £2 million support for the development of educational video-discs given by the British government in October 1984.[32] Such examples merely skim the surface of a level and extent of governmental concern in this broad area that has, at times, resembled hysteria.

Britain The picture in other areas of advanced technology is mixed, given the differences of outlook of governments and the different priorities accorded to the various technologies. The overall approach of the Thatcher Government in Britain has been particularly uncertain and uneven. Doctrine dictated official inactivity: reality has, however, compelled a number of last-minute efforts to revive areas of British technology that have been on the verge of submersion. In the years since acceding to power in 1979, the government initiated a number of ill-judged measures that had serious, if sometimes unintended, consequences. The resources, and role, of the National Enterprise Board were substantially reduced; the universities, and their advanced research, were shaken by a series of serious financial cuts; and the role and influence of the British Technology Group, the successor to the NEB, was further reduced in 1983.[33]

Despite the suspicion with which it was viewed by the British government, it was the NEB that was called upon to initiate a crash programme to save Britain's faltering biotechnology industry in 1980.[34] Once aroused, the Thatcher Government's concern with biotechnology continued and found further expression in the provision of £16m of financial support by the Department of Industry in November 1982[35] and the formation of a joint venture between the British Technology Group and private industry, Agricultural Genetics, to develop agricultural applications in this area.[36] However, advanced research in biotechnology has been one of the areas of endeavour that was also particularly badly hit by the British government's indiscriminate financial assault upon the country's universities.[37]

The British government also demonstrated interest in supporting a number of other areas of advanced technology, if not always as generously and as speedily as might have been desirable. Robotics have seen an unusual level of collaboration between British universities and industry, despite limited funding through the Science and Engineering Research Council.[38] The British government also injected some £3.5 million into the innovative robotics firm, Unimation: £1.5 million as grants from the Department of Industry and £2 million via the National Research Development Corporation.[39] Similar support has also been made available in the aerospace sector. The British government provided a £250 million loan to British Aerospace for its contribution to the projected Airbus A320[40] and a grant of £60 million to Rolls Royce for the development of the Airbus's engine.[41]

Japan The approach of Japanese governments contrasts sharply with the *ad hoc* meandering of British industrial policy. The Japanese Ministry of International Trade and Industry has, in combination with the Japan Development Bank, commercial financial institutions and the country's major enterprises, been able to orchestrate the systematic redevelopment of its industries in the post-war era and thence coordinate a spectacular advance into international markets.[42] The sectoral focus of this activity has been clear from the outset, with attention moving from such heavy industries as shipbuilding[43] to more consumer-orientated areas such as motor vehicles, and, finally, to the advanced sector industries of elecronics, computing, robotics and modern materials.[44]

The Japanese government is able to pursue its industrial intervention through a complex and often subtle set of institutions and practices. MITI itself is able to exercise considerable authority over Japan's major industries, drawing them into coordinated plans, involving the allocation of specific undertakings, or market shares, to individual firms. Rare has it been for firms, even those of considerable prominence, to reject such authoritative direction.[45] MITI has also been able to exercise influence through the Japanese financial system. MITI controlled the foreign exchange necessary to purchase imported technology during the two immediate post-war decades. It has subsequently continued to inspect financial applications made by industry to the Japan Development Bank[46] and retained the ability to set rates of depreciation on new investments that are favourable to the tax positions of firms.[47] Such devices can be employed discriminatingly to encourage desired sectoral developments.

MITI does not always have its own way, however. Its involvement in a sectorally advantageous cartel within the oil importing and distributing industry ultimately came to grief. In a case, now known as the Black Cartel Case, Japan's own Fair Trade Commission successfully challenged the arrangement in the Japanese courts.[48]

Despite occasional set-backs, MITI retains a central role in Japan's highly orchestrated assault upon the most promising industries of the future. A subsidiary of MITI—The Agency of Industrial Science and Technology—has been engaged in the attempt to pin-point the basic industrial technologies that will dominate the generation after the next one. In support of the attempt to achieve a dominant role in such industries, a £417 million programme of support has been devoted to a combination of government and private sector research and development in twelve areas, grouped into the three major fields of new industrial materials, biotechnology and new function electronic elements.[49]

Japan is making a special effort in the development of computer software, hitherto an area of Japanese weakness, with a programme of £8.5 million per year for seven years (from 1981) for relevant research.[50] Such efforts are supported by a range of financial incentives, including advantageous tax breaks, for firms that are prepared to invest in advanced technologies.[51] Such systematic efforts to secure competitiveness in important industrial areas can pay handsome, and relatively rapid, dividends, for a seven-year programme of £26 million of support has already seen the Japanese robotics industry achieve a substantial lead over Britain's.[52]

Industrial Rationalization
Many governments, and the EEC's authorities, have responded to surplus capacity in a number of major industries by authoritative measures of rationalization. The governments of a number of European countries have been active in promoting the rationalization of major industries, particularly those under governmental control or influence.[53]

Many Advanced Industrial Countries have promoted measures of rationalization within specific sectors of their industries. Britain witnessed a miners' strike of almost unprecedented duration and bitterness in resistance to such governmentally backed measures within their industry during 1984 and 1985. The French Socialist Government of President Mitterand found itself forced to accept programmes of employment reduction and capacity shedding in a number of industries, including car production, mining, steel, engineering and even some 'light' industries.[54] The Australian Labour Government of Bob Hawke declared itself in favour of reducing the number of car manufacturers with plants in Australia from five to three.[55] The EEC, overall, has adopted Europe-wide rationalization measures, particularly within the steel industry.[56] One of the smoothest rationalizations programmes was that of the Japanese shipbuilding industry, under the direction of MITI, during the late 1970s.[57]

Sectoral intervention in industry, however, encounters many of the dangers that confront other forms of governmental involvement in industry. Injudicious intervention can be both costly and futile. Attempts to defend industries that cannot be preserved at an acceptable economic cost might merely waste valuable resources, or inhibit their movement to more promising forms of employment. The problem facing policy makers is, however, that of differentiating those industries for which there are no realistic hopes from those that would have good prospects were they only to be given the time and opportunity for reconstruction. It is a dilemma which reflects the proposition, advanced earlier in this study, that many of the most important 'factors of production', upon which patterns of international competitiveness rest, are far from given but, rather, are the products of human decision and effort.

Regional Industrial and Development Policy
Selectivity is also available to governments in the form of the encouragement of industrial development in identified geographical areas and regions. The location of much of the Soviet Union's heavy industry reflects a concern to maximize

its distance from potentially vulnerable frontiers. The direction of US defence supply contracts to plants located in the southern states was based upon a wish to improve employment prospects in a traditionally depressed area of the country during the immediate post-war decades. French policy in the late 1960s and early 1970s was equally addressed to the problems of areas of the country, like Brittany, that had been the victims of relative economic stagnation.

Policies to stimulate industry and economic development within a country's regions may, however, be a complex and variable matter, as the British example during recent years indicates. Regional promotion has been attempted by central government and a growing number of organizations formed within the regions themselves. The approach of central government has varied considerably during recent years. The Thatcher Government has successively revised the character, and then the scale of support for, regional development schemes. A formal statement of government plans—a White Paper—of December 1983, indicated a switch of emphasis, under the 1982 Industrial Development Act, from capital-intensive schemes to those more clearly contributing to 'job creation' and heralded a reduction in the value of regional aid overall. The new emphasis upon selectivity also allowed the Industrial Development Unit, of the Department of Trade and Industry, to concentrate funds upon the more 'promising enterprises'.[58] 'Enterprise zones', marked by the removal of many usual controls and regulations, were also more to the taste of the government. Thus, in November, 1984, it announced the redesignation of a large number of areas of the country, with many losing their former status as 'development areas', and the further reduction of the funds for regional support.[59] Indeed, by January 1985, general financial constraints encouraged the government to impose a temporary freeze upon further grants under its regional aid programme.[60]

With a general economic recession, and a government that appeared rather unsympathetic towards regional development programmes, many of the more depressed areas of Great Britain turned to self-promotion. In some areas, organizations that had been established under earlier initiatives by central government, like the Scottish Development Agency, could be recruited for such regional endeavours.[61] Elsewhere, new bodies had to be established to meet the special needs of a number of particularly disadvantaged areas. The Greater London Council placed its faith in the ability of its new Greater London Enterprise Boad, with an annual budget of £32 million, to encourage the growth of jobs with good long-term prospects.[62] In the West Midlands, an area quite unprepared for the economic havoc of the early 1980s, the county council also restored to the establishment of its own Enterprise Board with an annual budget of £8 million.[63]

The problem with regional development schemes, however, is that they may amount to no more than expensive ways of relocating jobs from one area to another, or are merely subsidies for investments that were already planned by firms. Critics of such programmes argue that it would be more sensible, and substantially cheaper, to allow the new jobs to develop in the locations indicted by 'market forces'. Supporters of regional development schemes, however, continue to argue that efforts to secure employment in areas where economic infrastructure and established communities already exist makes equal economic sense when wider, and extremely important considerations, are included in the calculation.

There are a number of other policies that can assist a government in its efforts to promote industry. These areas of policy and practice vary in the extent of explicit governmental attention that they receive. They also vary in the degree to which they are judiciously managed by governments.

Energy Policy

The international competitiveness of a country's industry may be significantly influenced by the energy, and allied, policies that its government pursues. The low tax imposed in the USA upon petroleum products, including the fuel for motor vehicles has long had a number of important effects. Road transport costs have generally been extremely low in the USA, for industrialist and private motorist alike. Fuels for heating and the generation of energy, including natural gas, have also been maintained at a low price. The supplies of petroleum by-products for the synthetic materials' industry have also been relatively cheap by international standards and this has allowed the USA man-made textiles and carpeting industry to maintain a measure of international competitiveness.[64]

In marked contrast to the position in the USA, many argue that energy price policies have damaged the competitive prospects of much of British industry. The prices charged to industrial consumers by the state-owned electricity and gas industries have been determined by a variety of considerations. Governments have, at times, wished to minimize the subsidies that they have been asked to provide for such industries. On the other occasions 'market price' enthusiasms have held sway. More recently, the Thatcher Government's concern to minimize its budget deficit encouraged it to extract financial subventions from the profits of these public utilities. The consequence has been that the National Economic Development Council found, in a study of 1981, that some of Britain's largest industrial consumers might be paying as much as 20 per cent more for gas and up to 35 per cent more for electricity than their major competitors on the European Continent.[65] An earlier commitment to preserve the British coal industry may also have contributed to the higher electricity prices charged to British industry.[66]

Policy Towards the Financial System

Discussions of industrial development, and viability, have focused upon the role played by the financial systems within various countries. The early emergence of joint-stock banks, of share-holding, and a mechanism for the exchange of stock, considerably assisted the initial industrialization of Great Britain.[67] The subsequent reduction in the ability of Britain's financial apparatus to support her industrial effort, however, stands in marked contrast to the flexibility and imagination of the venture-capital system within the USA, or the systematic support for industrial developments provided by officially backed banks in Japan.[68]

Shortcomings in a country's financial system, as it relates to industrial investment and innovation, may be addressed directly or by-passed. The direct approach is to encourage, or compel, the financial sector to improve its procedures, attitudes and performance. The British government has encouraged a new system of unlisted shares exchange in Britain, in line with its faith in the long-term contribution of new and expanding businesses. The by-pass approach, in contrast, often involves the establishment of mechanisms for providing direct government funding for new investments. The establishment of Britain's National Enterprise Board (NEB), by the 1974–9 Labour Government, exemplified such an approach, the NEB orchestrated support for new departures in fields ranging from micro-electronics to the further development of the temporarily embarrassed areo-engine manufacturer Rolls Royce.[69]

Small Business Support
Systematic support for small businesses may be an additional measure that is particularly attractive to governments that believe that such enterprises promise much for the future of an economy. The Thatcher Government in Britain, reflected such a commitment by its appointment of a Minister with special responsibility for small firms.[70] This policy was subsequently elaborated through a variety of schemes designed to assist small businesses, including local Enterprise Agencies, a Department of Trade and Industry supported Small Firms Service and consideration of means of easing the financial pressures upon embryonic firms.[71] The EEC has also signalled its hopes for small businesses with its own support scheme, worth some 180 million ECUs.[72]

Science, Technology, Education and Training
Many governments have acknowledged the particular significance of those industries that employ the latest technologies. Such industries produce goods and services with a generally high income-elasticity of demand (i.e., are demanded more, proportionally, as the general level of global wealth increases); enable international competitiveness to be retained in the face of competition from new, and often low-wage-cost, producers; and last, but far from least, may

encourage the rest of industry to adopt more advanced techniques, to produce improved goods and to achieve greater general efficiency.

Successive new industrializing states have sought to secure access to, and the implementation of, the latest industrial technologies, from the Japan of the nineteenth century through to the Singapore[73] and Brazil of today. Education and training have, moreover, always played a central part in strategies directed towards the development of advanced technology industries. Britain's systematic failure to develop a sufficiently dynamic and technologically orientated education system during the late nineteenth century in this direction contrast markedly with the achievements of Germany, the USA[74] and Japan.[75]

The promotion of specific advanced technology industries falls under the heading of sectoral policy. Science, education and technology, however, are a matter of general salience within an economy. Many societies accord high status and relatively high salaries to their educators, with the notable exception of Great Britain.[76] Most are also concerned to see a steady expansion of the quality and quantity of educational provision at all levels, again with the notable exception of the Thatcher Government in Britain and its assault upon higher educational provision, and research,[77] and, despite its rhetoric of standards and salience, the resource base of much of the rest of the public sector education system.

Provision of training facilities specifically to industry is also a widespread concern. Private industry in many countries has a good record in this respect: substantially better than that of Britain. Indeed, Japanese industry assumes a considerable responsibility for the technical training of its more able entrants, who will have received a 'surprisingly' academic secondary and higher education.

Private provision of technical training is often supported by a range of public institutions of technical education. Acute concern with the general weakness of the provision for, and quality of, all forms of technical training has surfaced in Britain with impressive regularity. The 1980 report on the British Engineering Industry by Sir Monty Finniston highlighted the many shortcomings of engineering training in

Britain and called, in vain, for systematic improvements.[78] Thus, a report by the National Economic Development Council, in mid 1984, was still compelled to draw an unfavourable comparison between the training, and qualifications, secured by the average young British worker and his foreign counterparts and to appeal for a major initiative in improving training programmes and facilities.[79]

The remarkable feature of Britain's performance in the field of science, technology, education and training is that, despite the comparatively poor conditions under which her scientists and other educators work, the relative neglect of technological training and the general paucity of non-military research and development funding, the country has remained capable of generating a higher proportion of major technological advances and radical breakthroughs than any other Advanced Industrial Country.[80] The ability to convert basic innovation into internationally competitive production has, however, proved beyond the wit of much of British industry.

The Acquisition of Retention of Technology
The development and introduction of technology clearly constitue one path towards competitiveness in areas of advanced production. Technological progress may, however, be secured by importing innovation by one means or another.

Japan has practised a systematic policy of acquiring innovations, and advanced technologies, from abroad throughout the history of her industrialization. Her initial industrialization owed much to support, and supplies, from Great Britain. Her recent penetration of many world markets for technologically advanced goods has been heavily dependent upon the controlled licensing and/or copying of foreign innovations. MITI has been heavily involved in coordinating these efforts and has, indeed, often made the necessary financial and organizational facilities available to appointed Japanese firms. Japan has shown a remarkable capacity to improve and enhance the work of others, as with the development of more successful forms of the home video-recorder first introduced by Phillips of Holland. She has, however, remained keen to secure rapid access to foreign innovations, if necessary by the illegal means adopted by Japanese agents in America's 'Silicon Valley'.[81]

Policy measures that have the effect of drawing high technology industries into a community may be measures that have other, albeit allied, objectives. Regional development policies may thus have the effect of attracting advanced and/or dynamic industries from abroad to regions of unemployment and relative deprivation. The British government's recent concern to attract foreign direct investment from abroad reflects just such mixed motives, of assisting regional unemployment problems while introducing promising technologies and managerial practices.[82]

The Irish Development Agency has also been successful in recruiting high technology investment for the Republic of Ireland.[83] The Irish approach has been systematic, involving a ceiling on corporation tax, 100 per cent initial depreciation allowances for industrial buildings, grants of varying generosity depending upon the locality of the proposed investment and special bank facililties for small businesses.[84] This initiative has also been supported by the establishment of the National Institute of Higher Education at Limerick, to supply trained manpower, and general support in high technology, through such agencies as the Institute for Industrial Research and Standards and the National Board for Science and Technology.[85]

Efforts to retain a country's technological lead may involve strategic considerations, as with the USA's policy of denying Western micro-electronics and computers to the Soviet bloc,[86] or a wish to preserve a technological and, hence, competitive industrial advantage. The internal secrecy of many large firms, supported by the West's patenting system, goes some way to ensuring the latter objective, but such obstacles can be readily overcome by the determined. They also alienate many who believe that such protective measures are merely devices for perpetuating relative underdevelopment of the Less Developed Countries.

DISCIPLINE, RESTRAINT AND THE 'WORK ETHIC'

Governments may also be concerned to generate a social atmosphere that is conducive to economic dynamism and industrial competitiveness. Mrs Thatcher's much quoted evocation of 'Victorian values' is one expression of such a concern. Other societies have, however, their own means of securing analogous social and cultural conditions.

Many societies have been quite explicit in their promotion of attitudes, values and behavioural dispositions that are deemed to be appropriate to industrial effectiveness. Some societies, like the USA, have had to deal with the problem of building some form of community from successive waves of immigrants from all quarters of the globe. The ethos of the 'American way' reflected this concern: an ethos, moreover, that placed considerable emphasis upon the 'virtues' of acquisitiveness, competition and endeavour.

Japan has never been in any doubt that its educational and allied systems are to be devoted to building a society that is dedicated to the promotion of the nation-state in all its international dealings. The Meiji Restoration liberated a downtrodden feudal peasantry and prepared it for absorption into a militaristic social and industrial system. The heritage of such an experience, in today's supposedly peaceful Japan, is an obsessively conformist population, acutely attuned to the needs of an irrepressibly expansionist industrial system. Indeed, the concern to promote cohesion and uncritical national self-regard through the educational system has proceeded as far as to present school-children with a systematically distorted, highly censored, view of the country's atrocious behaviour during the Second World War.[87] Many Japanese leaders may be concerned about the suppression of creativity entailed by such a system, but it clearly provides a powerful springboard from which to construct a malleable industrial system.[88]

More specific measures may also be employed in the pursuit of a well-functioning industrial labour force. The development of a legal framework to govern industrial relations may be helpful, if constructed with care and caution. The contribution to harmony, and long-term efficiency, of the involvement of the Swedish government in industrial relations and wage bargaining during the post-war era has already been considered. The Swedish success in this direction reflects an approach that was designed, not merely to control industrial relations but to promote a wider social and economic consensus. A series of attempts have also been made, with somewhat less success, to place British industrial relations on a more satisfactory basis.

The 1964–70 Labour Government proposed an imaginative and wide-ranging plan for reforming and regulating the British industrial relations system, in the now famous 'In Place of Strife' White Paper. Deep divisions within the Labour Party, the union movement and, indeed, the Labour Government itself, finally buried the prospects of this initiative. The succeeding Thatcher Government, in contrast, had a clear and determined commitment to the control of trade union behaviour in pursuit of less disruptive industrial relations. The purpose of this policy was to restrain the ability of unions to call strikes and to limit the effectiveness of the picketing that unions might then employ to enforce strike activity.

The basic device employed in the Thatcher Government's industrial relations legislation was the exposure of trade unions to legal action by those affected by a strike: legal action to claim damages and/or to secure injunctions to prohibit 'improper' action. Reasonably effective in some relatively minor industrial disputes, this legislation was however, little employed during the famous miners' strike of 1984–5. Widespread recourse to the law would, it was feared, be unduly provocative and counter-productive. The industrial relations legislation was only used systematically by the Coal Board, in its attempts to compel the National Union of Mineworkers to hold an union-wide ballot on its strike action. However, the relative docility of many British trades unions during the early 1980s has, in many observers' view, been attributable more to the atmosphere created by recession and rising unemployment than to industrial relations legislation.

Legislation is not, however, the only means by which

governments can seek the creation of a docile work force. Many countries in the world have regimes that are quite happy to use considerable force, brutality and even widespread genocide to suppress trade union movement, and the progress of political dissent. The examples range from the systematic repression of effective trade unions and opposition parties in South Korea and Taiwan through to the widespread genocide unleashed by the late, unlamented military government of the Argentine.

HEALTH POLICY

A final area of governmental concern and possible policy is that of the general health and fitness of its population. Many LDCs have found that widespread disability amongst their populations exerts a most serious break upon development programmes. Undernourished people with endemic, debilitating diseases are not the most vigorous or responsive participants in the processes of rural regeneration or industrialization. The challenge posed by such problems is thus a priority for many contemporary governments and one in which they often turn towards international agencies for assistance.

A concern with popular health, nutrition and general fitness is not, however, peculiar to the governments of today's developing countries. Many of today's AICs have encountered serious problems in this area during their own development. Britain, during much of the nineteenth century, was compelled to confront the very serious problems of inadequate urban sanitation, appalling housing conditions, poor nutrition and widespread, curable disease that were blighting the lives of much of the working population and thereby reducing their economic effectiveness. Humanitarianism and the pursuit of economic efficiency can thus run hand-in-hand in the areas of popular health and fitness, as in education and training.

Health policy does, however encounter two significant problems. First, the extent of some disorders, and their considerable economic impact, is often overlooked. Thus the effect of back disorders, in terms of absence from work and reduced effectiveness when at work, is most serious in modern Britain but, understandably, little appreciated. Relative invisibility is, however, not the only difficulty in this area, for the second problem is that the range of treatment now available is extremely wide, often quite expensive and, regrettably, often of disputed effectiveness. A conflict thus arises between a wish to improve health and effectiveness by enhanced provisions, on the one hand, and a concern to avoid an ever more costly system of health and allied services, often of uncertain effect, on the other.

CONCLUSIONS

The purpose of this chapter has been to indicate the wide range of policies and practices that many modern governments characteristically adopt, and which may have a critical bearing upon the economic effectiveness and industrial competitiveness of their societies. This range of activities is an inevitable, and wholly legitimate, response to the pressures and demands under which governments operate in the contemporary world. They, and they alone, have the responsibility and the capacity, however constrained in practice, to ensure the well-being of their populations. International agencies remain seriously limited in their power and authority, while transnational corporations are, in the technical political sense, irresponsible.

Governments may, in practice, be faced with varying opportunities for policy and action. The governments of many LDCs remain seriously constrained by weaknesses, financial, industrial and organizational. Governments may, moreover, choose whether or not to exploit those opportunities with which they are presented. Prevailing doctrines, or variations in conditions, will influence such choices. However, the manner in which such measures may combine together to create a complex that is conducive to effective economic performance is worthy of the closest official attention, as is the strong possibility that once a society is impelled in a given direction it may develop a powerful momentum, whether in a beneficial or an adverse direction!

The industrialized countries of the West exhibit substantial variations in general economic and industrial policy. The USA of President Reagan is committed to a 'supply-side' revolution in which incentives, and the minimization of the constraints under which entrepreneurs operate, are seen to hold the key to economic growth, industrial competitiveness and future employment. In sharp copntrast, the British Labour Party has adopted a programme for the future regeneration of the British economy and industrial system based upon many of the devices surveyed in the last two chapters: substantial investments through public bodies and agencies; exchange controls and penalties upon those who wish to export capital; selective import controls; and, albeit with considerable circumspection, incomes policies.[89]

Beyond the reasonably conventional measures which the British Labour Party contemplates in the construction of its alternative economic and industrial programme, there are many other measures that can be adopted in the pursuit of improved performance, over the short or longer term. Many of these measures may be prompted by non-economic considerations and are at the very stuff of modern government. That they have substantial economic implications is unavoidable and a matter that warrants the most serious consideration by governments in all parts and of all persuasions.

NOTES

1. *See*, especially, H. G. Johnson (ed.), *The New Mercantilism: Some Problems in International Trade, Money and Investment*, (Oxford: Basil Blackwell, 1974); and Joan Robinson, 'The new mercantilism', in Joan Robinson, *Contributions to Modern Economics*, (Oxford: Basil Blackwell, 1978).
2. *See* B. Lapping, *The Labour Government, 1964–70*, (Harmondsworth: Penguin Books, 1970), Ch. 3.
3. On which, *see* Alan Budd, *The Politics of Economic Planning*, (London: Fontana Books, 1978)], esp. pp. 81–4.
4. On which, *see* M. Stewart, *Controlling the Economic Future*, (Brighton: Wheatsheaf Books, 1983), esp. pp. 38–43.
5. *See* J. A. Trevithick, *Inflation: A Guide to the Crisis in Economics*, (Harmondsworth: Penguin Books, 1977), esp. Ch. 5; and T. Cong-

don, *Monetarism: An Essay in Definition*, (London: Centre for Policy Studies, 1978).

6. Congdon *op. cit.*

7. *See* Stewart *op. cit.* esp. pp. 31–43.

8. *See* 'How money flowed abroad when the investment dam was opened', *Guardian*, 18 September 1981, p. 18; '£4.5 bn invested overseas in two years', *Guardian*, 22 January 1982, p. 18; and, 'Investment drain tops £10bn', *Sunday Times*, 20 June 1982, p. 49.

9. *See* 'Why the snake is looking so rattled', *Guardian*, 11 October 1981, p. 22.

10. *See* 'Join the EMS—forget about that overvalued dollar', *Guardian*, 26 February 1985, p. 26.

11. *See*: 'Groom for growth', *The Economist*, 17 November 1984, pp. 82–5; 'The ECU takes another stride', *The Economist*, 19 January 1985, p. 56; and 'Gaining currency', *The Economist*, 13 April 1985, pp. 60–2.

12. *See* the arguments in B. Gould, J. Mills, and S. Stewart, *A Competitive Pound*, (London: Fabian Society, 1977).

13. Budd *op. cit.* esp. Ch. 6.

14. *ibid.* Ch. 5.

15. *See*: A. Schonfield, *In Defence of the Mixed Economy*, (Oxford: Oxford University Press, 1984), esp. Chs. 5 and 7: and M. J. Wolf, *The Japanese Conspiracy*, (New York: Empire Books, 1983; and London: New English Library, 1984), esp. Ch. 8.

16. *See* 'OECD backs public investment', *Guardian*, 11 January 1985, p. 16.

17. *See* 'Wanted: strike-proof route to the continent', *Sunday Times*, 7 April 1985, p. 64.

18. *See* 'The man who curbs cartels', *Sunday Times*, 18 July 1982, p. 47.

19. *See* 'Reagan sets off a takeover explosion', *Guardian*, 15 July 1981, p. 19.

20. *See*: 'France's prices and incomes gamble', *Guardian*, 8 July 1980, p. 21; and 'French replace wage and prices freeze with "controlled freedom"', *Guardian*, 1 November 1982, p. 6.

21. *See* M. D. Hancock, 'The political management of economic and social change: contrasting models of advanced industrial society in Sweden and West Germany', in J. Rogers, Hollingsworth, *Government and Economic Performance*, (Beverly Hills: Sage, 1982).

22. *See* 'By all accounts they should be bust', *Guardian*, 9 October 1984, p. 22.

23. 'Lawson plots changes in jobs strategy', *Guardian*, 26 September 1984, p. 1.

24. *See* 'Britain to quit deal on minimum pay rates', *Guardian*, 26 March, 1985 p. 2.

25. 'Government throws BSC £1.5B lifeline', *Guardian*, 27 June 1980, p. 1 and back.

26. 'Taxpayers cash aid Laker', *Guardian*, 30 December 1981, p. 12.

27. 'Japan in "made in Europe" deal for VCRs', *Guardian*, 19 November 1983, p. 20.
28. 'EEC may double disc import duties', *Guardian*, 17 October 1983, p. 18.
29. 'Fibre-optics get £25m boost', *Guardian*, 28 July 1981, p. 20.
30. 'European standard on viewdata is emerging', *Guardian*, 17 March 1981, p. 16.
31. 'Ringing changes', *Guardian*, 14 June 1980, p. 22.
32. 'Britain gives a push to the video disc', *Guardian*, 16 October 1984, p. 20.
33. *See*, in particular: 'Governmental clips BTG's wings', *Sunday Times*, 27 February 1983, p. 57; and 'BASE moves in on research', *Guardian*, 10 November 1983, p. 18.
34. 'NEB called in to develop bio-technology projects', *Guardian*, 3 April 1980, p. 15.
35. 'Biotech boffins to get £16m', *Guardian*, 25 November 1982, p. 18.
36. 'New biotech venture formed', *Guardian*, 26 July 1983, p. 16.
37. *See* 'Drowned before the wave even breaks', *Guardian*, 20 June 1984, p. 19.
38. 'Universities help robot development', *Guardian*, 18 May 1983, p. 21.
39. 'Government aid for robot project', *Guardian*, 18 January 1983, p. 18.
40. 'A good gamble on the Airbus', *Sunday Times*, 4 March 1984, p. 66.
41. 'State aid and order boost aerospace firm', *Guardian*, 11 May 1984, p. 21.
42. *See*: Schonfield *op. cit.*; and Wolf *op. cit.*
43. G. C. Allen, *How Japan Competes: A Verdict on "Dumping"*, (London: Institute of Economic Affairs, 1975), pp. 28–9.
44. *See* M. Kikkawa, 'Shipbuilding, motor cars and semiconductors: the diminishing role of industrial policy in Japan', in G. Shepherd, F. Duchene and C. Saunders, (eds.), *Europe's Industries: Public and Private Strategies for Change*, (London: Frances Pinter, 1983).
45. For a discussion of the famous Sumitomo Case, *see* Schonfield *op. cit.* pp. 96–9.
46. *ibid.* p. 94; and *see also* Wolf *op. cit.* p. 209.
47. *ibid.* p. 94.
48. Wolf *op. cit.* pp. 206–7.
49. *See* 'Targeting for the twenty-first century', *Guardian*, 25 July 1983, p. 17.
50. 'Japan sets next target', *Sunday Times*, 29 November 1981, p. 72.
51. 'Japanese cash aid for high technology', *Guardian*, 19 July 1984, p. 6.
52. *See* 'Japanese robots are overtaking Britain', *Guardian*, 18 December 1980, p. 16.
53. *See* Shepherd, Duchene and Saunders *op. cit.* and *see also* S. Strange and R. Tooze (eds.), *The International Politics of Surplus Capacity: Competition for market shares in the world recession*, (London: George Allen and Unwin, 1981).
54. 'French shake-up could scrap half a million jobs', *Sunday Times*, 15 January 1984, p. 65.

55. *See* 'Changing down to rev up', *The Economist*, 9 June 1984, p. 76.
56. 'EEC maintains steel curb', *Guardian*, 17 November 1983, p. 18.
57. *See* Kikkawa *op. cit.* pp. 241–3.
58. *See*: 'Handouts under the counter', *New Statesman*, 31 May 1985, p. 810; and 'Getting the industrial balance right', *Guardian*, 14 December 1983, p. 16.
59. 'Scotland, Wales fear aid cuts will kill job hopes', *Guardian*, 29 November 1984, p. 2.
60. 'Freeze on aid to regions', *Guardian*, 17 January 1985, p. 1.
61. *See* 'Miracles north of the border', *Guardian*, 17 November 1982, p. 20.
62. 'Livingston's baby begins delivery of the jobs', *Guardian*, 2 February 1984, p. 19.
63. 'Socialist self-help key to recovery say the enterprising Midlands', *Guardian*, 6 October 1981, p.. 27.
64. *See*: 'Trade war truce may be short-lived', *Guardian*, 11 July 1980, p. 16; and 'Fibres quota heads list', *Guardian*, 16 October 1983, p. 15.
65. *See* 'Industry kicks at high energy costs', *Guardian*, 5 March 1981, p. 24.
66. 'Is coal scuttling British industry', *Sunday Times*, 5 December 1982, p. 60.
67. *See* B. Gillie, 'Banking and industrialization in Europe', in C. M. Cipolla (ed.), *The Industrial Revolution: The Fontana Economic History of Europe*, (London: Fontana, 1973), esp. pp. 261–2.
68. *See* 'Time to copy those foreign entrepreneurs', *Guardian*, 18 September 1981, p. 19.
69. 'The record shows the NEB did it one way', *Guardian*, 15 May 1979, p. 25.
70. *See* 'Seed corn falling on stony ground', *Sunday Times*, 30 October 1982, p. 62.
71. *See* 'Small firms bear job hopes', *Sunday Times*, 31 March 1985, p. 62
72. 'EEC to aid small firms', *Sunday Times*, 5 November 1984, p. 57.
73. *See* 'The Thatcher years of wasted brain power', *Guardian*, 10 April 1985, p. 19.
74. Corelli Barnett, *The Collapse of British Power*, (London: Eyre Methuen, 1972), pp. 103–6; and M. J. Weiner, *English Culture and the Decline of the Industrial Spirit, 1850–1980*, (Cambridge: Cambridge University Press, 1981).
75. *See* R. Storr, *A History of Modern Japan*, (Harmondsworth: Penguin Books, 1960), p. 113.
76. For an uncharacteristically critical review of the May, 1985 Green paper on Britain's higher education *see* 'Good education doesn't come cheap', *The Economist*, 25 May 1985, pp. 21–2.
77. *See* 'The strangling of science', *Sunday Times*, 5 February 1984, p. 72.
78. *See* 'Blueprint to guide manufacturers to prosperity'—a report on 'Engineering our future'— (The Finniston Report), *Guardian*, 10 January 1980, p. 16.
79. 'Britain "lagging in education for industry"',—a report on the NEDO

report 'Competence and Competition'— *Guardian*, 30 August 1984, p. 17.

80. *See* K. Pavitt, 'Technology in British industry: a suitable case for improvement', in C. Carter (ed.), *Industrial Policy and Innovation*, (London: Heinemann, 1981), esp. Table 7.4, p. 97.

81. *See*, for instance, 'Is it made in Japan—or stolen in California', *Sunday Times*, 27 June 1982, p. 49.

82. *See* 'Importing Technology: what's in it for Britain', *Sunday Times, 30 January 1983, pp. 68–9.*

83. For a general account *see* Wyn Grant, 'The political economy of industrial policy', in R. J. Barry Jones (ed.), *Perspectives on Political Economy: Alternatives to the Economics of Depression*, (London: Frances Pinter, 1983), esp. pp. 129–35.

84. *See* 'Special offer on high-tech products', *Guardian*, 24 February 1984, p. 21.

84. *ibid*; and 'Some of the best people are now wearing blue collars', *Guardian*, 24 February 1984, p. 21.

86. *See* 'Reagan's new trade ban scares Europe', *Sunday Times*, 11 March 1984, p. 22.

87. 'Professor says history censored in Japan's books', *Guardian*, 28 February 1985, p. 8.

88. *See* Wolf *op. cit*. Ch. 5.

89. *See* 'Labour's latest, exchange one control for another', *Guardian*, 22 November 1984, p. 26; and for a general, theoretical discussion *see The Alternative Economic Strategy: A Labour Movement Response to the Economic Crisis*, (London: Conference of Socialist Economists, 1980).

8 Secondary Neo-Mercantilist Policies and Practices in the International Sphere

INTRODUCTION

The international activity of modern states is directed by a range of motives. The 'economic' and the 'political' are inter-related in a complex manner. Economic capacities have often been developed as a basis of political and military strength, while international political and military manoeuvring has often been undertaken to preserve economic interests.

Many patterns of behaviour within the contemporary international system have such a dual character. Economic associations have complex connections with political relationships: complementary in the case of friendly states, a source of possible leverage in the case of political adversaries. Economic aid often has a complex association with the economic and politico-military interests of donor countries. The armaments industry now assumes such an important role in many economies that it has become a major source of exports and, hence, overseas earnings. Cultural connections, of all forms, have also become a popular means of promoting exports, however indirectly, and generating an atmosphere that is generally favourable towards a country's international economic interests.

CONTROL

The pursuit of control is, as has been argued throughout this volume, a central feature of international activity. Such control does not necessarily entail the coercion or disadvantage of others for it can be based upon mutually beneficial collaboration. However, conflicts of interest, and temptations to seek disproportionate advantage, are so frequent in international affairs that states are forced to look to their own resources, while treating cooperative arrangements with caution.

History has seen various forms of politico-military influence or control between states. The motives for such relationships have varied, but have often involved a complex of economic and politico-strategic considerations. Some Marxists see the pursuit of the economic interests of advanced capitalism as the source of the nominally political and strategic behaviour of modern capitalist states. However, classical mercantilist states, it can be argued, often pursued overseas economic assets as a means of enhancing their military capabilities and strength.

The patterns of control have also varied considerably. The widespread, and highly formal, imperialism of the late nineteenth century is but one example. Significant influence, if not outright control, has also been exercised through informal regions of economic influence. The overwhelming local economic strength of Germany, at various stages of her relationship with other states in Central Europe, has formed the basis of a pattern of regional influence.[1] Strategic communities, whether formalized by treaty or tacitly acknowledged in conventional behaviour, also generate patterns of political influence which may well encourage parallel developments in the economic arena. Such a process lies, in part at least, behind the changing focus of attention of Australia, and New Zealand, away from Britain and towards the USA during the post-war era.

The achievement of influence and control in international relationships may bring substantial advantages for the dominant state. Uncertainty is substantially reduced and, indeed, advantageous collaborative arrangements may be instituted. However, many specific matters may also be resolved to the advantage of the state that has influence and control. Subordinate states will hesitate from actions that are likely to alienate dominant partners, are more likely to accommodate their economic interests, and those of their national enterprises when they wish to operate locally, and are more likely to accord with their political views and strategic plans. Thus the Greece of Andreas Papandreou, while most radical in many of its dispositions and declared intentions, has refrained from actually withdrawing from the EEC.

ECONOMIC AID

Many states in the modern world provide other states, and their peoples, with various forms of aid. Such largesse ranges from emergency food to preserve the victims of famine to military equipment, and training, that may all too often contribute to the repression of peoples by their own governments. Between these two extremes there are, however, a number of forms of international aid that, irrespective of good intentions and effects, may provide the donor with a number of often subtle forms of influence, control and advantage over recipients.

Whatever the ultimate effects, it is possible that a good proportion of aid is motivated by a genuine wish to improve the conditions of the recipients. Such aid might be intended to support the economic development of a Less Developed Country, improve the general facilities available to its population or enhance the recipient's security. Non-governmental, humanitarian aid agencies maintain the purest reputations. Many forms of aid, however, have the effect, and sometimes the intention, of sustaining the economic and/or political influence of the donor over the recipient.[2]

The preponderance of international aid is provided on a bilateral, inter-governmental basis. The governments of donor countries provide aid to the governments of recipient countries in support of clear and specific programmes and projects, whether they be social, educational, economic or security and military. Bilateral aid relationships clearly provide the greatest possibility for direct influence. Over two-thirds of the economic and development aid provided by the world's AICs remains bilateral and under the Reagan administration this bias has been reinforced.[3]

The patterns and possible motives of bilateral aid are highly significant. The balance of all aid is highly biased towards a small number of recipient nations that are seen to be of particular strategic or economic significance. Perceived strategic significance seems to be central to the allocative decisions of the USA and such recent aid-donors as Japan,[4] while former imperial powers, like Britain and France, direct the bulk of their aid towards former colonies.[5] New economic sensitivities may also influence the pattern of aid disbursement. The aftermath of the 1973–4 oil embargo crisis thus saw a sudden surge of aid flows to a number of LDCs that were rich in important raw materials.[6]

The economic motives underlying such bilateral aid are various. Maintaining and enhancing the supplies of strategically sensitive materials and resources can, as has been seen, be a major consideration. Maintaining a hospitable environment for the operations, and assets, of a donor country's transnational corporations can be a further, and often linked, objective. All such purposes may be served by aid that supports the position of a sympathetic local elite. It is unsurprising, therefore, that much aid has been devoted to projects of great prestige value, or that favour the better-off urban dwellers, but that provide little, if any, benefit to much of the rural population.[7]

The neo-mercantilism of resource and asset protection can, moreover, be supplemented by the use of economic aid to promote a country's exports and, thence, its domestic industry. The general practice of 'tying' aid to purchases from the donor country has remained popular with some AICs, received renewed emphasis during the early 1980s and continued to generate controversy. British policy became more explicitly committed to the advantageous 'tying' of aid with the arrival of Mrs Thatcher's Conservative Government in 1979. The new Foreign Secretary, Lord Carrington, announced, in February 1980, that Britain must ' . . . give greater weight in the allocation of our aid to political, industrial and commercial considerations' and the Department of Trade was instructed to work in closer association with the Overseas Development Administration. In addition, the 'slush fund', established in 1978 to provide aid to countries that would not otherwise qualify, was enlarged and employed with greater vigour.[8]

The post-1979 shift in the orientation of British aid thus re-emphasized the neo-mercantilist flavour of much bilateral aid. In particular, this policy change amounted to an expansion of the proportion of British aid that assumed a bilateral form and the direction of a growing proportion to those more advanced LDCs that were likely to be interested in British exports of capital equipment, and allied goods.[9] Such manipulation of a country's aid programme may, however, encounter difficulties, particularly when other industrial countries engage in similar practices. In Britain's case, a decision not to contribute $2.5 billion to a Brazilian 'rescue package' in November 1983, merely opened the door to an additional $1.5 billion of 'tied' financing from the USA: a gain to US exporters at the direct expense of Britain's.[10]

Bilateral aid may, however, be preferred to the provision of resources for international and multilateral agencies, for reasons other than the ability to 'tie' such aid to donor country exports. Bilateral aid also allows the donor to practice greater general selectivity in the uses to which aid will be put, the countries to which it will be extended and, in some cases, the policies that will be required of the recipient.

The USA's administration, and a substantial body of opinion with Congress, during the early 1980s was suspicious of the policies of many of the multilateral agencies, including the World Bank, to which the USA had traditionally given substantial funds. These agencies were accused of a general profligacy, and a lack of political discrimination in the allocation of their resources.[11] Bilateral control of aid would, it was contended, overcome such shortcomings of multilateralism. Unfortunately, such attitudes encouraged the US government to threaten to withhold necessary financial contributions from some worthy multilateral organizations and thereby precipitated a number of minor diplomatic crises amongst the AICs.

In December 1983, the US government indicated that it would reduce its contribution to the seventh replenishment of the funds of the World Bank's 'soft loan' affiliate, the International Development Association (IDA), from $950 million to $750 million.[12] Such a *démarche* was unacceptable to other leading industrial nations, which embarked upon a series of consultations and proposals designed to pressure the USA to alter its position or, if that failed, to protect the IDA from the damage that it would otherwise suffer:[13] manoeuvring that proved successful in securing a change of the US position by May 1984.[14]

A saga of similar proportions, and equally serious implications, was precipitated at the end of 1984 by the unilateral decision of the USA to reduce its contributions to the United Nations' International Fund for Agricultural Development (IFAD)[15] and the subsequent unwillingness of some of the other richer nations, including Great Britain, to make good the whole of the resulting financial shortfall.[16]

It is the view of many analysts and critics, however, that 'neo-liberal' and 'neo-classical' suspicions of many multilateral aid agencies are largely misdirected. While multilateral agencies certainly reduce the amount of political and economic benefit that can be secured by any one donor country, the general advantage to the rich nations, as a group, may still be considerable. Indeed, many critics argue that the World Bank, its affiliates and the International Monetary Fund are major vehicles for maintaining the AICs' control over the LDCs.[17]

The World Bank and its major affiiates, the International Development Association and International Finance Corporation (IFC), are true multilateral aid organizations. These agencies are, however, under the sway of two influences which, in the view of critics, have given their policies an unduly conservative flavour. The first, and often decisive, influence is that exercised by the board of governors, on which the voting strength of countries is determined by size of financial contribution.[18] The staff of the World Bank may be permitted a good deal of independence over detailed policy. This discretion, however, can be exercised only against the background of the realities of political authority and, indeed, the patterns of financial influence that they reflect. A degree of conservatism in policy has resulted from these governing conditions.

A further, and significant, influence upon the activity of

the World Bank results from its practice of co-financing. The aid packages that the World Bank assembles from recipient countries are constructed from equal contributions from its own resources and loans from the international commercial banking system. To maintain its first class credit rating, the World Bank has had to be extremely cautious in the projects and programmes that it has approved and in the countries that it has been prepared to support.[19] An additional source of conservatism has thus been injected into World Bank activity by its dealings with the private banking system.[20]

The International Monetary Fund is not, technically speaking, an aid agency. Its initial purpose, under the Bretton Woods Agreement of 1944, was to monitor and support the fixed exchange rate system to which signatory states committed themselves.[21] The primary activity of the IMF, under the fixed exchange rate system, was, therefore, to provide help for states that were endeavouring to maintain the value of their currencies. Where necessary, the IMF was also able to impose conditions that it felt would help the re-stabilization of a country's currency, internationally. During the fixed exchange rate era, the IMF had extensive dealings with a number of the world's Advanced Industrial Countries.

The era that has followed the effective abandonment of the fixed exchange rate system has seen the IMF's attention increasingly focused upon the Less Developed World. The AICs have less need for the IMF's assistance now that floating exchange rates are tolerated, within certain limits. The mounting indebtedness of many LDCs has, in contrast, thrown them back upon the mercies of the IMF. The IMF has continued to approach the balance of payments, and associated currency, problems of the LDCs as if they were the result of short-term, frictional difficulties. Many would argue, however, that the problems of the LDCs are actually a product of economic underdevelopment, resultant difficulties and the wide-ranging development programmes that have, therefore, been deemed to be essential. The IMF is, therefore, involved in an aid relationship, by default.

The policies that the IMF has imposed upon countries that seek its financial assistance have, however, often failed to

reflect the realities of underdevelopment and the requirements of development. Indeed, the IMF's conditions for
loans are based upon conservative economic doctrines and
political views.[22] Radical regimes, such as that of Michael
Manley in Jamaica, have found it extremely difficult to obtain
timely loans from the IMF. Governments, regardless of
political complexion, that have been unwilling, or unable, to
implement IMF-approved economic and financial policies
have also been denied funds, as was the Argentine in
October 1983.[23] The IMF has also been heavily involved in
the negotiations on debt rescheduling, and interim financing,
for many of the LDCs that became most heavily indebted
during the late 1970s and early 1980s.

Political purposes are best, and primarily, served
through bilateral forms of economic aid. Broad strategic
interests, political affinities, moral issues and humanitarian
principles have all found expression in the direction of
economic aid. Recent examples have ranged across the
entire range of such considerations. Strategic issues, and
the inherent qualities of specific regimes, have been prominent in the determination of Japanese aid programmes,[24]
in the provision of $3 billion of military and economic aid
to Pakistan in 1981,[25] and in the EEC Council of Ministers'
decision, of October 1982, to withhold £30 million worth of
aid from Nicaragua.[26] Indeed, the Carlucci Committee,
working at the behest of President Reagan, produced an
explicit recommendation for a formal test of political
acceptability to be applied to potential recipients of US
aid.[27]

Moral and humanitarian issues have also exerted a visible
influence upon the determination of aid programmes. The
Reagan administration, swayed by 'born again' Christian
fundamentalism, declared itself in favour of withholding aid
from countries that permitted abortion or, indeed, aid
agencies that supported them.[28] In a somewhat different
vein, the EEC considered introducing a 'human rights' test
for the aid allocations to be determined by the negotiations
for a new Lomé Convention, between the EEC and its
associated African, Caribbean and Pacific group of LDCs,
in 1983.[29]

MILITARY AID

Military aid has a long, somewhat mixed and highly controversial history. A considerable portion of US aid, during
the post-war era, has assumed a military form. External
security and/or internal stability are the declared purposes of
such aid. Its effectiveness has been highly uneven, with some
major 'aid' programmes failing to maintain the position of
those being helped and the final balance being merely to add
to the sum total of destruction and misery wrought upon the
societies involved.

Whether the countries that are provided with military aid
are assisted is a matter of interpretation. Very few international situations actually present clear and unambiguous
evidence of unprovoked threat or aggression. Where such
evidence is lacking, the interpretation of the situation, and its
potentialities, rests with the analyst. It is open to argument as
to whether the stabilization, or not, of a given regime would
be beneficial and, indeed, to whom it would be beneficial.

What is clear, however, is that military aid suits the perceived interests of the donor countries and is governed by their
views of the situations into which they are prepared to inject
their martial bounty. The interests of a country in any international confrontation must accord with the strategic interests
of the donor country. The dispositions of a government must,
equally, fit with the perceived interests of a donor country if
assistance with internal security and stabilization is to be forthcoming. The interests of the donor country may, themselves,
be open to debate, as in the case of the wish of the Reagan
Administration to aid the Honduras-based opponents
(Contras) of the Sandinista regime in Nicaragua. However,
the majority of decisions about military aid are made by incumbent governments and reflect their views and peculiarities.

EDUCATIONAL AND CULTURAL NEO-
MERCANTILISM

Economic and military assistance are, however, no more
than the more obvious mechanisms through which states may

seek to establish influence, and control, or to use others as agents of their own interests. Subtle, but potentially profound, means are also available through the educational and other cultural contacts that societies are able to establish with others.

Educational contacts are ideal examples of those international relationships which embrace a mixture of motives. Societies that provide educational and training opportunities to the young of other countries often do so on the basis of a genuine wish to benefit both the individuals concerned and their home countries. Properly handled, however, such educational and training opportunities can bring a number of advantages. The student's familiarity with the language in which instruction is undertaken is substantially enhanced, usually at the expense of major international competitors (with the exception of the numerous English-speaking countries that engage in this area of activity). Where the training has a technical component, the student will become most familiar with the equipment of the host country and, therefore, more inclined to favour it on return to his, or her, home country. If the general experience has been agreeable, then the student might well develop a long-lasting sense of affinity for the host country.

Education and training in an industrialized Western country might also encourage the student to develop an affinity for the general culture of Western society. Whether or not this will prove beneficial for his, or her, home country in the long run, it may well encourage a more responsive political outlook and a taste for the goods which the West has specialized in producing. Rhetorical commitments aside, an impressive proportion of those leaders of LDCs who were educated in the West, or in Western-orientated institutions, do appear to have acquired a susceptibility to the material temptations of Western, capitalist culture. Clearly, then, Western governments that are interested in maintaining generally harmonious relations with the LDCs would be advised to promote suitable educational contacts.

The establishment of the appropriate linguistic competence and cultural orientation in an individual or, indeed, the educated section of an entire country, can be an extremely useful basis for other activities. Such a foundation can be reinforced, on a continuing basis, through books, magazines and other publications.

Societies also engage in quite self-conscious efforts to promote their images abroad. Elaborate organizations have been created by a number of countries to purvey favourable information about themselves and to facilitate hopefully advantageous contacts. The British Council is well-established in this area and has a record of considerable success. The US Information Service has become a major international presence during the post-war era. The Japan Foundation has also become increasingly active as it has been able to exploit Japan's considerable recent wealth to propagate a favourable image of Japan abroad and thereby disarm many who have become uneasy at that country's unrelenting assault upon the world's markets and industries.

Many other forms of cultural contact are, however, also capable of sustaining a form of 'cultural imperalism' that may be of benefit to Western states. It was the complaint of the Islamic radicals during the revolt against the Shah of Iran that his actions had encouraged just such a form of Western encroachment and the associated destruction of Islamic culture and society. Regimes within the Soviet bloc have prohibited the importation of 'blue jeans', and pop records, on similar grounds. Multinational corporations, by their presence, products and characteristic modes of conduct, have also been dubbed agents of western cultural imperialism in some host countries.

Some of the most powerful media of global cultural imperialism are the film and the television programme. The extraordinary power of Hollywood has long been witnessed in the audiences that gather in the most remote corners of the world to view films depicting gun-fighting cowboys in a largely imaginary nineteenth century USA, or the trials and tribulations of urban Americans. The television programme has amplified this somewhat Kafkaesque experience, with world-wide purchases of American 'soap operas' for local transmission. One of the most significant developments in this area is the arrival of satellite transmission, with its ability to allow direct transmission of television from one country to, in principle at least, any point on the earth's surface. Within the near future, anyone in the world who can acquire a television might therefore be able to watch, and wonder at, the latest episode of 'Dallas': a prospect that does not fill all governments or observers with unqualified joy!

THE MILITARY–INDUSTRIAL COMPLEX AND INTERNATIONAL ACTIVITY

A number of the world's industrial states also sell military equipment. Customers are primarily other countries, but sometimes militarily active groups and organizations. Some of these supplies are provided free, or on a concessionary basis, as military aid to like-minded or strategically important states. However, a massive international trade also exists in military equipment and it is a trade in which the governments of supplying and purchasing countries are necessarily heavily involved.[30]

One of the most interesting features of much of the international arms business, for the analyst of contemporary neo-mercantilism, is its quality of self-enclosure. Entry into this cyclical syndrome is, in a sense, arbitrary. However, a start is best made at its logical, if not empirical, point of initiation.

In the naive theory of armaments production, they are developed, produced and deployed to meet the security threats experienced by a society. The production of necessary armaments thus requires the development of a suitable system for research and development (R and D) and an industry capable of manufacturing the equipment that has been developed. Unfortunately, this system has two dynamic features of critical significance. First, security is primarily a function of the threat that is perceived to emanate, currently or potentially, from others.[31] Such perceived threat readily assumes a dynamic quality, given inevitable uncertainty about the intentions and current capabilities of others. Worst-case analysis is thus a constant temptation to security planners, who are disposed to define their country's military needs in terms of the largest assault to which they may be subjected. Britain's traditional Two Power Standard for the size of her navy exemplifies such a 'worst-case' outlook. The military capabilities of potential enemies are also open to expansion and/or improvement. The armaments of a country must, therefore, be improved and/or expanded *in anticipation* of such enhancements to the capabilities of others, for it will be too late to respond after opponents have exploited their newly introduced advantages.

The military–industrial complex harbours a second, and quite pernicious, source of dynamism within the industrial system itself.[32] Modern industrial societies are seized with an obsession with invention and innovation. The system of R and D and industrial production in the armaments' field shares this obsession. Novelties create markets for themselves by rendering existing equipment obsolescent. The existence and profitability of armaments industries is maintained by the constant generation of new orders. The R and D system is equally able to justify its size and continued existence by the endless production of novelties.

The truly pernicious feature of this process, however, is that innovation in the field of armaments generates its own demand. The armaments industry, like many others, devotes considerable efforts to persuading its potential customers that its newest products are essential to well-being. Members of the research and development community will be equally committed to promoting the virtues of, and necessity for, their latest projects and creations. On their side, the potential purchases within a country's armed forces and defence ministries will be open to the argument that innovations which have been introduced by their own industry may all too readily be introduced by the potential adversary. A strategic or tactical disadvantage may be avoided, therefore, only if the latest innovations are adopted with alacrity.

To sustain justification for a ceaseless process of development and procurement of armaments, it is essential to emphasize the possibilities of a relevant threat. A fear of the possible is thus bred and nurtured by the dynamic requirements of the industrial component of the military–industrial complex. It is also highly advantageous to those who wish to sell their ideas and products, and to those who wish to justify their increasingly expensive development and deployment, if a more tangible threat can also be identified. The military–industrial complex thus has a vested interest in defining enemies, who can then generate the necessary threats, whether actually as real or as substantial as is claimed. In a world which is already sufficiently dangerous, a system has been established within many modern states that has a commitment to the identification and, if necessary, the exaggeration of hostility and antagonism.

The armaments industry of many Advanced Industrial Countries has thus assumed an important, indeed often vital, place within the domestic economy. Some 50 per cent of Britain's total research and development expenditure has traditionally been concentrated in the military field. Such an investment of talent and resources cannot be written off purely against enhanced security, but generates a considerable pressure to produce tangible returns in the form of renumerative sales and earnings.

The role of the armaments industry within a national economy may also be highly significant. In the aftermath of the Falklands War, and at a time of economic recession, a package of British defence spending and purchases worth some £1 billion provided a major boost for a substantial segment of British industry, particularly in the fields of shipbuilding and electronics.[33] The bulk of successful tenders for defence contracts have also continued to go to British firms, despite a new 'open' tendering policy.[34] The choice of a new trainer for the Royal Air Force in early 1985 was finally swayed in favour of the Brazilian-designed 'Tucano', because it was to be assembled in the Belfast plant of the British company Shorts.[35] The situation in France is, if anything, even more extreme than that in Britain, for some 330,000 workers are employed directly in its armaments industries and the jobs of some 700,000 are estimated to be dependent upon that industry.[36]

Not only does the existence of a substantial armaments industry influence the basic strategic outlook of societies, it also creates a need for an international arms trade. Overseas sales often permit beneficial economies of scale and produce the revenues through which research and development costs can be compensated. Foreign arms sales are, therefore, an area of considerable cooperation between government officials, military personnel and industrial salesmen. The world-famous Farnborough Air Show is an outstanding example of such association and joint effort: an example which is followed by most of the major arms-manufacturing countries.

The joint promotion of a country's armaments goes far beyond the organization of fairs and showpieces. Considerable high-level political activity surrounds many large-scale procurement decisions, especially those for regional security organizations like NATO. Mixed teams of official and commercial arms salesmen also undertake frequent tours of more promising foreign countries, exploiting all manner of economic, political, economic and cultural connections in their efforts to secure orders.[37] Since most Advanced Industrial Countries maintain their own armaments industries, they often need to import only a limited number of items that fill particular needs. The most promising general markets are, therefore, within the Less Developed Countries that do not have the ability to meet most of their military requirements from domestic sources.

The efforts that AIC arms exporters make to secure sales in Less Developed Countries, and particularly the richer of the less industrialized countries, are considerable. The equipment that is offered may well be adapted to suit the particular needs of the intended consumer nations. British Aerospace developed an armed version of its Hawk training aircraft specifically to provide poorer Less Developed Countries with a cheap, multi-purpose fighter plane.[38]

There are also many financial and material inducements that international arms salesmen can use to secure orders from LDCs. The French are particularly determined, and supple, in their efforts to penetrate such markets. 'Soft loans', with long repayment periods and low interest rates, are made available to finance some 80 per cent of a range of co-operative manufacturing arrangements that France has concluded with a number of LDCs, including Egypt.[39] A long-term assault within the developing world has provided France with substantial markets: for its Mirage jets within the Arab countries, for air-defence systems for countries like

Saudi Arabia, and for Aerospatiale's now notorious 'Exocet' missile. In sum, France has managed to develop an export market for its exports which netted it some $4.9 billion during the first six months of 1984 alone.[40]

Determined efforts to secure initial orders for a country's military equipment are not justified merely in terms of the initial boost to earnings and employment. Military equipment requires considerable quantities of replacements and spare parts to remain functional. Much of it also consumes ammunition which may be specific to given equipment, or to the munitions supplied by a specific country. Continuing orders of considerable value thus flow from initial sales of armaments to another country. Moreover, if those armaments prove satisfactory, and a generally harmonious relationship is established between the two parties, the purchasing country may be more disposed to order other items of equipment from the supplying country on future occasions, particularly if that new equipment is in some way suited to the existing equipment.

Complementing the officially supported sale of armaments, is a somewhat more unorthodox global trade in armaments. This business facilitates a significant proportion of the international movement of armaments and covers shipments that range from those that are actively prohibited by the governments of the source countries, through to those of which the source government publicly disapproves but is privately willing to tolerate, if not actually support. South Africa has, in the past, been the beneficiary of this shadow armaments trade and, by many accounts, the Argentine was a further beneficiary during the Falklands Conflict.[41]

Advanced military technology and equipment is, however, a succubus that may threaten to consume the very economy that sustains its development and procurement. Modern combat aircraft are particularly expensive to develop and manufacture. International collaboration to produce new models is, therefore, a possibility which is particularly attractive to groups of countries that have other reasons for wishing to foster such joint ventures. Five of the major European nations have thus undertaken a project to develop a new fighter aircraft and thus overcome competition from the

USA. A successful development of a 'home-built' plane would protect local employment and generate business estimated to be worth up to £3,000 million.[42]

The relationship between the defence systems, strategic dispositions, armaments industries and arms sales efforts of many Advanced Industrial Countries (and some of the Newly Industrialized Countries) is thus complex, cyclical and of considerable significance. There are some analysts who see this complex as a major cancer within the contemporary global system. Whatever the contribution and consequences of this system, however, it is clear that it has a major influence upon the economic well-being of a number of societies and, in turn, upon their external economic relationships and behaviour.

CONCLUSIONS

The purpose of this chapter has been to indicate the range of international behaviour that states may undertake which, despite having little apparent connection with such practices as protectionism, may nevertheless have profound significance for the promotion of national economic well-being. Such behaviour ranges from the provision of 'aid', through the relative subtlety of educational and cultural contacts, to the somewhat cruder promotion of international arms sales.

Aid, in most of its common forms, has been identified with the maintenance of control and influence over recipient countries. Donor countries may not intend, or even be aware of, this facet of their efforts. This effect may, nevertheless, be real and fully perceived by the recipients. However, it is clear that the pursuit of influence is intentional in many forms of aid. Bilateral aid is particularly vulnerable to manipulation by the donor.

Multilateral forms of aid have sometimes been thought to be free from manipulative possibilities. However, many critics of the IMF, the World Bank, and the World Bank's affiliates have identified a strongly conservative bias in their policies and practices: a bias that has, moreover, seriously damaged the interests and developmental prospects of many of those LDCs that have been involved with these organizations. The overall effect of most forms of international aid is thus, in the view of many critics, to ensure the economic and strategic interests of the donor countries throughout much of the less developed world.

Educational and myriad cultural contacts allow societies to exert a low-key, but often highly significant, influence over the 'hearts and minds' of the populations and, in particular, the leading members of other countries. Linguistic competence, cultural affinity and acquired tastes may all assist exports and the preservation of other economic interests. At their extreme, such sources of influence may amount to a form of cultural imperialism which is all but irresistible, save to those communities that consciously seek to resist and expel such 'contaminants', as with contemporary Iran.

The armaments industry has, finally, come to occupy a highly significant place in the domestic economies of a number of the world's industrialized countries. The implications of this presence go far beyond the contribution such industries make to domestic economic activity, and employment prospects. The scale and costs of developing and producing modern military equipment are such as to compel manufacturers, and their patron governments, to seek economies to scale based upon substantial export orders. The promotion of foreign arms sales is thus an activity in which governments, and their officials, participate energetically and deploy the full range of inter-governmental inducements. A parallel trade in private arms sales also flourishes with, it may be suspected, a degree of tacit governmental toleration.

Few, then, are the areas of international activity in which states, and their authorities, engage that are entirely divorced from the promotion of domestic economic well-being. Governments vary in the degree to which they recognize, and choose to exploit, the opportunities that are open to them. The exploitation of such opportunities may, moreover, be undertaken with varying levels of subtlety and sophistication. However, international relationships in the contemporary world remain the province of neo-mercantilism: real and enduring irrespective of liberal rhetoric.

NOTES

1. *See* the interesting and seminal discussion in Albert O. Hirschman, *National Power and the Structure of Foreign Trade*, (Berkley: University of California Press, expanded edition, 1980), esp. pp. 34–40.
2. *See*: David Wall, *The Charity of Nations: The Political Economy of Foreign Aid*, (New York: Basic Books, 1973), Ch. III; and Joan M. Nelson, *Aid, Influence and Foreign Policy*, (New York: Macmillan, 1968), Ch. 1.
3. *See* 'Reagan—the wicked witch of the North', *Guardian*, 6 January 1985, p. 13.
4. *See* 'Staid aid', *Guardian* 18 January 1980, p. 7.
5. *See* R. D. McKinley and R. Little, 'A foreign policy model of the distribution of British bilateral aid, 1960–70', *British Journal of Political Science*, Vol. 8, pp. 313–32.
6. *See* H. Munoz, 'Strategic dependency: relations between core powers and mineral-exporting periphery countries', in C. W. Kegley and P. McGowan, *The Political Economy of Foreign Policy Behavior*, (Beverly Hills: Sage, 1981).
7. *See* C. R. Hensman, *Rich Against Poor: The Reality of Aid*, (Harmondsworth: Allen Lane, 1971), esp. Ch. 5.
8. *See* 'Aid funds buy work for British industry', *Sunday Times*, 1 November 1981, p. 53.
9. 'Tory aid switch "hurts poorests"',, *Guardian* 21 June 1982, p. 16; and 'Development aid tops £1 billion', *Guardian* 23 February 1983, p. 22.
10. 'US threatens Britain's British trade', *Guardian*, 11 November 1983, p. 18.
11. *See* 'US aid strings tighten', *Guardian*, 1 February 1985, p. 9.
12. 'Debt pressure squeezes the poorest', *Guardian*, 13 December 1983, p. 22.
13. 'Europe and Japan snub Reagan', *Guardian*, 23 December 1983, p. 13.
14. 'US agrees support for IDA funds', *Guardian*, 18 May 1984, p. 13.
15. 'US squeezer,' *Guardian*, 2 November 1984, p. 17.
16. 'Soft loan fund avoids collapse', *Guardian*, 4 March 1985, p. 21.
17. *See*, especially: T. Hayter, *Aid as Imperialism*, (Harmondsworth: Penguin Books, 1971), esp. Ch. 2; and Cheryl Payer, *The Debt Trap: the IMF and the Third World*, (Harmondsworth: Penguin Books, 1974).
18. On the organizational principles of these organizations *see* J. H. Richards, *International Economic Institutions*, (London: Holt, Rinehart and Winston, 1970), esp. pp. 88–95.
19. 'World Bank borrows $8.5bn', *Guardian*, 17 July 1982, p. 20.
20. *See* Hayter *op. cit.*
21. *See* Richards *op. cit.* Ch. 2.
22. *See*, especially, Hayter *op. cit.*
23. 'IMF withholds loans to Argentina', *Guardian*, 13 October 1983, p. 18.
24. *See* 'Staid aid', *Guardian*, 18 June 1980, p. 7.
25. 'Pakistan accepts $3 bn aid', *Guardian*, 16 September 1981, p. 7.

26. 'EEC attacked on withdrawal of aid', *Guardian*, 14 October 1982, p. 8.
27. 'Reagan hits out with a fistful of dollars', *Guardian*, 9 December 1983, p. 12.
28. 'US to cut aid to abortion nations', *Sunday Times*, 24 June 1984, p. 23.
29. 'EEC may apply rights lever', *Guardian*, 19 May 1983, p. 7.
30. For a general survey *see* Anthony Sampson, *The Arms Bazaar*, (London: Hodder and Stoughton, 1977).
31. *See* Barry Buzan, *People, States and Fear: The National Security Problem in International Relations*, (Brighton: Wheatsheaf Books, 1983).
32. On the 'military–industrial complex' *see* S. Lens, *The Military–Industrial Complex* (London: Stanmore Press, 1971).
33. 'How industry won the peace', *Sunday Times*, 19 December 1982, p. 45.
34. *See* 'MoD cash targeted at electronics', *Sunday Times*, 5 May 1985, p. 66.
35. On the background *see* 'Four-war dogfight', *Sunday Times*, 8 April 1984, p. 68.
36. *See* 'Making a killing', *The Economist*, 20 October 1984, pp. 78–9.
37. Sampson, *The Arms Bazaar op. cit.* esp. Ch. 10.
38. 'Cheap hawk aimed at Third World markets', *Guardian*, 3 September 1984, p. 7.
39. 'Making a Killing' *op. cit.*
40. *ibid.*
41. *See* G. Thayer, *The War Business: The International Trade in Armaments*, (London: Weidenfeld and Nicolson, 1969), esp. Chs. 2 and 3.
42. *See* 'Britain drain threatens new plane project', *Sunday Times*, 1 July 1984, p. 2.

Part V
Summary and Conclusions: The Faces of
Contemporary Neo-Mercantilism

9 Economic Realism and Neo-Mercantilism in Action

INTRODUCTION

The discussion in Part IV indicated the range of policies, practices and conditions that may have a significant effect upon economic activity, industrial vitality, international competitiveness and, hence, the general well-being of any society. Popular discussion has tended to concentrate upon the protection and direct support of industry. This, however, fails to do justice to the richness, complexity and, indeed, murkiness of much of contemporary reality.

Contemporary governments are presented with wide-ranging, and far-reaching, opportunities for involvement in, and contribution to, their societies' industrial systems. All of these opportunities have been exploited at some time, by some government, somewhere. Rare, however, have been attempts to exploit the entire range of possibilities simultaneously. The contribution that governments have made to the development of their countries' economies and industries have, in contrast, been selective in their utilization of policy options. The choices of options have, moreover, reflected the peculiarities of given societies.

The conclusion, therefore, is not that any one policy, or set of policies, offers an ideal which can be prescribed for any society that wishes to enhance its industrial performance and economic well-being. Neither should it be thought that a survey of past, and present, practices reveals a consistency of approach amongst those governments that appear successful in enhancing economic effectiveness. Rather, the argument herein is that various patterns of support can be invaluable in promoting economic development and international competitiveness. In contrast, many societies that have not achieved notable economic success might well be advised to adopt one or more of the policies, and practices, that have proved effective in similar contexts. The consistent application of such policies may be the only way of fulfilling governments' responsibilities to promote the general economic well-being of their citizens in a world of chronic turbulence and uncertainty.

This chapter will, therefore, be devoted to an examination of the practical effects that governmental policies in a number of countries within the advanced industrial (capitalist) West have had upon industrial developments during recent years. The selection of the micro-electronics/computing industry reflects the central role that it plays, and will continue to play, in the economic and industrial future of much of the world. The subsequent brief discussion of the French and British boat-building industries is then offered as a contrast, for it reveals, in part, the unintended, yet serious, consquences that can follow from ill-advised policy departures.

THE MICRO-ELECTRONICS AND COMPUTING REVOLUTION

A number of advanced technologies promise to transform tomorrow's world. Technologies to exploit renewable energy sources, biotechnology and advanced materials technologies all carry profound implications. Many of these new technologies are now interconnected in their development and deployment. However, all have depended, in their initial development and their subsequent application, upon the capacity for analysis, calculation and control that has been furnished by the spectacular revolution in micro-electronics, and computing, of the post-war era.

It is the very capacity of micro-electronics and computing to transform so many aspects of modern life that locates it centrally within the complex of contemporary economic, industrial and technological developments. Modern micro-electronics have transformed many branches of tactical and strategic weaponry, lie at the heart of many new consumer products, have wrought profound changes in many areas of production technology, and are facilitating a cumulative transformation of many service industries, ranging from banking through to the communication of news and information. A technology that carries implications ranging from the threat of destabilizing the nuclear deterrence balance, to the reversal of the recent relocation of some forms of industrial production to the Developing World is such as to warrant the closest governmental attention and concern.

The USA and the first phase of the micro-electronics revolution

Fundamental research in the emergent field of micro-electronics was not confined to the USA, during the immediate post-war years. Moreover, one of the most impressive initial advances in computer construction was achieved at Manchester University, England. However, it was in the USA that the micro-electronics revolution germinated and flowered.

Many factors contributed to the undeniable lead seized by the USA in micro-electronics in the 1950s, 1960s and early 1970s: some being necessary for such a major industrial breakthrough, others merely complementary. Some of the necessary conditions were common to both the USA and other countries, like Great Britain, that were to fall by the wayside in the race towards a micro-electronics dawn.

The modern micro-electronics industry is quintessentially 'knowledge based'. The major advances in the design and manufacture of micro-electronic components were made by the recipients of extremely high levels of scientific and technological education. The existence of an educational system, and particularly a university system, capable of producing such innovators was, therefore, the first necessary condition: a condition that was amply satisfied in the case of the USA of the 1950s and 1960s.

Industrial innovation also requires a strong, and effective, entrepreneurial response to the possibilities created by basic research advances. Two sources of such entrepreneurship in the field of micro-electronics existed within the USA. Some large companies, like the Bell Telephone Company, supported substantial research and were prepared to ensure the rapid exploitation of its fruits. The pioneering development of the transistor by William Shockley and his team gave both Bell, and the USA, an invaluable lead in this vital area.[1]

The second source of entrepreneurship was to be amongst the very scientists and technologists who were to become the pacemakers in the never-ending process of technological advance. Many US scientists and technologist seemed not to share the distaste for business and commerce manifested by many of their European colleagues. Many thus left the research laboratories of universities, and larger firms, to form the small, personally owned companies that were to dominate the integrated circuit industry (and California's Santa Clara Valley—the 'Silicon Valley' of world fame) during its formative years.[2]

Transistors were the harbinger, though not yet the ultimate consummation, of the approaching micro-electronics revolution. The semiconductor technology, upon which the transistor was based, is common to both discrete transistors and the now ubiquitous 'chip'. A 'chip' is, essentially, no more than an integrated set (or circuit) of transistors grouped together within one small block of silicon, or other suitable material. Progress in the integration of transistors was substantially accelerated by a third feature of the USA in the early 1960s: the sudden fear of an adverse 'missile gap' between it and the Soviet Union, coupled with an increased enthusiasm for the conquest of space.

The launching of the Soviet Union's Sputnik satellite in 1957 came as a considerable surprise, and something of a shock, to many in the USA. It demonstrated both a significant level of Soviet technical competence and the substantial lifting capacity of Russian rockets. US military and civilian leaders thus determined that progress in micro-electronics might forestall a Soviet advantage in miniaturized control and communications technology and bring the possibility of improving the accuracy, and hence the capabilities, of the US's lighter rockets.

The early support that had been given to the development of the transistor by the US military[3] was now to be followed by massive funding for research and development on integrated circuits.[4] 'Throwing money' upon an extremely fertile soil in this manner was bound to elicit some notable successes. Moreover, the military provided a more-or-less guaranteed market, at fixed and generous prices, for any worthwhile products that resulted from the fire-storm of research and innovation that was being stoked by official money and encouragement. The later cut-throat price competition did not therefore affect the early micro-electronics industry[5], and the USA government, through its military agencies, was thus able to stimulate and sustain a vital industry during the critical years of its infancy.

The continued development of the US micro-electronics industry also owes much to the existence of a substantial, and effective, indigenous venture capital market. The combination of favourable tax concessions with the enterprising outlook of many individuals and firms, has ensured continued investment in promising ventures in the US micro-electronics and computing industry, as well as in other areas of advanced technology.

A suitable mix of demand-side and supply-side conditions thus provided the USA's embryonic micro-electronics industry with a fertile soil in which to grow. The growth of this industry has also been lionized as a supreme example of the potentialities and achievements of an unfettered and vigorous competitive free-enterprise system, particularly in its capacity to germinate those small, innovative firms that create new industries. However, this survey has already highlighted the significant role played by 'big government' in the form of the USA's military and space establishment.

The subsequent development of the US micro-electronics industry has also been instructive. Innovations in any one area of micro-electronics have, after an initial and often quite short period of gestation, usually proliferated throughout the industry. The pace of competition in the industry has, therefore, been hectic. With innovative products barely recovering their development costs, the few highly profitable firms have been paralleled by many that have teetered constantly on the precipice of financial disaster. Particular difficulties have been experienced during the periodic phases during which production has expanded but demand has stagnated, if not actually declined.[6]

Such a competitive maelstrom has stimulated a slow, but perceptible, movement towards consolidation and concentration within the mainstream of the micro-electronics industry. The tendency has been towards the emergence of a smaller number of larger firms which increasingly dominate both 'chip' manufacturing and the production, and supply, of 'end-user' systems. This process of 'horizontal' consolidation and integration has, however, been reinforced by a further, and quite peculiar, characteristic of the micro-electronics and computer industry.

The steady, and often rapid, advance of power and capability of integrated circuits has facilitated an unusual form of vertical competition. Firms that operated initially at one level of the industry have been able to develop their products so as to mount a challenge, albeit partial, to firms that have previously been dominant at a higher level. IBM remained for many years the undisputed leader, indeed quasi-monopolistic giant, in the US computer world and an all but irresistable force globally. A direct challenge to IBM has never yet been undertaken successfully at the highest levels of the mainframe business, despite heroic failures like that of Amdahl. Indeed, an indigenous mainframe computer industry has been sustained in many countries, outside the USA, only by the adoption of systematic neo-mercantilist practices by their governments. However, the progress of the micro-electronics revolution was such as to produce mini-computers of sufficient power to challenge the role of IBM mainframe computers in many situations. This challenge from below was mounted by such mini-computer firms as Digital and Wang. The response of the mainframe producers was, with some delay, to take the market for 'smaller' business machines more seriously and to make efforts to secure some share to the market at this level.[7]

A second and, equally profound, shock to the major powers within the computer world was, however, to emerge from even deeper recesses within the industry. The sudden appearance of the personal computer during the late 1970s brought substantial computing power to a potentially enormous market, at a price that was, by historical standards, ludicrously low. The USA's Apple Personal Computer heralded this new, and remarkable, phenomenon and was soon to spawn a burgeoning industry. The arrival of the ultra-cheap home computers of the mid 1980s merely marked the final stage of a seemingly irresistable process.

Competition from below has thus been a major stimulus to a process of 'vertical' consolidation and integration in which firms that have traditionally operated at one level of the industry seek entry into another. The outstanding example of this process was the late, and reportedly reluctant, production of its Personal Computers by IBM.[8] This form of movement 'down market' has, however, been accompanied by a further form of industrial integration.

The very competitive dynamic which has characterized the micro-electronics component industry has contributed to instability and an unreliability of supplies which, at times, has been quite serious for established producers of systems.[9] A number of firms have, therefore, absorbed established chip manufacturers to complement their existing work in the design and manufacture of systems and to ensure regular supplies of necessary components,[10] including IBM's acquisition of a stake in the chip maker Intel in 1982.[11]

Ferocious competition continues between the major US components and systems manufacturers in the field of micro-electronics, computers and allied systems. However, the process of consolidation has been enhanced by the 1982 decision of a number of the leading US firms in the computing and integrated circuit industries to collaborate in a $25–35 million a year research project—Semiconductor Research Cooperative—designed to maintain the USA's lead in this area over such competitors as Japan.[12] This venture was followed by the decision, in mid 1983, to establish a jointly-funded $50 million a year Microelectronics and Computer Technology Corporation in Austin, Texas, to develop a 256K 'superchip'.[13] Such industry-wide ventures reflect the more exclusive arrangements between erstwhile competitors like Texas Instruments and National Semiconductors who agreed, in May 1984, to share the otherwise prohibitively costly research and development of a 32 bit microprocessor for the forthcoming generation of personal computers.[14]

International Responses to the Micro-Electronics Revolution

Japan Japan, with typical prescience, was early to appreciate the central significance of the semiconductor, integrated circuit industry. The Japanese electronics and electrical industry relied overwhelmingly upon imports of integrated circuits from the USA during the 1960s. However, the Ministry of International Trade and Industry (MITI) had identified the critical importance of the industry and negotiations were held with the six leading Japanese electronics firms during the early 1970s. By 1975, a plan had been agreed for the coordination of a joint venture in the production and marketing of random access memory (RAM) chips.[15]

MITI's plan for Japanese memory chips involved the 'targeting' of the world market for memory chips. Leading firms were paired together in cooperative research and development ventures, to avoid wasteful competition;[16] extensive financial support was made available through generous grants, subsidies, tax credits and loans;[17] the embryonic micro-electronics industry was heavily protected by a variety of non-tariff barriers;[18] the rapid internal diffusion of techniques and knowledge was encouraged;[19] and the successful assault upon international markets was thus ensured.[20]

The fruits of the programmed Japanese assault upon the world's memory chip market were rapidly achieved. A substantial place in the US market itself was secured for Japanese 16K memory chips by the start of the 1980s.[21] Against a background of considerable suspicion that industrial espionage had secured illegitimate access to the fruits of US research, Japanese firms proceed to gain some seven per cent of the market in their next target sector—64K RAM memory chips—and push US manufacturers into rapid retreat.[22] US chip manufacturers then effectively abandoned the race for the next market—that for 256K RAMs—to the Japanese,[23] and their $500 million, MITI organized, development programme.[24]

The US industry has now been alerted to the dangers posed by Japan. The joint research and development programmes, mentioned in the preceding section, are one response to this problem. However, the Japanese are equally determined to persevere with their systematic attack. MITI has targeted the development of the 'fifth generation' of 'intelligent' computers, for which it has organized a $500 million, ten-year research programme.[25] 'Fifth generation' work, which involves developments in both computer hardware and software, is also to be complemented by a $100 million scheme to produce a range of super-fast computers.[26]

The Japanese are far from being dazzled by the highest peaks of micro-electronics and computer technology for they remain equally keen to dominate the personal computer industry. MITI was again able to arrange a highly sensible understanding between eight of Japan's leading electronics firms to adopt a common operating system for all their personal computers: the MSX standard. This innovation is designed to overcome the classic problem of the incompatibility of different makes of personal computer, the consequential difficulties in linking them together in networks and the lack of transferability of software (programmes). The MSX range has not, in the event, made a major impact upon the European market but it remains an example of the coordination and joint effort of which the Japanese industry is capable.[27]

Responses outside Japan The reaction to the micro-electronics revolution outside Japan was initially somewhat muted. There was a general lag in the adoption of technological innovations[28] and many of the leading firms that had developed a chip-making capacity, like Britain's Marconi and GEC, opted to concentrate upon high-value, low-volume, custom-made chips.

The significance of the more obvious applications of modern micro-electronics was, however, more widely appreciated. The survival of local computer firms was widely supported through a range of policies, as with Britain's International Computers Limited, which had been formed with governmental encouragement and which then enjoyed a near-monopoly of official orders. Comparable policies and practices were adopted in France and West Germany to stimulate the emergence of 'national champions' in the computer field during the 1960s and 1970s.[29]

Developments by the late 1970s had, however, demonstrated the critical importance, and pervasive influence, of micro-electronics in all their areas of application, from home video-games to the industrial control processes. The issue, however, was whether the preservation of industries that used micro-electronics also required the maintenance of an industry capable of designing and producing general purpose micro-electronic components (memories and unspecialized microprocessors). Micro-electronics was seen to be an expensive, highly risky industry which would never produce more than marginal profits. Some believed that it would be preferable, therefore, to rely upon imported micro-electronic components and concentrate upon industries that incorporated such devices in high-value products.

The strategy of abandoning general purpose micro-electronics, however, encountered a number of difficulties. First, general purpose micro-electronics, despite considerable risk and relatively modest unit profits, could be seen to be a major business of the future, with massive annual markets. Second, there were fears that European applications industries would remain vulnerable to interruptions of supplies of components from their foreign manufacturers under a number of circumstances, most probably periodic shortfalls in capacity during which manufacturers would favour local, or even linked, applications industries. Third, the existence of a components-manufacturing industry locally might have a number of beneficial spill-over effects upon the national applications industries. Finally, there was signs within the industry of a trend for the manufacturers of end-user systems to become closely involved with the designers of micro-electronic components, and particularly microprocessors, at the initial stages of their development, to ensure a product that was optimal for the intended application. Clearly, such initial consultation and participation would be considerably eased if systems designers and chip designers were located in the same country.

European Responses The debate over the desirability of retaining a general micro-electronic chip-making capacity formed the background to the responses within Europe during the late 1970s and early 1980s. Many countries have made an effort to preserve some presence in the micro-electronics industry, in addition to stimulating a healthy applications capability, including computers.[30] The EEC also orchestrated a regional response, with a joint programme on advanced intelligence research.

Britain Britain has continued to extend official support for its 'national champion' computer company ICL. In the late 1970s, however, intense interest was focused upon the general development and impact of micro-electronics and modern 'informatics'. From relaxed neglect, British policy makers were seized by acute concern about the strategic centrality of this group of complementary industries.[31] Action was to follow, but action that was often too little, too late and irresolutely pursued.

Britian's response to the micro-electronics and computer-based revolution has been the subject of a regular series of critical official reports. These reports have all identified, and lamented, the failure of government, educational system and industry to respond adequately to the challenges with which they have been faced. The clarion call was raised by the Government's Advisory Council for Applied Research and Development (ACARD) in its 1978 report 'The Applications of Semiconductor Technology': a report which identified Britain's past neglect and recommended a comprehensive response embracing action by government, industry and the educational system.[32] A series of specialized and general reports subsequently reiterated such criticisms and appeals.

The failure of British manufacturers of electrical resistors to exploit the possibilities offered by micro-electronics was criticized in a NEDO report of August 1981.[33] 1981 also saw two reports by the National Economic Development Council that remained highly critical of Britain's general performance and called for a systematic policy involving enhanced assistance through purchasing policies[34] and a supportive framework of general economic policy.[35]

Déjà vu would, however, have been experienced by the reader of reports issued by the NEDC and other investigative bodies during subsequent years. The 1982 report by the Electronics EDC, 'Policy for the UK Electronics Industry', identified the transformation of this wide-ranging industry's balance of payments surplus of £100 million in 1975 into a deficit of over £300 million by 1980; pin-pointed a number of areas, including 'informatics' and derivate industries, in which Britain had strengths sufficient to hold future promise; and, again, called for a systematic and supportive policy.[36] However, in late 1984, alarm calls at Britain's fast-faltering performance were still being sounded by the NEDC's information technology committee[37] and NEDO's electronic components committee.[38]

A laggardly British response to the 'challenge of the chip' did not, however, exclude any policy or action. The 1974–9 Labour Government identified the problem and initiated a response, of sorts. The succeeding Conservative Government, of Mrs Thatcher, was doctrinally disinclined towards an interventionist policy in any area but was compelled to make a tacit 'U' turn by the realities of this industrial sector.

In 1978, the then Labour Government decided to support the British micro-electronics industry. Early in that year it was decided that the National Enterprise Board should provide £50 million of support for the establishment of a new British micro-electronics firm, the initial target of which would be the development and commercial production of a 64K memory chip.[39] This policy of selective concentration led to the establishment of the ultimately successful firm Inmos. Established firms were also supported and in February 1979 it was announced that a £7 million grant was to be given to support the establishment of a joint chip-making venture between GEC and the American firm Fairchild.[40]

Mrs Thatcher's incoming Conservative Government, in 1979, had some difficult decisions to face in the area of state support for the micro-electronics and allied industries. Doctrine denied the value, indeed acceptability, of such governmental intervention. The serious requirements of Britain's industries, however, dictated caution with regard to any potentially precipitous reversals of the policy adopted by the preceding government. Considerable nail-biting and public anguishing thus resulted but could not impede the steady drift of policy towards continued support, however grudging, for the British industry.

In July 1979, the new Conservative Government agreed to cumulative grants of £14 million for a chip factory to be built by the USA's National Semiconductor Company in Greenock, Scotland.[41] By September 1979, the Thatcher Government had announced that it would continue with the general micro-electronics industry support programme, worth some £125 million, of the preceding government.[42] Before the year was out, £1.4 million of funds from the semi-official Science and Engineering Research Council had also been provided for the production of specialized micro-chips in the Universities of Edinburgh and Southampton: part of a wider effort to enhance the work of the universities in this area.[43] The fate of Inmos, and Britain's place in the production of general purpose memory chips, was, however, still in doubt.

The National Enterprise Board was clear in its recommendation to the government that Inmos be provided with its second £25 million grant. However, the then Secretary of State for Industry, Sir Keith Joseph, aroused widespread alarm by delaying his response.[44] The final decision was positive, however, and by March 1980 the neo-liberal Thatcher Government was committed to continued support for the Inmos venture.[45]

The story of Inmos proved to be one of the Thatcher Government's more meandering sagas. The firm achieved considerable success with its first product, a 16K chip. By July 1982, it had received some £95 million of public grants and loans to assist it in this achievement. However, there were soon signs of renewed governmental reserve towards such support. Further funds were required to develop larger chips and a request for some £10 million was addressed to the government.[46] Patrick Jenkin, who had replaced Sir Keith Joseph as Industry Secretary, proved more responsive than his predecessor and, in January 1983 it was announced that Inmos would receive an additional £15 million.[47]

Despite its continuing financial support for Inmos, the Thatcher Government was also committed to the doctrine of 'privatization'. With Inmos firmly established by 1983 it was, therefore, targeted for sale to the private sector by a government whose acute need for revenue now complemented its ideology.[48] The problem remained, however, as to whom this sale might be made, for Inmos had been developed as a means of securing a British presence in the manufacture of general purpose chips. Its offer for sale, however, raised the possibility that it would be purchased by foreigners. Indeed, by June 1984, controversy focused upon the offer of £58.5 million by the American AT&T for the manufacturing facilities, but not the development team, of Inmos: an offer which the new Secretary of State for Industry, Mr Norman Tebbit, was initially unwilling to rule out.[49] Ultimately, however, a seventy-six per cent stake in Inmos was acquired by Britain's Thorn-EMI, in July 1984, for £125 million.[50]

The government's attention during the early 1980s was now focused exclusively upon Inmos. A Minister of Information Technology was created in November 1980,[51] and its short-lived incumbent, Mr Adam Butler, was replaced by Kenneth Baker in January 1981.[52] A plethora of schemes, many heralded by the previous Labour Government and generally rather modest, were then introduced: to stimulate education in micro-electronics and computer skills,[53] to reinforce support for the Microprocessor Applications Project (MAP),[54] to advance computer-aided industrial design and manufacture,[55] and to encourage innovative developments in computer software.[56]

The needs of Britain's micro-electronics and informatics industries continued to exert a compelling pressure upon the Conservative Government. In March 1984, it was felt necessary to revive a scheme which had originally been introduced by the previous Labour Government—the Microelectronics Industry Support Programme—but then substantially reduced on the arrival of its Conservative successor.[57] The focus of MISP was now to be orientated more towards the smaller firms in the industry.[58]

Two particular issues were of particular significance in the evolution of the Thatcher Government's approach towards micro-electronics and the computer industry. The first was that of the continuing difficulties experienced by Britain's 'national champion', ICL. The second stemmed from a recognition, prompted by the publication of a report by a committee chaired by British Telecom's John Alvey, that a British involvement was essential in the international 'race' to produce the so-called 'fifth generation' of computers which would exhibit marked levels of artificial intelligence.

By the early 1980s, ICL, Britain's sole mainframe computer manufacturer, was in serious financial difficulties. Substantial support was necessary if it was both to survive and to maintain a secure place in the market. The government recognized the strategic role of ICL and felt obliged to continue its financial support for the firm.[59] In an ultimately successful effort to restore its competitiveness, ICL also embarked upon an ambitious programme of collaboration with Japan's leading mainframe producer, Fujitsu.[60] By 1984, however, the government's instincts had reasserted themselves and ICL was offered for partial privatization. The main bidder for a share of ICL was, however, to be a British subsidiary (STC) of the American giant ITT[61] and approval for such a contentious sale was given only under strict conditions.

The fifth generation of computers was the second major issue to confront the British government during the mid 1980s. John Alvey's committee had reversed earlier thinking which, under the influence of Sir James Lighthill, had encouraged the neglect of artificial intelligence research and projects designed to produce 'knowledge-based systems'. Now, however, under the twin stimuli of a number of promising research programmes, and the looming threat of a Japanese assault in this area, the Alvey Committee recommended a strenuous effort, supported by some £350 millions of public money.[62] By July 1983, these recommendations had resulted in the formation of a directorate to oversee the Alvey Programme of joint research by industry and universities, and the spending of the recommended funds.[63]

The range of the Alvey Programme has been considerable. It has supported the development of manufacturing facilities to generate forthcoming generations of ever more powerful micro-chips.[64] It also authorized a variety of programmes in chip development and artificial intelligence research, despite some significant difficulties in orchestrating the necessary cooperation between industry and universities.[65] The Alvey Programme is also the British link with the Europe-wide Esprit programme on advanced computer research.[66]

The British government has thus engaged in wide-ranging support for the British micro-electronics, computing and allied industries. It has also sought to influence the industry's long-term pattern of development, by its decisions on the fate of such central enterprises as Inmos and ICL. The Alvey Programme has crystallized the government's concern with, and commitment to, the future condition of Britain's micro-electronics based industries.

France French governments, throughout the 1970s and early 1980s, were concerned to support and promote an indigenous micro-electronics and computer industry. With its tradition of state intervention in industrial developments, the French government found it natural to provide financial support for the industry and to participate in shaping it over the longer term.[67]

In 1978 the French government committed itself to a five-year, £15 million a year programme of support for an indigenous micro-electronics industry, albeit born of collaboration with industrial leaders from the USA. The initial plan, therefore, was for a joint venture between France's 'national champion', Thomson-CSF, and the USA's Motorola.[68] At the start of 1980, the French government then determined upon a highly imaginative, if not uncontroversial, scheme to replace the conventional directories of its telephone subscribers with on-line terminals that would permit continuous up-dating of details of telephone numbers. The manufacture of these terminals was, moreover, to be confined to French suppliers including, inevitably, Thomson.[69]

The policies of President Mitterand's Socialist Government focused upon the possibilities of strengthening France's micro-electronics and computing industry by combining general support with rationalization. In October 1982 the government committed itself to a five-year programme of some £14 billion of aid for the electronics industry and, in

November, orchestrated a market-sharing plan in which Thomson-CSF would concentrate upon mini-computers and CII-Honeywell Bull on the middle range and mainframe sectors.[70] Rationalization was then promoted through governmental approval for the recently nationalized Thomson's proposals to take a 75 per cent controlling share in Germany's Grundig, an agreement which followed earlier intervention to prevent a tie-up between Thomson, Britain's Thorn-EMI and the failing German AIG-Telefunken company.[71]

Italy The pattern of official Italian support for, and involvement in, its domestic micro-electronics and computer industry has been characteristic of its general approach to industrial intervention.[72] A leading role in electronics has been played by the subsidiary—Stet—of the state holding company Institute per la Reconstruzione Industriale (IRI). A subsidiary of Stet—SGS-Ates—has, with dynamic management, internal reorganization and substantial injections of R and D finance, secured an expanding and increasingly important presence in the world's micro-electronics industry.[73]

Germany Germany benefited from an early appreciation of the importance of the micro-electronics revolution and the development of a coherent response. The German industry, and its 'national champion' Siemens, was assisted by the development of a specific plan for semiconductors in 1974 and public financial support on a scale equal to that made available elsewhere in Europe. The focus has been upon the adoption of innovations made elsewhere: a focus that has allowed Germany to reduce its adaptation time in the micro-electronics industry.[74]

Ireland For a country that has not had a particularly strong record in the more advanced branches of modern industry, the Republic of Ireland has achieved much in the fields of micro-electronics and computers. This success has been a direct product of the programmatic policy adopted by the Republic towards the attraction of inward investment by advanced technology firms.[75]

The Irish development plan included a long-term target of attracting micro-electronics and computer firms. Efforts were made during 1979 to add additional American, and possibly Japanese, firms to its pioneering chip-manufacturing deal with Mostek. The establishment of a chip-making laboratory in an Irish university was part of the package of inducements to such inward investment.[76] Considerable success has been achieved through such an approach, with such world-famous micro-computer manufacturers as Apple establishing plant within the Republic of Ireland.

The European Economic Community The European Economic Community (EEC) has developed its own community-wide approach to micro-electronics, computing and allied industries, additional to those of its member states. The policy formulated at Community level has encompassed two main elements: a competition policy, aimed at enhancing market prospects, and an embryonic policy for community-wide coordination of research and industrial development.

The EEC's competition policy has been directed, in part, towards weakening the monopolistic position that a number of US firms have threatened to establish in advanced technology industries. The position of IBM in the computer industry has been of particular concern, with the EEC Commission bringing an anti-trust case agains IBM in the European Court of Justice to prevent it 'abusing' its dominant position within the European market. The purpose of this action was clearly to protect the opportunities of European computer producers.[77] By mid July, 1984, this issue had been resolved by an out-of-court 'pact' between IBM and the Commission, in which IBM agreed to accelerate the disclosure of the technical details of its new products, and hence assist European manufacturers of IBM-compatible 'peripherals', and to accept continuous monitoring by the Commission.[78]

The EEC's approach to micro-electronics was also motivated by a concern to avoid the kind of chip famine that was experienced by Europe during mid 1984,[79] as well as the failure to secure beneficial 'spill-over' effects. The then EEC Commissioner for Industry, Viscount Davignon, had developed his European Programme for 'Informatics' with just such objectives. His programme included proposals for common computer equipment standards throughout Europe, extensive use of government purchasing power, and coordinated research and development, particularly in micro-electronics.[80]

Initial progress on a concerted EEC assault in the fields of micro-electronics and computing had, however, been rather slow and hesitant.[81] By the end of 1982 the EEC had, however, secured agreement on the Esprit programme for a £2.5 billion programme of research and development in micro-electronics, advanced computers, robots and computer-aided design. With financing shared equally between the Community and industry, the aim of this programme was to secure 30 per cent of the world's information technology industry for Europe by the early 1990s[82] and thereby reverse the steady decline of its position in these industries.[83]

THE GLOBAL POLITICAL ECONOMY OF THE MICRO-ELECTRONICS AND COMPUTING REVOLUTION

The common theme in the responses of all countries to the micro-electronics and computing revolution of the late 1960s, 1970s and 1980s is a recognition of its critical significance. Disagreements have arisen over the precise implications that these interrelated developments will have for the industrialized countries and for the pattern of 'North–South' economic relations. That these implications will be profound is, however, rarely disputed.

The impact of the micro-electronics revolution upon the industrialized societies will be felt both in what is produced and in how it is produced. Within manufacturing industry, new products will emerge, the performance of many established products will be significantly enhanced through the introduction of micro-electronics, and, by no means least, the means of producing many goods will be transformed. Home video-games exemplify the new micro-electronics based products. In the motor vehicle industry, micro-electronic ignition systems are replacing the older mechanical arrangements, while micro-electronic controlled robots are transforming many phases of vehicle production.

While such particular possibilities and implications are reasonably clear to most observers, controversy continues over the general effect of the micro-electronics revolution upon societies. The impact upon employment is at the heart of this issue. Some believe that micro-electronics will replace a wide range of skilled jobs, thereby condemning a significant proportion of the working populations to unemployment or low-paid, low-skill service jobs. Such concerns were already being expressed before the advent of the policy-induced world recession of the early 1980s.[84]

Many have disputed the argument that the micro-electronics revolution heralds a future of mass unemployment within the advanced industrialized countries. The initial counter-argument was that this new technological advance would, in fact, increase the total number of jobs available, by increasing the numbers employed in the industries that built micro-chip based capital equipment and in the new consumer industries that would be based upon applications of micro-electronics.[85]

The optimistic view of the employment effects of the micro-electronics revolution would, however, require the satisfaction of a number of quite demanding conditions, for even partial fulfilment. World demand for all the goods and services affected by, or introduced as a result of, this transformation would have to rise at a rate sufficient to compensate the increases of productive efficiency in labour-shedding industries and services. Moreover, any affected society would have to ensure that it continued to secure its established share of the world trade of the goods and services affected, or introduced. Failure to satisfy such conditions would have a significant effect upon domestic employment. While many inhabitants might discover new more renumerative, and more rewarding, occupations, many others would experience de-skilling or protracted unemployment. The impact upon a country's socio-economic structure, social harmony and political stability of this latter possibility might, moreover, be both substantial and portentious.

The practical difficulties of fulfilling either, or both, of the conditions for preventing increased unemployment have contributed to, though not been the sole cause of, the rising unemployment experienced by many established industrialized countries during the 1980s.[86] Their intrinsic difficulty also lies behind the form of 'supply-side' economic policy, espoused by Mrs Thatcher's Government in Britain, in which a 'solution' to mass unemployment is seen to lie in the acceptance by the unemployed of low-skilled employment in the service sector of rates of pay so low that they barely exceed subsistence.

The impact of the micro-electronics revolution upon economic relations between the 'North' and the 'South' are also controversial: controversial in a manner that has some bearing upon the debate about employment effects within the Advanced Industrial Countries. Two contrasting viewpoints have, again, emerged on this issue. The first is that the advent of micro-electronics presents Less Developed Countries with an unprecedented opportunity to 'leapfrog' in their economic and industrial development. Micro-electronics, in this argument, amplify the possibilities for adopting and exploiting the latest productive technologies, and thereby stealing a competitive advantage over the established industrial societies. What Japan was able to achieve with such spectacular success in the late nineteenth and twentieth centuries might be even easier for the newly industrializing countries.[87]

Such a view may, however, be somewhat naive with regard to a number of critical realities of the global distribution of economic, industrial and financial power and of technological capability. It is these asymmetrical realities that attract the attention of adherents to the alternative view of the impact of the micro-electronics revolution upon North–South relations. Rather than enhancing the developmental prospects of the LDCs, advanced technologies might merely allow many of the AICs to recapture, or retain, manufacturing industries that had previously been in the process of relocation to the lower labour cost regions of the world.

From hesitant beginnings,[88] such views have now become widespread.[89]

The dangers of AICs retaining or recapturing 'old' industries through the application of advanced production technologies are exemplified in one industry of particular interest to the South: that of clothing and textiles. Here, computer-aided design and computer-controlled cutting and assembly threaten to restore a competitive edge to the AICs. Areas of the industry that had previously been moving to low labour cost competitors may now be recovered and a significant contribution to the development of many LDCs lost.[90]

The damage to specific industries, in which considerable developmental hopes had been placed, is but one of the problems with which the micro-revolution and explosion of informatics' capability has confronted the LDCs. They also face a wider danger of intensified dependency as the major 'informatics' corporations in the North develop, and operate, even more powerful systems of global information gathering, transmission and processing. Significant mergers between computer and telecommunications firms have been taking place within the AICs. STC's fusion with ICL in Britain is but a weak reflection of the portents attendant upon IBM's interest in satellite communications or the move of American Telephone and Telegraph into computers.[91] Many in the South are apprehensive of a future in which such conglomerates operate world-wide information-processing systems to which the authorities of those nation-states that are often the subject matter of such information may obtain access, if at all, only at prohibitive costs.

The economic (and military) strategic implications of the micro-electronics revolution, and the industry that it has spawned, are such as to have stimulated two notable reactions. The first is the massive effort being made by some governments within the 'Third World' to promote an indigenous computer industry: an industry that, it is hoped, will reduce their future level of technological dependency. Brazil, though not alone, has been notable in this respect. The Brazilians have long maintained a '*mercado reservado*' policy of reserved markets for certain products[92] and used this facility to protect, and promote, a local computer-manufacturing capability.[93] Government support was also forthcoming for the acquisition, by the local Matias Machline, of the US-owned Philbrase–Philco micro-electronics factory.[94] Brazilian policy reflects a long-standing recognition of the critical role that capability in this industrial area has for national economic and military sovereignty.[95]

The second effect of the widening recognition of the strategic implications of the micro-electronics revolution has been the growing concern of the US government to inhibit the outflow, and general diffusion, of relevant technologies.[96] The declared justification for a policy of imposing increasing restraints upon the export, or re-export, of advanced technology has been that of denying such equipment to the Soviet Union and its Eastern allies. There have, however, been suspicions that the motives for such restrictions are as much economic as they are military.[97]

The contemporary revolution in micro-electronics and informatics thus has the most considerable significance for the global economy. Employment patterns and prospects within many of the world's most industrially advanced countries may be profoundly affected. The impact within the AICs may, moreover, be regional as well as sectoral. Those in Britain who live in the South-East, and therefore within Europe's 'golden triangle' of industrial prosperity, might be substantially advantaged, while those in the more 'peripheral' regions might face steadily worsening prospects. This regional and sectoral impact within AICs may, moreover, be extended and amplified when the implications of the revolution of advanced information technologies impose themselves fully upon the general pattern of North–South economic relations.

Given the range and intensity of their impact, responsible political authorities are therefore compelled to pay the greatest attention to the strategically central microelectronics and computing industries. It is hardly surprising, therefore, to discover the breadth and depth of official involvement in the development of such industries within the great majority of the AICs and, indeed, the intense concern expressed by the leaders of many of the world's LDCs.

THE YACHT-BUILDING INDUSTRIES IN BRITAIN AND FRANCE

From the profundities of the micro-electronics and computing revolution, a shift of attention to the yacht-building industries in Britain and France provides a substantial contrast. However, the yacht-building industry has a number of interesting characteristics which are themselves worthy of examination in any study of political economy. A comparison of the experiences of the British and French industries during the last decade is also highly instructive with regard to the effects that policy, whether intended or incidental, may have upon the well-being of an indigenous industry.

The modern yacht-building industry is interesting in a number of respects. While not requiring quite such high skills as the earlier construction of wooden boats, the manufacture of modern glass-reinforced plastic (GRP), steel or alloy yachts remains a relatively labour-intensive and skilled activity. Boat building is also precisely the kind of industry that might be expected to experience steadily growing demand in societies that are supposed to be moving towards more leisure-orientated life-styles. The vitality of this particular industry is, however, particularly susceptible to the effects of public policy in a number of areas, whether or not those effects be directly intended.

The contrast between the British and the French boat-building industries during the 1970s and 1980s has been marked: a fitful, and often tenuous, struggle for survival within the British industry, a relatively smooth and steady pattern of progress on the French side. Government policy and action have had a significant influence in both cases.

The British yacht-building industry has always contained large numbers of relatively small-scale builders, with a bare few firms that produced boats in any volume. The collapse of small operators is to be expected in all industries, as they encounter numerous obstacles to continued viability. The British experience is full of such examples of small-scale failure. What is significant in the British case, however, is the way in which government policy has intensified the problems faced by the entire industry, including its largest and most prestigious members. Two major shocks were experienced during the 1970s and early 1980s, both resulting from government policy. The first was the imposition, albeit relatively short lived, of a 'luxury' rate of Value Added Tax upon such items as boats in the late 1970s; the second was the combination of high exchange rate and high interest levels that resulted from the initial monetarist enthusiasms of the Thatcher Government on its accession to office in 1979.

The 'luxury' VAT rate seriously depressed demand for boats at a time when foreign competitors, and particularly the French, were not afflicted by such impediments. The disastrous consequences of the early Thatcherite monetarism then dealt a severe blow to two groups of firms within the industry: those that were committed to developing and maintaining a substantial export market; and those that had borrowed heavily to improve their model range or production facilities. By a stroke of great misfortune, one of Britains's leading builders of medium-sized yachts—Westerley's—found itself in both situations simultaneously. A firm that had responded to exhortations to improve its products and seek export markets had, by its progressive investments, exposed itself to the effects of maladroit government policy, and condemned itself into the hands of the receiver, albeit with ultimately happy results.

The British yacht-building industry has also been disadvantaged by a general failure of recognition of those neo-mercantilist practices that can promote the well-being of domestic industries and by a more specific lack of appreciation of the local needs of the boat-building industry, and its home clients. The general problem derives from the general reluctance of British governments to exploit the advantages that can be obtained for domestic industries, and that are commonly secured by many competitor nations, by protectionist devices of a tariff or non-tariff character.

The more specific long-term problem faced by the British yacht-building industry has been a reluctance to respond to the need for more facilities, particularly marinas, for boat owners. Local authorities have retained control of the planning permission required by developers of marinas and similar facilities. Such local authorities have often, with the support of relevant government departments, been disposed to deny development permission on one 'worthy' ground or another. With inadequate provision of coastal yachting facilities, home demand for new boats was depressed and the British yacht-building industry denied a timely, and much needed, stimulus.

The contrasting experience of the French yacht-building industry is instructive. French governments during the 1970s identified yachting as a worthwhile activity for a society that would assume a growing leisure orientation and as an industry that offered good employment prospects and the possibility of export earnings. The policy implications of this view were many. The development of marinas along France's various coastlines was actively encouraged, with the removal or reduction of many obstacles. Imports of foreign-built boats were systematically obstructed by non-tariff barriers. These non-tariff barriers have been operated within a legal framework—the '_Marine-marchande_'—which allows French authorities to engage in the minute scrutiny of every aspect of a boat that seeks import authorization. Regulations nominally applied to ensure safety have thus be used to subject importers of foreign-built boats to substantial delays, if not outright obstruction.[98]

A serious imbalance in the trade in sailing yachts between Britain and France has resulted from the clear asymmetry of treatment and experience of the industries of the two countries. French yacht builders have been able to sustain an extensive, and largely unobstructed, export drive within the British market. In contrast, the British builders of sailing yachts have experienced the demand-dampening effects of inadequate coastal facilities and a number of the sharp shocks from government policies. Their domestic market, moreover, has remained open to foreign competitors. The result is that a British industry which continues to manufacture sound and innovative products continues to face unequal competition. Signs of a growing appreciation of the significance of the boating industry as a leisure market and as a potential source of employment in areas that are often somewhat depressed economically have, however, been indicated by the joint commitment of the Welsh Tourist Board, Development Board for Rural Wales and the Welsh Development Agency to an ambitious £18 million scheme for the development of some twelve new boat marinas around the otherwise poorly served Welsh coast.

The comparative examples of the British and French yacht-building industries illustrates the range of both policies and measures that may affect the vitality of a domestic industry. It also indicates the attention that judicious governments should assign to the promotion of even the most unlikely industries in a world of changing life-styles, growing competitive pressures and obstinate, if not chronic, unemployment.

CONCLUSION

A survey of the sources, and responses to, the modern micro-electronics revolution reveals much that is of pertinence to an Economic Realist, economic nationalist or neo-mercantilist approach to the contemporary global political economy. Additional insights also emerge from a brief examination of the contrasting experiences of the British and French yacht-building industries during the 1970s and 1980s.

An extremely wide range of governmental policies and actions may have a significant, if not determinate, effect upon indigenous industries, their development, promotion and preservation. Governments have often adopted these policies and practices without a full appreciation of their consequences. However, where governments have identified the significance of a given industry, analysed its requirements, and then adopted policies that satisfy such requirements, considerable results have often been achieved. The Japanese micro-electronics and computer industry and the French yacht-building industry have both born witness to the effectiveness of such supportive policies. Where, in contrast, governments have failed to appreciate the full consequences of their policies, or felt compelled towards unhelpful actions, then substantial damage can be inflicted upon local industry and major opportunities lost, perhaps irretrievably.

The need for such neo-mercantilist policies and practices is created by the nature of the real world. In both its economic and political aspects, the world fails to conform with the assumptions, or basic methodology, of neo-classical economic theory and its 'neo-liberal' enthusiasts. Equilibrium does not emerge, stability is not ensured and the well-being of the populations of all countries does not develop in the wake of a world-wide equalization of the returns to factors of production[99] and the equitable distribution of efficiently produced goods and services.

The real world is turbulent, afflicted by chronic uncertainty and replete with temptations to defect from collaborative, and mutually advantageous, arrangements. Such realities eventually impose themselves upon even the most intransigent of neo-liberal governments. Little exemplifies this better than the conversion of the British government of Mrs Thatcher to substantial support for exports, in the wake of the loss of the contract for the second bridge over the Bosporus to heavily subsidized Japanese competitors.[100]

Governments are faced with wide-ranging opportunities to promote the well-being of their industries and peoples. Not all will suit all situations, and not all are universally successful. Failures will be experienced, as with the ill-fated support by the British government of a project to build Lear Fan jets in Belfast.[101] However, failure is a common experience in all walks of life and for all kinds of institutions, be they governments or private enterprise.

One of the most difficult decisions facing governments, however, is the extent to which collaboration will be attempted with other states. Where successful, such collaboration can be invaluable. Where ill conceived, commitments to international cooperation can be seriously counterproductive. However, the advantages that can be secured from effective collaboration are such as to encourage some seasoned observers to foresee the emergence of regional blocs within the world economy. In such a world, Britain's place would be firmly within an essentially self-regarding Europe.[102] However, the problems that afflict all international cooperation are all too evident within the attempts to form an European Community. Its fate, therefore, remains uncertain.

The conclusion, then, is that the reality of the contemporary world economy faces societies, and their governments, with many opportunities and difficulties. As ever, it is the skill with which governments can exploit the opportunities that will determine the well-being of societies and, therefore, their ability to make a positive contribution, ultimately, to the well-being of others.

NOTES

1. *See* the seminal study by E. Braun and S. MacDonald, *Revolution in Miniature: The History and Impact of Semiconductor Electronics*, (Cambridge: Cambridge University Press, 1978).
2. *ibid.* esp. Ch. 9.
3. *ibid.* pp. 80–2.
4. *ibid.* pp. 91–3.
5. *ibid.* pp. 112–13.
6. *See* a report in the *Guardian*, 31 January 1983, p. 15.
7. *See* 'Big, blue, booming', *Sunday Times*, 17 February 1983, p. 65.
8. *ibid.*
9. *See*, for instance, 'Queues form in US chip famine', *Sunday Times*, 12 February 1984, p. 68.
10. *See* 'AT&T tries again for slice of Inmos', *Guardian*, 11 February 1984, p. 18.
11. 'IBM takes stake in Intel', *Guardian*, 23 December 1982, p. 12.
12. 'US forms link to keep lead in electronics', *Guardian*, 3 March 1982, p. 14.
13. 'Rivals team up to fight the Big K', *Sunday Times*, 3 July 1983, p. 58.
14. 'Texas Instruments joins forces with National Semiconductors', *Guardian*, 9 May 1984, p. 24.
15. *See* M. J. Wolf, *The Japanese Conspiracy*, (New York: Empire Books, 1983; London: New English Library, 1984), Ch. 4.
16. *ibid.* p. 70.
17. *ibid.* pp. 73–4.
18. *ibid.* pp. 77–8; and *see also* 'All's not fair in the chip war', *Guardian*, 21 April 1982, p. 15.
19. *ibid.* p. 87
20. *See*: Braun and MacDonald *op. cit.* pp. 159–60; and Ian M. Mackintosh, 'Micros: the coming world war', in T. M. Forester (ed.), *The Microelectronics Revolution*, (Oxford: Basil Blackwell, 1980), esp. p. 90.
21. *See* 'All's not fair in the chip war' *op. cit.*
22. Wolf *op. cit.* p. 84.
23. *ibid.* pp. 85–8.

24. *See* 'Rivals team up to fight the Big K' *op. cit.*
25. *See*: 'Vaulting into the fifth generation: Japan goes for no. 1', *South*, (September 1983), pp. 21–2; and 'Coming shortly—the world domination machine', *Guardian*, 12 October 1983, p. 20; and 'Computer drive', *Guardian*, 15 April 1982, p. 14.
26. *ibid.*
27. 'Japan's soft options', *Sunday Times*, 20 May 1984, p. 66.
28. *See* Giovanni Dosi, 'Semiconductors: Europe's precarious survival in high technology', in G. Shepherd, F. Duchene, and C. Saunders, *Europe's Industries: Public and Private Strategies for Change*, (London: Frances Pinter, 1983), esp. pp. 217–18.
29. *See*: R. Ballance and S. Sinclair, *Collapse and Survival: Industrial Strategies in a Changing World*, (London: George Allen and Unwin, 1983), p. 151; and Dosi *op. cit.* p. 227.
30. *See* Dosi *op. cit.* esp. pp. 227–9.
31. *See* 'New technology revolution is passing Britain by, officials tell Government', *Guardian*, 16 July 1980, p. 14.
32. Advisory Council for Applied Research and Development, *The Applications of Semiconductor Technology*, (London: HMSO, 1978).
33. *See* 'The chicken and egg in miniature', *Guardian*, 19 August 1981, p. 15.
34. *See* 'Neddy attacks computer policy', *Guardian*, 15 April 1981, p. 14.
35. 'Call for electronics strategy', *Guardian*, 27 October 1981, p. 16.
36. Electronics Economic Development Committee, *Policy for the UK Electronics Industry*, (London: National Economic Development Office, 1982).
37. *See*: Report in *The Economist*, 8 September, 1984; and 'UK facing "Third World Status"', *Guardian*, 3 September 1984, p. 16.
38. *See* 'Action on electronics demanded', *Guardian*, 6 December 1984, p. 23.
39. *See* 'State puts £50m in electronics', *Sunday Times*, 28 May 1978, p. 53.
40. 'Chip factory gets £7 million grant', *Guardian*, 2 February 1979, p. 14.
41. '14M state aid for micro-chip factory', *Guardian*, 24 July 1979, p. 21.
42. 'Microelectronics aid stay', *Guardian*, 29 September 1981.
43. 'Two campus chip centres launched', *Guardian*, 21 November 1979, p. 15.
44. 'Inmos wants quick Sir Keith decision', *Guardian*, 29 January 1980, p. 19.
45. 'Joseph approves £25M for NEB's Inmos microchip', *Guardian*, 8 March 1980, p. 18.
46. 'Taxpayers may chip in £10M at Inmos', *Sunday Times*, 4 July 1982, p. 50.
47. 'U-turn as Inmos gets £15m', *Sunday Times*, 2 January 1983, p. 15.
48. 'Inmos is poised for sell-off', *Sunday Times*, 3 July 1983, p. 53.
49. *See* 'Tebbit will not rule out Inmos takeover', *Guardian*, 22 June 1984, p. 16.
50. 'Thorn-EMI wins control of Inmos', *Guardian*, 13 July 1984.

51. 'Infotech minister gets Whitehall brief', *Guardian*, 6 November 1980, p. 19.
52. 'Baker gets down to spreading the word', *Guardian*, 7 January 1981, p. 14.
53. *See* 'Chalk and Chips', *Guardian*, 24 January 1981, p. 19.
54. 'MAP to get chips money', *Guardian*, 1 April 1981, p. 17.
55. '£6m official push for computer', *Guardian*, 28 October 1981, p. 18.
56. '10 million more for software', *Guardian*, 30 April 1982, p. 17.
57. 'More government hitech aid to go to small firms', *Guardian*, 6 March 1984, p. 22.
58. 'UK's ailing microchips wait for a shot of Misp2', *Guardian*, 20 March 1984, p. 23.
59. 'ICL's rehabilitation gets an extra boost', *Guardian*, 28 November 1981, p. 20.
60. *See* 'Will Fujitsu help the ICL balancing act', *Guardian*, 8 October 1981, p. 19.
61. *See* 'Kinnock fear over £391m bid for ICL', *Guardian*, 27 July 1984, front and back.
62. 'Making the most of intelligence', *Guardian*, 2 December 1982, p. 13.
63. 'Britain in race for superbrain', *Guardian*, 24 July 1983, p. 49.
64. 'Super chips get £63 m grants', *Guardian*, 10 August 1984, p. 16.
65. 'Microchips squeezed in town vs gown battle', *Guardian*, 13 March 1985, p. 23.
66. *ibid.*
67. *See* Dosi *op. cit.* p. 229.
68. 'France seeking computer chips deal', *Guardian*, 13 September 1978, p. 4.
69. *See* 'Ringing the changes', *Guardian*, 24 January 1980, p. 22.
70. 'France boosts computer cash', *Sunday Times*, 14 November 1982, p. 53.
71. *See* 'French teamwork against Japan', *Guardian*, 20 November 1982, p. 18.
72. *See* Dosi *op. cit.* p. 229.
73. *See* the report in *The Economist*, 8 December 1984, pp. 73–4.
74. *See* Dosi *op. cit.* p. 227.
75. *See*, for instance, the reports in *Guardian*, 24 February 1984, pp. 21 and 22.
76. 'Dublin seeks chip making partners', *Guardian*, 10 April 1979, p. 24.
77. *See* 'Europe wins first round of fight with IBM', *Guardian*, 12 November 1981, p. 16.
78. 'IBM to settle out of court', *Sunday Times*, 29 July 1984, p. 49.
79. 'Investment failure by Europe worsens the microchip famine', *Guardian*, 21 May 1984, p. 21.
80. *See* 'EEC "must run to catch up in micros"', *Guardian*, 23 October 1980, p. 18.
81. *ibid.*
82. 'Esprit puts d'accord into Europe', *Sunday Times*, 19 December 1982, p. 44.

83. *ibid.* and *see also* 'Europe's technology gap' *The Economist*, 24 November 1984, pp. 99–100.
84. *See*, especially, C. Jenkins and B. Sherman, *The Collapse of Work*, (London: Eyre Methuen, 1979).
85. For a discussion, *see*: S. Nora and A. Minc, *The Computerization of Society: A Report to the President of France*, (Cambridge, Mass.: MIT Press, 1981), esp. Ch. 3; and 'Look at how the jobs debate has wobbled', *Guardian*, 18 October 1983, p. 18.
86. *See* a report on an APEX study, 'New technology "destroying jobs"', in *Guardian*, 27 February 1984, p. 17; and details of a report by the Policy Studies Institute, 'Microchips account for 34,000 lost jobs', *Guardian*, 2 March 1984, p. 23.
87. *See*, for example, Arthur C. Clarke, 'Third World 1001', *South*, (November 1981), pp. 13–15.
88. *See*, in particular, J. Rada, *The Impact of Micro-electronics*, (Geneva; ILO, 1980); and H. K. Hoffman and H. J. Rush, 'The impact of micro-electronics on the Third World', in A. R. Riddell (ed.), *Adjustment of Protectionism: The Challenge to Britain of Third World Industrialization*, (London: Catholic Institute for International Relations, 1980).
89. *See* 'The last road to survival', *South*, (February 1985), pp. 79–80.
90. *See*, for instance, 'Hi-tech scissors poised over the garment trade', *South*, (August 1983), pp. 60–1.
91. *See* 'What big teeth', *The Economist*, 4 May 1985, pp. 13–14.
92. 'Supermini versus the superpower', *South* (May 1983), pp. 64–5.
93. *ibid.*
94. 'Big noises on the micro scene', *South*, (April 1984), p. 65.
95. *See* 'Brazil chips away at the giant', *South* (May 1984), pp. 63–4.
96. *See*, for example, 'Undercover agents chase seepage in Silicon Valley', *Guardian*, 19 May 1981, p. 20.
97. *See* 'The trade war peril in US hitech controls', *Guardian*, 14 March 1984, p. 23.
98. *See*: 'Plumbing the new depths at the Boat Show', *Sunday Times*, 9 January 1983; and letter to *Yachting World*, April 1984, p. 40.
99. For a discussion of such equalization of factor returns *see* Chris Edwards, *The Fragmented World: Competing Perspectives on Trade, Money and Crisis*, (London: Methuen, 1985), esp. pp. 17–39.
100. *See* 'Thatcher U-turn on export loan', *Guardian*, 22 May 1985, p. 32.
101. 'Britain will lose £57 m in collapse of Lear Fan', *Guardian*, 27 May 1985, p. 20.
102. *See*: the arguments of D. P. Calleo and B. J. Rowland, *America and the World Political Economy: Atlantic Dreams and National Realities*, (Bloomington: Indiana University Press, 1973) esp. Part V; and Dudley Seers, *The Political Economy of Nationalism*, (Oxford: Oxford University Press, 1983), esp. Chs. 11 and 12.

Select Bibliography

Allen G. C., *How Japan Competes: A Verdict on 'Dumping'*, (London; Institute of Economic Affairs, 1978).

Ballance R. and Sinclair S., *Collapse and Survival: Industry Strategies in a Changing World*, (London: George Allen and Unwin, 1983).

Bell D. and Kristol I., *The Crisis in Economic Theory*, (New York: Basic Books, 1981).

Blackaby F., *De-Industrialisation*, (London: Heinemann, 1978).

Blake D. H. and Walters R. S., *The Politics of Global Economic Relations*, (Englewood Cliffs: Prentice-Hall, 1976).

Braun E. and MacDonald S., *Revolution in Miniature: The History and Impact of Semiconductor Electronics*, (Cambridge: Cambridge University Press, 1978).

Buzan Barry, *People, States, and Fear: The National Security Problem in International Relations*, (Brighton: Wheatsheaf, 1983).

Calleo D. P. and Rowland B. J., *America and the World Political Economy: Atlantic Dreams and National Realities*, (Bloomington: Indiana University Press, 1973).

Carter Charles (ed.), *Industrial Policy and Innovation*, (London: Heinemann, 1981).

Eichner A. S. (ed.), *A Guide to Post-Keynsian Economics*, (London: Macmillan, 1979).

Ellsworth P. T., *The International Economy*, (New York: Collier Macmillan, 3rd edn., 1964).

Gomes L., *International Economic Problems*, (London: Macmillan, 1978).

Gordon-Ashworth F., *International Commodity Control: A Contemporary History and Appraisal*, (London: Croom Helm, 1984).

Green F. and Nore P., *Economics: An Anti-Text*, (London: Macmillan, 1977).

Hartley K., *Problems of Economic Policy*, (London: George Allen and Unwin, 1977).

Hindley Brian and Nicolaides Eri, *Taking the New Protectionism Seriously*, (London: Trade Policy Research Centre, 1983).

Hirschman A. O., *National Power and the Structure of Foreign Trade*, (Berkeley: University of California Press, 1945; expanded edn., 1980).

Rogers Hollingsworth J., *Government and Economic Performance*, special edn. of *The Annals*, (Beverly Hill, Cal.: Sage, 1982).

Hutchinson T. W., *Knowledge and Ignorance in Economics*, (Oxford: Basil Blackwell, 1977).

Johnson H. G. (ed.), *The New Mercantilism: Some Problems in International Trade, Money and Investment*, (Oxford: Basil Blackwell, 1974).

Barry Jones R. J., *Perspectives on Political Economy: Alternatives to the Economics of Depression*, (London: Frances Pinter, 1983).

Barry Jones R. J. and Willetts P., *Interdependence on Trial: Studies in the Theory and Reality of Contemporary Interdependence*, (London: Frances Pinter, 1984).

Katzenstein P. J., *Between Power and Plenty: Foreign Economic Policies of Advanced Industrial States*, (Madison, Wis.: Wisconsin University Press, 1978).

Keohane R. O., *After Hegemony: Cooperation and Discord in the World Political Economy*, (Princeton: Princeton University Press, 1984).

Kindleberger C. P., *Power and Money: The Politics of International Economics and the Economics of International Politics*, (New York: Basic Books, 1970).

Knapp John, 'Economics or political economy', *Lloyds Bank Review*, (January 1973), 19–43.

Knorr Klaus, *Power and Wealth: The Political Economy of International Power*, (London: Macmillan, 1973).

Krasner S. D., *International Regimes*, (Ithaca: Cornell University Press, 1983).

Morgenthau Hans J., *Politics Among Nations: The Struggle for Power and Peace* (New York: Alfred Knopf, numerous edns.).

Nora S. and Minc A., *The Computerization of Society: A Report to the President of France*, (Cambridge, Mass.: MIT Press, 1981).

Oslon Mancur, *The Logic of Collective Action: Public Goods and the Theory of Groups*, (Cambridge: Cambridge University Press, 1965).

Riddell A. R. (ed.), *Adjustment of Protectionism: The Challenge to Britain of Third World Industrialisation*, (London: Catholic Institute for International Relations, 1980).

Robinson Joan, *Contributions to Modern Economics*, (Oxford: Basil Blackwell, 1978).

Samuels W. J., *The Economy as a System of Power*, 2 volumes, (New Brunswick: Transaction Books, 1979).

Schumpeter J. A., *Capitalism, Socialism and Democracy*, (London: George Allen and Unwin, 5th edn., 1976).

Seers, Dudley, *The Political Economy of Nationalism*, (Oxford: Oxford University Press, 1983).

Shepherd G., Duchene F. and Saunders C., *Europe's Industries, Public and Private Strategies for Change*, (London: Frances Pinter, 1983).

Schonfield A., *In Defence of the Mixed Economy*, (ed. Z. Schonfield), (Oxford: Oxford University Press, 1984).

Simpson D., *The Political Economy of Growth*, (Oxford: Basil Blackwell, 1983).

Stewart M., *Controlling the Economic Future: Policy Dilemmas in a Shrinking World*, (Brighton: Wheatsheaf Books, 1983).

Strange Susan and Tooze Roger, *The International Politics of Surplus Capacity: Competition for market shares in the world recession*, (London: George Allen and Unwin, 1981).

Tucker R. W., *The Inequality of Nations*, (New York: Basic Books, 1977).

Wolf M. J., *The Japanese Conspiracy*, (New York: Empire Books, 1983; and London: New English Library, 1984).

Index

264